TRACING THE SPIRIT

The Woodstock Theological Center was established in 1974 by the Maryland and New York Provinces of the Society of Jesus to explore contemporary social and political issues from a standpoint of Christian faith. Located in Washington, D.C., this independent institute works in collaboration with university faculties and other groups. Through this interdisciplinary approach, the Center offers research, seminars, symposia and publications on such problems as ethics and nuclear power, faith and justice, human rights, moral and religious values in government, religion and politics, Christian values and American capitalism.

PUBLICATIONS OF THE CENTER

Religious Freedom: 1965–1975. A Symposium on a Historic Document, edited by Walter J. Burghardt, Woodstock Studies 1, Paulist Press, 1976.

The Faith That Does Justice: Examining the Christian Sources for Social Change, edited by John C. Haughey, Woodstock Studies 2, Paulist Press, 1977.

Personal Values in Public Policy, edited by John C. Haughey, Woodstock Studies 3, Paulist Press, 1979.

Claims in Conflict, David Hollenbach, Woodstock Studies 4, Paulist Press, 1979.

Above Every Name: The Lordship of Christ and Social Systems, edited by Thomas E. Clarke, Woodstock Studies 5, Paulist Press, 1980.

Human Rights in the Americas: The Struggle for Consensus, edited by Alfred Hennelly and John Langan, Georgetown University Press, 1982.

Human Rights and Basic Needs in the Americas, edited by Margaret E. Crahan, Georgetown University Press, 1982.

Inequality and the American Conscience, Christopher Mooney, Woodstock Studies 6, Paulist Press, 1983.

TRACING
THE
SPIRIT

Communities,
Social Action, and
Theological Reflection

Edited by
James E. Hug, S.J.

PAULIST PRESS
New York/Ramsey

Library of Congress
Catalog Card Number: 82-62419

ISBN: 0-8091-2529-3

Published by Paulist Press
545 Island Road, Ramsey, N.J. 07446

Printed and bound in the
United States of America

Contents

Introduction

In small pockets across the country, something new is stirring. Small groups of people committed to working for a more just social order are setting aside important meeting time for prayer, for stories of faith, for reflection on Scripture passages, for discovering "our story within the Scriptures and Scripture within our story." There are neighborhood groups, city-wide coalitions, base communities, small churches. There are religious communities, parish staffs, peace and justice centers, national offices and lobbying groups. They are sifting through the complex realities of their daily social struggle for traces of the Spirit.

What does that mean? What traces does the Spirit of God leave? Jesus tells Nicodemus, "The Spirit blows where it wills, and you hear the sound of it, but you do not know where it comes from or where it is going." Can we learn to recognize those sounds and trace its movements? How?

And what does this have to do with social action? These seem to be the language and concerns of Christian spirituality. It is no secret that two of the groups in recent Christian history that have had great trouble understanding and trusting each other are the social activists and those working in spirituality. Is something bringing them closer together now?

Drawing out a link between Christian faith and socio-political life is not, in itself, anything new. Christians have claimed God as their support for everything from legitimation of the Roman Empire to the Crusades to a nuclear freeze and unilateral disarmament. The hand of God has been identified in the civil rights legislation of the 1960's and the New Federalism of the 1980's. The Suffering Servant has been identified with the poor and marginalized of the first and third worlds ... and with transnational corporations. The problem remains, as it has for centuries, how to be honest and discerning with God.

1

Theological Reflection

Still, there is something new going on here—something quite new and intriguing, and potentially revolutionary. It is bringing social activists to concern about spirituality and theology at the same time as it is bringing centers of spirituality to send people into the inner city and into rural areas marked by poverty and oppression for a privileged experience of God.

It seems to be rooted in the realization that God is revealing and being discovered in action. The place to meet and contemplate the living God is in the work going on to redeem and renew the world in the image of the Word.

Various approaches are being used in the attempt to trace the Spirit in social realities and movements. Some are simple and preliminary, some developed and elaborate. They have precedents—perhaps even some historical roots—in movements such as those spawned by the Jocists (YCW, CFM, YCS, etc.) or by the Catholic Worker. Still, they represent a new phenomenon in contemporary Christian life, one well worth serious consideration. It goes by different names in different communities and different parts of the world. One commonly used descriptive term can serve as a catch-phrase for the whole variety: *Theological Reflection.*

The focus of this book, then, is theological reflection on experience as it is (or can be) carried on in small communities of people engaged in the struggle for social justice.

This theological reflection is a new phenomenon in Christianity from a number of angles. It differs from traditional forms of theology in where it is done, what its starting point is, how it is done, who does it, what its goal is, and what its criteria for truth are.

Traditionally theology has emerged from two locales. It has come from the libraries and classrooms of universities or from the seminaries and the private studies and meeting halls of Popes and bishops. It has been academic or ecclesiastical—or, more usually, some combination of the two. The theological reflection we're considering here is coming from the streets, from shacks, from the living rooms where small communities and coalitions are being drawn together by the struggle for justice.

Ordinary people with little or no formal theological training, with little or no ecclesiastical status or power, are the "new theologians." They are people like those in the neighborhoods of the South Bronx and the rural poverty pockets of Mississippi and Appalachia who—though they frequently find social analysis foreign to their experience and difficult—are right at home finding guidance from their faith for understanding their problems and living their lives with hope.

The conscious starting point for theological reflection is different as well. It usually does not begin with Scripture study or research into the writings of the Christian tradition. It begins in action—suffering, working, struggling, imagining, lobbying, organizing, building. It begins in pain and in the hunger and thirst for justice. It begins with personal stories about that experience and action.

Its processes are not the usual processes of academic or ecclesiastical theology. It moves from experience and story-telling to looking for patterns and trends. It sifts society, looking for the roots of suffering. It responds to the shreds and traces of justice that give it hope, that reflect the presence and activity of God.

The explicit goal of theological reflection is not a dogmatic statement or a contribution to academic theology. Its goal is pastoral and practical: it aims at transformation of social structures and institutions and at fuller personal integration and conversion.

As a result, its criteria for truth and value are practical as well. This theological reflection is "true" and successful when it liberates the fullest living of the Christian spirit possible in the context, the fullest and most aware response to what the Spirit of God is doing here and now and inviting us to do.

The Woodstock Project

In the spring of 1980, the Woodstock Theological Center launched a project to study the theological reflection being done in small communities struggling for justice. A taskforce was established to draw upon a wide range of ecumenical expertise. Under the direction of Thomas E. Clarke, S.J., it set out to learn about theological reflection from groups that were doing it. It hoped, as it listened and asked questions about their theological reflection, to get a clearer image of what the groups were doing and why they were doing it. Stimulated by those discussions, the members of the taskforce wrote the essays that comprise this book. These essays represent efforts by a group of professional theologians to listen, to describe and clarify different facets, dimensions, and implications of what they have heard, and to offer some cautious suggestions from their own perspective for doing theological reflection well.

A taskforce of professional theologians called together to reflect theologically on theological reflection? At first it sounds like a breakthrough to new pretzel-twists of theological navel-gazing! A breakthrough sure to produce the perfect cure for any insomnia that might afflict social activists—an update of the legendary theological concern about angels and pinheads: "How many forms of theological reflection can dance on the head of the social justice movement?"

The real promise of the taskforce project, however, is far more significant. Karl Rahner has called attention to the opening of a new epoch in Church history, the first since St. Paul moved Christianity beyond the Jewish community. If not aborted, it will see the emergence of Christianity as a world Church, replacing its current status as a Western, European Church spread around the world. It will see Christian faith take on cultural forms and expressions much more capable of communicating its reality and its social vision to local peoples—and therefore much more faithful to its true spirit. It may be that theological reflection rooted in local communities will be an important midwife in the birthing of these new forms of Christian life and faith. The promise of deeper understanding of that process and of the chance to help facilitate it is very alluring.

A study of theological reflection holds out another significant area of promise. As I mentioned earlier, it promises the possibility of reconciling two traditionally divided and suspicious groups in the Christian Churches, those involved in personal spiritual renewal and those involved in social action and social renewal. By focusing upon the presence of God working for social transformation in today's world, it calls forth the contemplative side of social activists and the active side of spiritual contemplatives—building upon the strengths of each and calling each beyond their weaknesses.

The Communities

So, in early 1980, the Woodstock taskforce began a series of interviews with various communities and action/reflection groups in and around Washington, D.C. More than twenty-five people representing at least sixteen groups or organizations contributed to the process. In addition, one of the members of the taskforce, Al Hennelly, S.J., interviewed members of base communities in Central America to explore the relationship between the theological reflection developing in those communities and that present in the United States.

A profile of several of the communities interviewed can be found in Chapters 2 and 3. Limitations of space prevented our describing all those we interviewed, so we tried to offer a representative sampling. Our gratitude, however, extends equally to those whose help could not be described or acknowledged there—to the Campaign for Human Development, Christian Life Communities, the Colloquium of the Jesuit Secondary Education Association, the Interreligious Taskforce on U.S. Food Policy, the Leadership Conference of Women Religious, the Conference of Major Superiors of Men, the Center for a New Creation, the Washington office of the Presbyterian Church in the U.S.A., the Southeast Vicariate Cluster of Washington, D.C., and the Center of Concern.

The selection of the communities or action/reflection groups was made on practical grounds. These were groups known to members of the Woodstock taskforce and available in the area for consultation. Limited resources made a wider casting of our net unfeasible.

As a result, our survey cannot claim the status of a scientific sociological study. Using a distinction developed by Tom Clarke in Chapter 1, we could say that it builds upon experiential data rather than empirical data. It describes and reflects upon the experience of a certain group of people in order to stimulate our own reflection upon our own experience.

The fact that so many of the groups interviewed are based in the nation's capital immediately suggests a warning. The experience of groups that make up a Washington office for a national constituency is unrepresentative in two seemingly contradictory ways. First, it tends to be fed by the concerns and activities of grassroots communities from around the country. As a result, it reflects a much broader range of experience than is usual for a small community. On the other hand, as national groups concerned with national issues, these communities tend to be rooted in no single local context. Precisely in their links to a variety of local communities, they lose immediate touch with their own grassroots. Since the experience of national groups was such an important part of the stimulus for the reflection that follows, it is especially important that readers constantly test its assumptions and conclusions against their own experience.

The Process

The interviews were only one element in the process undertaken by the Woodstock taskforce. The taskforce met monthly to explore the issues involved and to ferret out our own presuppositions. We surveyed and discussed recent literature on theological methodology. With the help of one of the taskforce members, Bob Kinast, we kept an eye on the development of new forms of theological reflection in seminaries and theological schools across the United States and in Toronto. Throughout the process, a plethora of memos bearing suggestions, critiques, imaginative dreamings, précis, and scenarios enriched the atmosphere.

In the fall of 1981, the first drafts underwent serious scrutiny and revision. Each essay was fully discussed by the whole taskforce. In addition, each was sent to four or five different action/reflection groups who responded generously with criticism and suggestions. Enriched by mounds of feedback, the taskforce members revised their work. Some of the critiques were incorporated into the revisions and the chapters are considerably better as a result. Others were not or could not be followed. Final responsibility for what is in the essays belongs to the authors, of course. But we are very grateful for the help given the taskforce by those who read and responded to the chapters of this book when they were in their first draft form. If this work is not theology done by people at the grassroots, it is certainly theology stimulated and refined by them.

In the spring of 1982, the second drafts were gathered and the final processes of editorial collation and revision took place.

The Result?

What did we learn about theological reflection in the context of social justice ministry? In thumbnail form, it is reflection on experience understood in the light of religious experience by involved communities moving toward conversion and/or action. Let's unpack that just a little.

REFLECTION—By emphasizing the reflective dimension of this process, we mean to insist that it does not proceed by deduction from authoritative books or statements to speak to current issues. It begins with contemporary experiences and proceeds indirectly by analogy between these experiences and the experiences from which the religious tradition and its teachings were shaped.

ON EXPERIENCE—This is the experience of the contemporary local community itself. It may be the experience of its own identity or of its social context. It may be the experience of its struggles, suffering, successes or failures. It is the action and passion of ordinary people in everyday life.

UNDERSTOOD—This reflection on experience usually begins in the swapping of stories. Deeper understanding emerges only when we mull over the stories and ask some probing questions. How are the stories alike? unlike? What patterns are revealed? Who has power and how is it being used? What values are at stake? This type of theological reflection makes use of sociological, psychological, economic, cultural, political, and historical tools of analysis to whatever degree is possible. And it uses them to approach the present reality from the perspective of the poor and oppressed.

IN THE LIGHT OF RELIGIOUS EXPERIENCE—The principal light for understanding and judging the experience is the religious experience found in the lives of its members. That experience, in dialogue with the religious experience revealed through the Scriptures and the religious tradition, guides the response of the community to its present situation.

BY INVOLVED COMMUNITIES—The involvement is a central element in theological reflection. The deep personal engagement of the people in the issues at stake gives them a privileged sense of the revelation of God, the traces of the Spirit, present. So-called "emotional distance" or "scientific objectivity" is considered a delusion and a hindrance rather than an ideal or a help.

MOVING TOWARD CONVERSION AND/OR ACTION—The goal of this theological reflection is Christian life rather than Christian truth—or, perhaps better, it is lived Christian truth rather than articulated Christian truth.

A Caution

When theological reflection unfolds as it is sketched here and elaborated on in the essays of this volume, a tension is present that should be noted. It is a tension between the understanding given by social analysis (used as a broad term for the variety of analyses mentioned) and that given by religious experience. It is fairly widely recognized now that the social sciences are not value-free. The implicit values governing their perspectives may blind them to certain facets of reality. So a difficult question will always haunt those engaged in theological reflection: Do the assumptions and the reigning logic of the social sciences effectively control the selection from our recollections of our own religious experience and from the experience recorded in the Scriptures and the tradition? In other words, does the social analysis control the religious interpretation of the situation? Or is it possible for religious faith to criticize and modify those analyses? Is there openness to transcendence, to the possibility of surprise? Or are the results of social analyses taken too simply to be "facts"?

The caution, then, is intended to warn groups and communities to be explicit and clear about what holds the final effective authority in their processes of theological reflection. The spiritual energies at the heart of theological reflection should be religious. They will embrace the insights and energies available through the social sciences, but not uncritically. The "bottom line," the place our feet should be firmly planted, is our lived sense of the traces of the Spirit before us.

This Volume

As the Table of Contents indicates, this volume is divided into three main parts. The division is based upon our understanding of theological reflection. Each of these parts has its own brief introduction giving advance clues to the contents of its chapters. It might help, nonetheless, to give an overview of the three parts here.

Part I relates various aspects of the experience upon which the members of the Woodstock taskforce reflected. It presents our starting points and points of reference in the hope that these will enable readers to understand our work more clearly and assess more accurately what elements of it fit their own situations and what adaptations need to be made.

Part II begins our analysis. The first two chapters attempt to discover the appropriate atmosphere and context for approaching the narrative data of Part I. The final two represent a very small sampling of the types of analysis that can help us understand our stories of experience in a more penetrating way.

Part III is comprised of essays designed to bring the analyzed experience under the light of Christian religious experience, that of the Church today and that of the earliest communities.

None of these three parts is complete. We have no illusions that we have captured this movement adequately or understood it fully. This is not a definitive work on theological reflection; it is not even a full systematic treatment. It is too early in the life of the movement to attempt to synthesize its significance.

We do feel, however, that we have gained valuable insights through our process over the last two years. We want to give voice to them here in the hope that they will get people talking more about

Theological Reflection—and, more than talking about it, doing it themselves. This is our way as theologians of responding to the traces of the Spirit that we are uncovering.

The success of this project owes more to Tom Clarke, S.J., than to any other single individual. Tom's experience, intuitions, and fertile imagination generated it. His persistent research, organizational efforts, and interviews—all undertaken with tireless enthusiasm—shaped it until it was viable and healthy both as a project and as a small Christian community. It is no exaggeration to say that without Tom Clarke this project and this volume would not be.

Tom would be the first to insist, however, that the success of this project depends on many people—more than can be named here. I have already mentioned our gratitude to the action/reflection groups and small communities we interviewed—those mentioned earlier in this introduction and those profiled in Chapter 2. We drew as well upon the experience of a wide variety of occasional consultants. Ms. Jude Howard's seemingly endless work of typing and photo-copying moved our process into this product with great patience and graciousness. Substantial subsidies from the New York and Maryland Provinces of the Society of Jesus, the Raskob Foundation, and the Woodstock Jesuit Community made the project financially feasible. I want to express our sincere gratitude to them all.

Finally, special thanks are due to the members of the taskforce. They contributed many long hours and great talent to listening, writing, and criticizing each other's work. Through the process they formed a community of friends, sharing prayer and food, hard work and laughter. This fact in itself is probably the surest confirmation that they have been successful in tracing the Spirit.

James E. Hug
Woodstock Theological Center
December 15, 1982

Part I

Experience

God's revelation. What images dc these two words evoke in you? The New Testament stories and parables? The Bible? The mystical experiences of the great mystics?

The essays in Part I invite us to look closer to home at something far more ordinary and inconspicuous. They ask us to consider whether we revere our own experience as God's revelation too—our personal experience, each other's experience, the experience of our contemporaries. Do we treat it with the care and seriousness we direct to the Bible or the eucharistic presence of Jesus?

In the first chapter of this section, Tom Clarke looks to his own experience as a theologian. He shows how, in the last two hundred years, experience has come to be recognized as a prime source of God's revelation. This insight is generating what Clarke sees as a new way of theologizing. This "new way" brings together sense and sensibility, memory, story, and dreaming imagination in an effort to discover and cooperate with God active here and now in the creation of a more just and graced society.

Clarke's insight that any "theory or plan that has lost living contact with the story which generated it will eventually lose its power to shape life constructively" guided this project. The Woodstock taskforce listened to the stories of a variety of small communities engaged in work for social justice. Chapter 2 gathers the highlights of several of these stories. Bill Newell focuses particularly on their efforts at integrating some form of theological reflection into their lives and works. His chapter describes the principal experiential base for the theological reflection of this project. It will be important for you to note the ways that the stories there reflect your experience and the ways they do not.

In the third chapter, Al Hennelly broadens our experiential

foundation by surveying the base community movement—especially in its roots in Latin America. In many instances, their base communities and their approach to theological reflection have had more time to mature than our own. Hennelly attempts to evaluate the applicability of their experience to the largely middle class churches of the United States. Can we fairly simply adopt their patterns? Or must U.S. theological reflection be marked by distinctly regional characteristics? What might they be?

In the final chapter of Part I, we expand the dialogue on experience in theology even further. Bob Kinast takes us back into a formative home of traditional theologizing—the seminary—to look at the development of theological reflection in ministry preparation in recent years. He contrasts that style of theologizing with traditional theological education and with the theological reflection developing in the action/reflection groups and base communities. His discussion helps clarify issues of central concern, while his critical survey of the contemporary literature on models of theological reflection and his own suggestions provide some practical guidelines for more effective, penetrating theological reflection on experience.

1

A New Way: Reflecting on Experience

Thomas E. Clarke, S.J.

Theological reflection, as a distinctive way of theologizing, is by more or less common consent a reflection on experience. Therefore that is what this opening essay will be.[1] In view of the important role of story in theological reflection, I will situate my remarks within a sketch of part of my own theological journey.

A quarter century ago I was completing my third year as professor of dogmatic theology at Woodstock College, a Jesuit seminary situated in the Maryland countryside. It was perhaps the most prestigious Roman Catholic seminary in the United States at that time. John Courtney Murray, Gustave Weigel, and Walter Burghardt (and later Joseph Fitzmyer and Avery Dulles) were eminent members of its faculty. But in 1957 Woodstock's style of theology, with the exception of what was happening in Scripture classes, was still predominantly Tridentine. I wince a bit now as I think of what I then took for granted: Latin manuals supplemented by mimeographed professor's notes, also in Latin; lectures partly in Latin, partly in English; the handing on of timeworn texts, proofs, problems; the centrality of "Denzinger" (the massive Latin collection of Church documents), as much used by professors and students as the Bible itself.

It was an in-between period in seminary theology; more radical change would come in the late 1950s and early 1960s. But the seeds of renewal had been sown. Back in the late 1940s I had done my own seminary studies at Woodstock, and in my own private reading, divorced from what was happening in the classroom, had found my excitement in reading some of "the new theology" then developing on the Continent, notably in France. I was thrilled with what I was able to pick up of the remarkable renaissance taking place in biblical, liturgical, patristic, pastoral, and ecumenical circles. De Lubac's *Surnaturel,* echoes of the daring thought of Teilhard de Chardin, and the visionary pastorals of Cardinal Suhard fed both my mind and my devotion. Such reading, however, was strictly extracurricular, and for close to a decade failed to show up in my classroom activity, either as student or as professor.

There is no space here to detail my personal theological journey since 1957. Being more scavenger than scholar, and, as I have come slowly to appreciate, being primarily pastoral in my orientation, I took some of the major developments of theory and practice in the Church of the Vatican II era as grist for the mill of my personal reflection. Particularly through ministry with women religious, my understanding of theology—of my own theologizing, that is—gradually changed. I cannot claim to be a twice-born theologian, and the habits of another era still operate in me. But my status has changed. I am no longer a seminary professor and no longer a "research fellow" (a title that has given me many a chuckle). I am in the process of becoming an unattached pastoral reflector. With many others, I think I see emerging in the contemporary Church a new way of theologizing which the shorthand formula "theological reflection" attempts to describe. Mine is not the task, in this volume, of analyzing this new way comprehensively. I wish only to depict one of its constitutive elements, namely its strong and explicit reference to revelatory experience.

Since I see theological reflection as a new way in theology, I do not consider it a substitute for other ways. It does not replace, for example, the theology of seminaries or other centers of training for ministry, or the theology expounded in both Christian and secular universities. Still less do I feel obliged to disparage these latter. In fact, much of what I will be saying here has been picked up along the way from work done in academic circles, and by such seminary professors as Karl Rahner, Bernard Lonergan, and Avery Dulles.

The three parts of the essay will correspond to three realizations which have come to me through the years, partly from reading and discussion and partly from pastoral engagements. The first part will contain an overall appreciation of how experience came in the course of several centuries to its present importance in theology. The second part will dwell upon some of the primary specifications and amplifications of the theme of experience. The key notion here will be that of divine revelation as mediated through human experience, but I will also attend to the dynamic interplay of memory and imagination, story and dreaming. And I will situate them in broader social and cultural contexts through attention to "signs of the times." The third part owes much to my actual experience of theological reflection in formally structured processes.[2] It will offer suggestions for groups interested in theological reflection on experience. The movement of the essay, then, is from the historical/descriptive to the analytical/reflective to the pragmatic/pastoral.[3]

I

It is only in the last decade or so that I have learned how human experience has come to a place of special honor in contemporary theology and pastoral practice. It may be helpful here to set this development within a broader cultural context. Let me use four terms—humanization, modernization, secularization, historicization—to describe several facets of the profound change that has taken place in Western consciousness since the Renaissance and Reformation. Powerful currents have conspired to produce a complex "mindset" in which the importance of the human subject, individual and corporate, is highlighted. A turn from "classical" to "historical" consciousness reduced the influence of metaphysics and accented the importance of learning from experience. Scientific inventiveness embodied in technological creations showed how the life of the senses and perception of natural phenomena could, when combined with imaginative and rational skills, transform human beings from toolmakers into wonder-workers. Freud, Jung and others made human subjectivity itself a focus for empirical research and experimentation. Sociology and anthropology cast a similar light on the mechanics and dynamics of life in society. Particularly in the United States, democratic populism and pragmatism combined to produce an almost religious conviction that the way to the future lay in honoring fresh human experience. Out of such developments has emerged a modern consciousness which tends to believe what it sees, trust what it can empirically verify, and love whatever corresponds to the witness of human experience.

In such a context there emerged a tendency toward the polarization of two cultures, one characterized by scientific objectivity and the progressive rationalization of human endeavors, the other marked by recourse to the aesthetic and artistic facets of the human.[4] It seems appropriate, then, in speaking of the role of experience, to distinguish between its *empirical* and its *experiential* referents. The empirical is primarily concerned with data, the factual, the accurate description of inner or outer phenomena. It allies sense (and instrumental extensions of the senses) and reason in an effort to understand and shape reality with as much detachment from personal feeling and group bias as possible. The experiential referent, in contrast, draws on sense and other experience with a frank acceptance of the "reasons of the heart." It revels in what is unique, personal, subjective. Not clinical experiment but story-telling and artistic creation are its chosen vehicles.

Empirical and Experiential

This distinction of empirical and experiential is important for understanding the character of theological reflection. When I was a scholastic theologian at Woodstock three decades ago, the challenge presented me by my colleagues in Scripture and Church history was to pay more attention to the empirical side of things. I tried, with other theologians, to validate theology as a scientific discipline by developing models and tools similar to those employed in the physical, behavioral, and social sciences. Especially as Christian theology attempted to gain serious status within the American university, it was drawn to present itself as inductive, empirical, objective, secular, and detached.

But, even as I tried to heed such a call to modernize my way of theology, I began to experience a contrasting call. As the pastoral orientation of seminary theology began to receive more emphasis, and particularly as the Latin American experience of basic communities and theological reflection began to make itself heard in North America, it was the *experiential* approach to experience that beckoned and challenged me as a theologian.[5] Temperamentally, this was more appealing to me than the empirical. I still find it difficult to be greatly concerned about mere facts, but the "reasons of the heart" and the recourse to personal history as sources of one's wording of the Gospel message have increasingly attracted me.

This attraction in turn led me to a new perspective on the history of Christian theology since the Reformation. There had been a polemical time when the anti-scholastic aspect of the Reformation and the insistence of Luther that what really counted was not whether Jesus was both God and man (which Luther did not deny) but whether he was such "for me" were put down in Catholic circles as mere subjectivism. But I came to see that the first person singular need not be excluded from theological discourse. I gained some little acquaintance, too, with Friedrich Schleiermacher's situating of the starting point of theology in the feeling of absolute dependence, and I saw in this a most influential way of asserting the value of personal human experience for theological understanding. Karl Barth's challenge to the liberal currents stemming from Schleiermacher took the form of a sharp contrast between God's revelatory word and the initiatives of human religion (with the former of these as normative). This was a salutary caution against a betrayal of the primacy of God's gracious initiative, but it did not reverse the trend toward experiential accents in theology. Some exposure to Paul Tillich's "method of correlation" and his close integration of religion and culture (culture providing Christian faith with the form of the questions which it needed to answer in any given era) opened me still further to a posture of listening to my own experience within the various contexts which helped to form me.

So far as the history of modern Catholic theology was concerned, I had been brought up—at least so far as the "Denzinger theology" I imbibed in the 1940s was concerned—to view the Modernism of the turn the century as a subjectivistic and Protestantizing camel's nose under the Catholic tent. But eventually my exposure to the "new theology" of the post-World War II period made me see in it a new and irrepressible wave of the consciousness that had surfaced unsuccessfully through the Modernists. Here again the honoring of human experience was a central affirmation. In the years just before the Second Vatican Council, a growing exposure to Karl

Rahner, as well as listening in on what Avery Dulles was saying at Woodstock about the historical and experiential character of revelation, brought my understanding of revelation and grace much closer to my own personal experience of faith. It was around these two themes of revelation and grace, as well as around the Christological discussions of the human consciousness of Christ, that my own personal assimilation of an experiential theology took place.

Through the 1960s and 1970s more specific currents confirmed this orientation: Johannes Metz's powerful elaboration of the role of "dangerous memories," together with his espousal of a "narrative theology"; treatments of the "theology of story" by such American figures as Sally TeSelle and John Shea; attention to theological imagination in the writings of William Lynch, Julian Hartt, and Walter Brueggemann, among others.

Pastoral Currents

But it was not only the work of outstanding academic or professional theologians which made a difference for me. Both directly and indirectly I was exposed to various pastoral, spiritual, and psychological movements and ideas which highlighted the importance of experience, memory, imagination, story, and "discerning the signs of the times." To name only a few of these: personal journal keeping; the retrieval of "personal salvation history" by individuals in prayer and retreat experiences; "faith sharing" by small groups, usually including personal interpretation of the Scriptures; the charismatic movement with its encouragement of individual and communal listening to the inner voice of the Spirit; the revival in Jesuit circles of the practice of individual and communal "discernment of spirits"; the development in Latin America of basic communities employing simple forms of a praxis/reflection method; the use of experiential exercises for renewing and energizing groups and organizations through the sharing of personal stories, the retrieval of communal "myths," and the imaginative exploration of the future. And so pastoral experience was confirming what I was hearing from respected circles of professional theologians: that the time had come for a way in theology which took the "I" and the "we" out of the mothballs to which they had long been consigned by previous eras in theology, both within the Tridentine seminary and within the modern secular university.

As I have said, I do not consider this new way to be in basic conflict with the other ways. In fact, in the second part of this essay I will be drawing largely upon the results of research done over a period of decades by theologians whose dominant milieus were the seminary or the university. As much as possible, however, I will attempt to shape the several notions so as to make them more accessible and helpful for those whose call is to theologize within pastoral communities situated at various junctures between the Church and contemporary society and culture.

II

The key term, I believe, is *revelation*. For many years at Woodstock I simply assumed the truth of the thesis that Christian revelation had ceased with the death of the last apostle. Even today I would not say that the thesis was simply incorrect. It contained in fact an important truth. John of the Cross' celebrated dictum—that God, having spoken once for all in the Word, has nothing more to say to us—beautifully captured the definitive import of what happened at Nazareth, Bethlehem and Calvary. Yet, if we take the mission of the Holy Spirit seriously, we must *also* say that God continues to be revealed in us—to Christians and to every human being. Without faith no one can be saved. Without revelation faith is impossible. Centuries of struggle with the problem of the "salvation of the infidel" (a misnomer, we now see) has finally brought theology to a coherent view in which the uniqueness of Christ as Savior, the role of the Church in salvation, and God's love for *every* human being are all maintained.

No one has contributed more to the formulation of such a view than Karl Rahner. Rahner has made a key distinction in his theological anthropology between transcendent and categorical revelation and has linked revelation and grace closely. Every situation in which human beings are called to respond to values is considered by Rahner to contain the potential for a graced, salvific response to the triune God who is revealed in that situation. All human engagement contains a Yes or a No to God's self-offering in love. The important point here is that the whole gamut of human experience is seen as mediating divine revelation.

Experience and Consciousness

However it is easier to say *experience* than to define it. It is, in fact, as a primordial notion, not properly definable at all. But some effort to circumscribe its sense in the present context is necessary. I understand it here as designating those aspects of human behavior which have to do with the *perception* of reality, with *receptiveness* toward the real in all its dimensions. Experience is our encounter with life—or at least the initial phase of encounter, the point at which we feel the *touch* of life. Though the person experiencing is not passive or inert, the term points to the quasi-infinite capacity of each person or group of persons to receive whatever is.

Like all primordial terms, this one is elusive and admits of various degrees of inflation and contraction. For purposes of this essay, the following are some of its more important qualifications:

1. Though the primary subject of experience is the individual person, it is also true that human beings can share a *common experience.*

2. *Experience* and *consciousness* are not synonymous, yet they are intimately linked. It is not possible to discuss the distinction in detail, but here are a few observations which may be helpful. The object of experience can be within us or outside of us, whereas consciousness, properly speaking, designates awareness of the self as subject. Perhaps, too, the term consciousness points more directly toward a *state* of the subject, whereas experience points toward the *exercise* of awareness. It should also be said that not all experience is conscious, at least in the ordinary sense of this term.

What makes the relationship of experience and consciousness theologically significant is that it is through experience—revelatory experience—that the Christian consciousness is shaped and developed. Here it is helpful to recall the pioneering work of Emile Mersch and Teilhard de Chardin, among others, who introduced the language of consciousness into Roman Catholic theology. Largely because of them we have become accustomed to speak of the consciousness of the Christian as Christic, ecclesial, global, and cosmic.[6]

We might distinguish Christian experience and Christian consciousness, then, by asserting a reciprocal relationship between experience as the concrete, here-and-now encounter with reality, and consciousness as the mentality or posture, shaped by previous experience, which in turn affects the character and the quality of each new moment of revelatory experience.

3. It is clear that the kind or, rather, the level of human experience which concerns us here is its deepest level, the point at which it is indeed revelatory of the divine. For this the term faith-experience, rather than the term religious experience, is preferable. The latter term connotes a felt dimension of numinosity in an experience, and so restricts the scope of what is being described. But the theological insight which we are espousing here is that *all* human experience, numinous or not, is potentially revelatory of the divine. This is, obviously, an important point for groups engaged in theological reflection in the context of mission and ministry, especially within the secular society.

The Experience of Time

But as long as we say merely "experience" and "consciousness" we have not yet expressed what is distinctively human about them. God and angelic beings are conscious and experience reality. It is historicity, understood as existence in time—the capacity for experience of past, present, and future—which characterizes the human spirit-in-the-world. Temporality is a critical notion for understanding and exercising theological reflection on the basis of experience.

The human person/community experiences reality at once in a time-bound and yet time-transcending way. This is our greatness among the creatures of earth, the mark of our humanity, and the source of both the pathos and the grandeur of human existence. We experience past, present, and future in their "circumincession," that is, in their mutual indwelling, their reciprocal shaping of one another. At no moment are we ever exclusively energized or healed from just one of the three. Our experience of the present transforms our remembrance of the past. When the future is imaged in hope or fear, it is rendered already present, powerfully affecting both our attentiveness and our remembrance. If *sense,* inner and outer, is a term

which aptly designates our experience of the *now*, *memory* represents
our ability to render the *past* present, and *imagination* does the same
for the *future*. And so sense, memory, imagination are the intimately
intertwined forms of our distinctively human experience. Or, to use a
familiar threesome, our Christian experience is intrinsically constituted by *loving* sensing (presence, or, in Simone Weil's term, "paying
attention"), *faithful* remembrance, and *hopeful* anticipation.

The central instance of the experience of time is sensing or attending to what is present. This may sound like a truism but, especially in a culture which tends increasingly to blunt sense and
sensibility, it becomes more difficult for people to be energized by attentiveness to what is happening. The previously made distinction
between the empirical and the experiential needs to be recalled here;
I am talking especially about the experiential. The building up of an
authentic Christian consciousness in any individual or community is
contingent on the quality of paying attention. The spiritual tradition
of the Church has made much of this exercise, when it speaks of acts
of the presence of God, the sacrament of the present moment, and
when it employs the adage, *age quod agis* (do what you are doing).[7]

The Role of Memory

The role of *memoria* was prominent in patristic and medieval
theology, most strikingly in the trinitarian speculations of Augustine
and Aquinas. *Anamnesis* (remembrance) is of primary importance in
liturgical theology. Tridentine theology was without the modern anthropology which would have enabled it to draw creatively on the
power of memory. Definitions of the Church, for example, tended to
focus on dogmatic belief, moral code, and sacramental and disciplinary structure. But is it not just as clear that the Church is continually
being reconstituted by the remembrance of Jesus Christ, particularly,
as Metz has developed, the remembrance of his suffering (*memoria
passionis Christi*)? Would it be an exaggeration to say that were
Christians all suddenly stricken with radical amnesia, the Church
would literally cease to exist? It is essential, then, that we give to
holy remembrance its crucial role in energizing individuals and
groups engaged in theological reflection.

Sharing the Story

This understanding of the importance of memory leads us to appreciate just how the recovery and sharing of story are a constitutive element in the total process of theological reflection and how the current interest in "narrative theology" and "theology of story" is relevant to our pursuit. There are many ways of letting the past energize us, but the most characteristic and powerful would appear to be story telling. Our best example is the central Christian celebration of *anamnesis*—the Eucharist. What happens at the heart of each Sunday celebration, the "Eucharistic Prayer"? What is it that effects the "real presence" of the risen Christ in the sacrament and in the community which celebrates it? It is not a dogmatic affirmation or the promulgation of a moral or disciplinary code but simply the telling of the story, once more, in *this* time, in *this* place, for *this* assembly of disciples. "The night before he suffered, he took bread. . . ." And as it is the sharing of the remembered story which ritually reconstitutes the Church, so it is by way of sharing stories, individual and communal, that the community engaged in theological reflection in any sector of its life and ministry is energized.

What is in question here is a substantive quality of the human. Each of us in and through the stories that we remember and share is an embodied story. Story is the appropriate term for human existence as that existence is exercised dramatically in the flow of time. It is the very nature of the human to *be* narrative and, in this sense, mythic. It is from the flow of narrative that our more rational and pragmatic constructs and designs derive their vitality. Every theory or plan that has lost living contact with the story which generated it will eventually lose its power to shape life constructively.

One value of accenting the vehicle of story in the exercise of ecclesial *anamnesis* is that it highlights the *creative* character of the remembrance being exercised. Human memory is not to be reduced to a sophisticated computer programmed for the retrieval of factual data. We can faithfully remember who we were and what we did only from the standpoint of who we are and what we are doing. The advances of recent decades in the area of biblical hermeneutics have helped us here. If the present is being continually reconstituted by the past, the past in turn is—inevitably and legitimately—being re-constituted by the present. The witticism, "The past ain't what it used to be," conveys an essential human truth. A sound interpreta-tion of the faith of the primitive Church as expressed in the New Tes-tament is fully possible only to those engaged in an authentic struggle for faith today. This is an important facet of the famed "her-meneutical circle," which cogently expresses how remembrance of things past and attention to the present are interdependent.[8]

The Role of Imagination

If memory and story are the vehicles by which the past ener-gizes the present, imagination is the means which brings the power of the future to bear on present struggle. Even more than memory, imagination has until recently been a Cinderella ignored by theolo-gians. Here again theological anthropology helps us to root our un-derstanding of revealed truth in a sound grasp of human experience. Dreaming—by day as well as by night—is an essential ingredient of the healthy human being. When this power in individuals, groups, cultures, becomes blocked or distorted, trouble lies ahead. Violence, someone has said, is due to a failure of imagination.

So too the Church lives by dreaming hope just as much as by faithful remembrance. Without the power to imagine the absolute fu-ture of God and its anticipations within the historical process, the Church would literally cease to exist. The revival in our day of a healthy Christian eschatology, particularly in its social or public as-pect, is a major enrichment of the life of the Church. It was a stroke of brilliance on the part of the bishops at Vatican II to include in the Constitution on the Church a full chapter on the eschatological na-ture of the Church. The vitality of the Church in any individual, group, or era will be largely dependent on and proportionate to the grace of dreaming hope accepted by Christians.

This ability to create a genuine future through the use of dream-ing imagination is interdependent with memory's power to recreate the past authentically. This is a good place to note that not all re-membering and imagining are life-giving. Metz's distinction of "dan-gerous memories" (recollections which undermine the power of present oppression) and "nostalgic memories" (deadening enslavement to fictitious "good old days") is here pertinent and calls for a parallel distinction touching the use of imagination—between "dream" and "illusion," perhaps. It is also worth noting—and how tragically is this verified by psychopathology and sociopathology—that people deprived of a past worth remembering have no future worth aspiring to. "We ain't been written down"—the anguished reaction of some Appalachian folk when told that their birth records had disappeared—poignantly echoes the cry of the poor everywhere. To be deprived of one's story is the most ruthless form of oppression. Individuals, groups, peoples whom society through racism, sexism, classism has denied ownership of a distinctive story will inevitably be tempted to despair of themselves and to exercise violence toward others. The key factor would seem to be the link between grateful remembrance and dreaming hope.

This is where the power of the prophetic spirit is brought to bear on situations of hopelessness, as Walter Brueggemann has shown. True prophecy is a dynamic movement which combines criticism of the oppressive present, graced remembrance of the past, and the liberating exhibition of alternative futures to convert potentially destructive energies into the saving waters of life. This may be a human secret which both Christianity, with its bias toward the poor, and Marxism, with its depiction of the role of the proletariat, have in very different ways been able to discern.[9]

The Experience of Society and Culture

So far these observations on the experiential roots of theological reflection might be taken as touching only the private aspects of experience. But no human being is an island, and solitude is not the only place where experience is revelatory. There is another dimension of human existence which we express in such primordial terms as society and culture. Though the subject is vast, I need to make a few remarks about the way in which theological reflection draws on the exercise of attending, remembering and imagining as these are concerned with the larger dimensions of life.

A good entry is made through the phrase "signs of the times." Pope John XXIII and Vatican II gave it a sense notably different from its New Testament usage. It has become almost a jargon term in current pastoral theology. In the present context, it serves to situate the experiential component of theological reflection within society and culture. The concept "signs of the times" implies that God and God's call are being revealed not merely through the stirrings of individual hearts or even through the shared aspirations of groups, but also through the powerful movements and ideas of our society and culture. Ecumenism, the empowerment of the laity, and the demand of women for full equality are a few of the examples given in official Church documents. To these could be added a host of others: the peace movement, the ecological movement, the widespread attraction to prayer and solitude, etc. In each sign there is question of some societal reality through which God is calling Christians in a special way.

What we have said about the temporality of experience suggests how theological reflection might relate to signs of the times. There will be question, first of all, of paying attention, listening with a certain immediacy to what is happening in our society and culture. What happens to people—to us—as they—as we—listen to rock music, or shop in a supermarket, or watch commercials on TV? What is the message from God contained in such influences from our culture? Do such influences tend to render us more or less human, more or less committed to the Gospel?

Second, what we have said about memory and story suggests that we need to listen to signs of the times with a consciousness of history, a sensitivity to how things came to be the way they are, and an openness to being energized by a return to our roots. The women's movement affords a good example. We are all, men and women, being invited not only to an acceptance of structural and attitudinal changes regarding the relationships of women and men, but also to listen to the retelling by women of the story of those relationships.

And, third, our approach to signs of the times will be experiential to the degree to which it enlists the power of Christian imagination for dreaming of alternative ways for humans on earth. The peace movement, for example, strikes at the despairing assumption that there will always be war among sovereign nations. It was such a daring imagination which prompted Paul VI to cry out to the assembled leaders of the world in his United Nations address of October 4, 1965, "No more war! War never again!"

Ecclesial Space and Time

There is a further aspect of societal experience which relates to theological reflection. Primarily, at least, theological reflection as a new way in theology is taking place within particular communities, such as the ones described in William Newell's essay in Chapter 2 of this volume. Such communities are situated, we may say, in ecclesial space and time. In the first aspect, ecclesial space, their efforts to discern faithfully signs of the times often put them in tension with the larger institutional and hierarchical Church. In the second aspect, ecclesial time, the tension is with tradition. The question which communities commonly have to face is this: How can we be faithful to our own experience, that is, to our experiential encounter with God revealed through signs of the times, without being alienated from the larger Church which reads the signs from a different, even clashing, perspective and without being alienated from the Christian tradition? The question is too serious and complex to be dealt with adequately here.[10] But what has already been said prompts the remark that this twofold tension, when it arises, needs to be dealt with first of all at the level of experience, memory, story, dream, and not only at doctrinal, moral or juridical levels.

As regards ecclesial space, this means that when difficulties arise, the first recourse should be simply to paying attention to the partner in conflict, to contrasting experiences, to diverse stories and to the variety of dreams. Such an approach, while it will not guarantee eventual harmony, will foster it better than if the first response to conflict is at the level of concepts or regulations.

Where there is question of situating the fresh experience of communities in ecclesial *time,* it may help to follow a process which sees the *traditioning of experience* and the *experiencing of tradition* as mutually interdependent. By "the traditioning of experience" I mean the broadening and correcting of today's revelatory experience through experience of the normative context of the Christian heritage. For example, what modifications of humanizing tendencies in Christology might be made when one measures the spontaneous views of a particular Christian community against the views of similar communities in Rome or Ephesus in the first century, or Alexandria or Antioch in the fourth century? By the "experiencing of

tradition" I mean dealing with those views of ages past not only at
the level of doctrinal formulation but also at the level of the stories
which formed the basis of the doctrines. Consider how, for example,
popular devotion to Mary as Mother of God led to the Council of
Ephesus' formal declaration in this regard. A defensive repetition of
the *dogma* of Chalcedon without a care to retell the *story* of Chalcedon is not only futile but destructive.

Summary

It may be well to bring this central part of the essay to a close
with a brief summary. If theological reflection is a new way emerging
in theology it is so partly because of its immediacy to the faith experience of the ecclesial communities who practice it. Working from
the supposition that God reveals to us through the whole gamut of
individual, group, and societal experience, theological reflection proceeds in an experiential more than a deductive or even empirical
way. It pays attention to what individuals and communities are experiencing here and now. It situates this present experience within the
flow of time through remembrance and story. And it draws upon the
power of imagination to suggest alternative attitudes, behaviors, relationships, structures. In dealing with "signs of the times," it does so
in a primarily experiential way. So, too, when conflict occurs between such reading of signs and that of the larger Church of space
and time, it deals with such conflicts in a predominantly experiential
way.

III

How can the key notions (revelation, experience, etc.) just discussed become enfleshed in the actual exercise of theological reflection? In the remarks which follow there will be no effort to outline a
complete method or process. For one thing, we have been dealing
only with the experiential aspect of the total process of theological
reflection. Any proposal of method would have to take place after
the contribution of social analysis had been discussed and attention
given to the decision-making aspects of the process.[11] In addition,
much more actual experience of theological reflection by groups

struggling to do it will probably be needed before a coherent method is possible.

What I am proposing here, therefore, is something quite modest: a partial checklist, with some observations, of elements which ought to be found in any theological reflection on experience.

Prayer and Worship

First, there is the key element of prayer and worship, on which John Haughey's essay will enlarge.[12] I say key element because we are dealing with reflection on *revelatory* experience in the proper sense. God is speaking to us and we are listening and obeying. It is true that genuine worship and even prayer in a radical sense takes place whenever people act in faith and love. But we are less than perfect creatures, and finding God and God's call to us in the flow of life requires special times and places for more deliberate and conscious exercise. The degree and forms of such exercise will vary according to the character and needs of the community or group. NETWORK, for example, represents quite a different endeavor from the Church of the Saviour. The degree of pluralism within a group, the churchly or secular milieu in which it functions, and accordingly the kind of language appropriate for its domestic dialogue and apostolic witness will help to determine its forms and style of prayer and worship. One thing we may say is that the power and value of such prayer and worship is in disposing the community to listen for the voice of God in all that it experiences as well as in creating solidarity within the community itself. Ideally, such listening will take place in solitude, friendship and society (Thoreau)—that is, in prayer that is individual, interpersonal, and societal.[13] The last of these, in the form of ritual worship, has the special value of bringing the power of symbol, sensibility, memory, and imagination to bear on the life of the community, energizing it for alert listening and courageous response.

The Role of Scripture

Second, intimately linked with prayer and worship is the important role of God's word in Scripture. Listening to the signs of the times will be more efficacious if it is allowed to interact with the sacrament of the biblical word of God. When we read the Bible, alone or with others, we are involved in a return to roots, in the adventure of "dangerous memories."[14] Reading the Bible also impels us to engage in dreaming hope, particularly when we turn to the eschatological, prophetic, and apocalyptic passages in which both Old and New Testament abound.

The Experiential and the Empirical

Third, it is important that a reflecting community's attention to what is happening in society sometimes takes place in an experiential, and not only in an empirical way. This is not to minimize the importance of a solid empirical, statistical and analytical base for the social analysis which is essential to theological reflection. But the empirical needs to be complemented by the experiential. For example, a community reflecting on world hunger with a view to ministry in that area will need both an exposure, through books, articles or lectures, to the social, political, economic, and ecological dimensions of the problem, *and also* to have some personal and communal experience of what it means to be hungry. A communal fast and an "insertion experience" of living with poor people for a period of time are examples. Such a complementarity of the empirical and the experiential is important, and different individuals and groups need to be sensitive in finding the appropriate balance between the two. Some individuals and groups are tempted to be too exclusively detached, objective, analytical, while others are tempted to jump into the struggle emotionally without a calm appreciation of sound theory and the importance of practical, well-informed strategies.

Interweaving Stories

Fourth, it is important that the stories of individuals, groups, and larger society be interwoven with one another. By way of example, let us say that a few new members are being received into a community centered on providing food for the hungry and on changing economic structures to this end. The story process here would include: (1) an opportunity for new members to share what it was in their personal histories that led remotely or proximately to their joining the community; (2) a review of how this particular community came to be formed around the food and hunger question; (3) a situating of these two types of story within both the American story and the Christian story. This might include a common reflection on the story of sin and grace in America's treatment of the hungry, attention to the meals of Jesus portrayed in the Gospels, the example of saints of other eras, the development of the Church's teaching on justice, etc.

Dreaming

Fifth, there should be moments of futurizing when critical judgment is suspended so that individuals may share their dreams in freedom and so that the community may come to envision new possibilities for itself. Critical judgment has its essential place, of course. But when a group is too exclusively inclined by the temperaments of its members or by a dominant corporate spirit toward rationality and practicality, it can cut itself off from rich possibilities and from the energizing experience of dreaming together.

CONCLUSION

By way of conclusion, I wish to make a few remarks about some distinctive values to be found in theological reflection on experience. When a new way emerges in theology and proves itself by its perseverance, it is obvious that it has been called for by certain needs not being fulfilled in other ways. Those other ways have their own distinctive values, of course, and develop their own characteristic traits in pursuing those values.

From observation of the movement of theological reflection, my impression is that two of its primary constituents are the immediacy of its reference to human experience and the degree to which this experience, precisely as revelatory experience, becomes a source for the theological endeavor. It is true, of course, that every mode of theolo-

gizing depends on human experience. Where else would theology of
any kind derive its data? But not all ways in theology resonate equally with the personal experience which is mediated through sense and
sensibility, memory and story, and dreaming imagination. More specifically, dogmatic theology as exercised in seminaries and other ad-
juncts of the official Church, and academic theology as practiced in
universities, would, often at least, be positively hindered in achieving
their specific goals were they to feature such an experiential approach. The primary *situation* of theological reflection as an historical phenomenon is neither the seminary nor the university but the
basic Christian community. It is only to be expected that it will have
very different characteristics from the theologizing which takes place
in these two other locations. For it seeks to realize specific values
which are different.[15]

A first value which this resonance with experience gives theological reflection is the energizing of the theologizing community itself for its communal response to the signs of the times. Less focused
than the other two ways—seminary and university theology—on the
achievement of theological statement as a content, this way generates
a distinctive word whose primary value is not orthodoxy or new insight but incentive to authentic action—*orthopraxis.*

This first value leads to a second one. A way in theology which
is experiential in the manner described is ordered to, or at least results in, the *transformation* of the reflecting community and its members. Once again it is the immediacy of this orientation which
distinguishes this way from the other two. This is not to say that holiness of life, authentic discipleship, is irrelevant to the quality of exercise of those forms. But, intent on other immediate values, their
methodologies allow for a certain bracketing of concern for holiness
and discipleship. The way in theology which we name theological reflection knows no such bracketing. Within the sharing of personal
faith-experience which helps to constitute it, it lives continuously
with the need for continuing and total conversion to Christ.

And, third, this new way in theology differs from the other two
in the immediacy of its orientation to Christian *solidarity.* When the
term *theological reflection* is taken abstractly, it admits of exercise by
individuals in isolation. But as an historical phenomenon, theological

reflection is primarily the work of communities and groups. And its highly experiential character gives it the power to foster, with greater immediacy than other ways, that solidarity in Christian mission and ministry which is the distinctive sign of discipleship (Jn 13:35; 17:23).

APPENDIX

Sample of a Group Exercise

Let us say that a parish group or religious community is devoting a day or weekend to the issue of world hunger. The following would be the broad lines of one or two exercises, toward the beginning of the program.

1. Reading of one of the Gospel passages on the multiplication of the loaves.

2. In solitary prayer and reflection, each one asks: What particular experience(s) of sharing food and drink do I recall with most gratitude? With most pain or regret?

3. In small groups people share the fruit of this reminiscence, and, without "reporting from the groups," the resonances of such sharing are made known in the entire assembly.

Later in the program, after some input of social analysis and advertence to the social teachings of the Church, an exercise such as the following might be had.

1. Reading of a pertinent Scripture passage.

2. Each one in solitude addresses the question: "What would my life be like in the matter of food and drink if I were fully responsive to the Lord's call as I now experience it?"

3. In small groups, people share what has occurred in solitude.

4. In the same small groups, the same question is asked from the viewpoint of "we" (the entire parish or religious community).

5. The results are shared by way of report with the entire assembly, which then deals with the question: What are some immediate, concrete steps we wish to take toward the realization of our hopes?

NOTES

1. Being both partial and provisional in dealing with the relationship of experience and theological reflection, the present essay cannot offer an integral and firm view of what theological reflection is and how it differs, especially with regard to experience, from theology in general and from more familiar forms of theology. But readers may be helped in grasping what follows if I say from the outset that the term "theological reflection" for me is an instance of synecdoche—that is, the use of a term designating a part of a whole for the whole itself. The whole in question is a new *way* of theologizing, significantly different from other ways such as those called dogmatic (or magisterial) theology, academic theology as practiced in universities, etc. The distinctiveness of this new way can be described from several standpoints. First, its *locus* or situation is not the seminary, the university campus, the Roman curia, but some kind of basic Christian community. Second, its primary *agent* is not the professionally trained theologian, research scholar, or someone juridically entrusted with a canonical mission to theologize in immediate service to the hierarchical Church. Rather it is the basic community, its members theologizing together in virtue of the baptismal and confirmational imperative to render an account to themselves and others of their faith. Third, its *goal* is pastoral action or praxis of the community within the Church as it touches the world. Fourth, its *method,* appropriate to the locus, agent and goal, may be broadly described as a *common Christian reflection on revelatory experience (including especially the "signs of the times") interpreted with the help of social analysis and on the basis of Scripture and tradition, with a view to Christian action in the world.* One model expressing this type of method is that developed by the Center of Concern for the "Convergence" meeting of the major superiors of men and women religious in Cleveland in 1977. The model is designated as "the pastoral circle" or "the circle of praxis." It is constituted by a circular movement from *experience to social analysis to theological reflection* (understood as one component of the total process) *to pastoral planning.* See the description of the model, with extensive development of the social analysis component, in Joe Holland and Peter Henriot, *Social Analysis: Linking Faith and Justice* (Washington, D.C.: Center of Concern, 1980).

2. My chief debt in this regard is to the skilled consultants of Management Design, Inc. (MDI), a Cincinnati-based firm which has created out of a largely Jungian base several process models which admirably integrate the diverse energies to be found within each person and within groups and organizations. I owe much also to Sister Mary Magdala Thompson, R.S.M. and Dr. W. Harold Grant with whom I have worked for several years in Jungian

programs aimed at integral development. Our retreat/workshop will appear in a paperback entitled *From Image to Likeness: A Jungian Path in the Gospel Journey* (Ramsey, N.J.: Paulist Press, 1983).

3. Here are some of the writings on which I have drawn for the present essay or which may be helpful to readers:

Braxton, Edward K. *The Wisdom Community.* New York: Paulist, 1980.

Brueggemann, Walter. *The Prophetic Imagination.* Philadelphia: Fortress, 1978.

Carr, Anne. "Theology and Experience in the Thought of Karl Rahner." *The Journal of Religion* 53 (1973): 359–376.

Driver, Tom F. *Patterns of Grace: Human Experience as Word of God.* San Francisco: Harper & Row, 1977.

Dulles, Avery, S.J. *Revelation Theology: A History.* New York: Herder & Herder, 1969.

Lamb, Matthew. "Dogma, Experience and Political Theology." *Concilium* 113 (1979): 79–90.

Metz, Johannes. "The Future in the Memory of Suffering." J. B. Metz (ed.). *New Questions on God. Concilium* 76. New York: Herder & Herder, 1972.

Metz, Johannes. "A Short Apology of Narrative." J. B. Metz and J. P. Jossua (eds.). *The Crisis of Religious Language. Concilium* 25. New York: Herder & Herder, 1973, 84–98.

Moran, Gabriel. *Theology of Revelation.* New York: Herder & Herder, 1966.

Neumann, Karl. *Der Praxisbezug der Theologie Bei Karl Rahner.* (Freiburger Theologische Studien 118). Freiburg: Herder, 1980.

Niebuhr, H. Richard. *The Meaning of Revelation.* New York: Macmillan, 1941.

Niebuhr, Richard R. *Experiential Religion.* New York: Harper & Row, 1972.

Rahner, Karl. *Foundations of Christian Faith.* New York: The Seabury Press, 1978.

Schillebeeckx, Edward. *Christ: The Experience of Jesus as Lord.* New York: Seabury, 1980.

Schillebeeckx, Edward and van Iersel, B. (eds.). *Revelation and Experience. Concilium* 113. New York: Seabury, 1979.

Smith, John E. *Experience and God.* New York: Oxford University Press, 1968.

TeSelle, Sallie McFague. *Speaking in Parables: A Study in Metaphor and Theology.* Philadelphia: Fortress, 1975.

Tracy, David. *Blessed Rage for Order: The New Pluralism in Theology.* New York: Seabury, 1975.

Tracy, David. *The Analogical Imagination: Christian Theology and the Culture of Pluralism.* New York: Crossroad, 1981.

4. C. P. Snow, *The Two Cultures: And A Second Look* (2nd ed.) (Cambridge: University Press, 1964).

5. For a fuller discussion of contemporary pastoral theology in ministerial formation and its implications for theological reflection, see Chapter 4 by Robert Kinast. For more on theological reflection in Latin American basic Christian communities, see Chapter 3 by Alfred Hennelly, S.J.

6. See E. Mersch, *The Theology of the Mystical Body,* trans. Cyril Vollert (St. Louis: Herder, 1951). Teilhard's *The Divine Milieu* (New York: Harper & Row, 1960) and *The Phenomenon of Man* (New York: Harper & Row, 1959) are the best known illustrations of his use of the category of consciousness. I am grateful to Monsignor Joseph Gremillion for calling my attention to Pope John Paul II's treatment of the Church's consciousness in his first encyclical, *Redemptor Hominis* (March 4, 1979). See nn. 3, 4, 7, 11, 14, 18, 21.

7. A striking treatment is that of Simone Weil in her essay, "Reflections on the Right Use of School Studies with a View to the Love of God," in *The Simone Weil Reader,* ed. G. Panichas (New York: McKay, 1977), pp. 44–52.

8. See Sandra M. Schneiders, "Faith, Hermeneutics, and the Literal Sense of Scripture," *Theological Studies* 39 (1978), 718–736.

9. One aspect of the bias toward the poor, the claim of a hermeneutic privilege for the poor, is examined by Monika Hellwig in Chapter 6.

10. Various facets of this question are dealt with in the essays by Jouette Bassler, Avery Dulles, and James Hug.

11. For more on social analysis, see the booklet by Joe Holland and Peter Henriot entitled *Social Analysis: Linking Faith and Justice* (mentioned at the end of note 1 above) and Joe Holland's essay in this volume, "Linking Social Analysis and Theological Reflection." For more on the decision-making aspects of the process, see the following essays by Avery Dulles, Larry Rasmussen, and James Hug.

12. See Chapter 5, "The Role of Prayer in Action/Reflection Groups." There is also a discussion of the place of prayer in James Hug's essay in Chapter 13.

13. I have taken this triadic approach to prayer in "Toward Wholeness in Prayer," in William R. Callahan and Francine Cardman (eds.), *The Wind*

Is Rising: Prayer Ways for Active People (Quixote Center, Hyattsville, Md., 1978), pp. 18–20.

14. The chapters by Jouette Bassler and Avery Dulles are examples of embarking on this adventure. See Chapters 9 and 10.

15. See Robert Kinast's fuller discussion of these issues in Chapter 4.

2
The Reflection Groups

William L. Newell

Beginning from the insights and intuitions described in the previous chapter about the birth of a new way of theologizing, members of the Woodstock Theological Center taskforce set out to interview a variety of groups engaged in work for social justice. The intent was to learn from the groups about their forms of reflection. These groups, then, provided the experiential base stimulating and guiding the theological reflection of the taskforce. Having just reflected on the importance of experience and narrative, it seems appropriate here to present a brief description of the groups. This chapter introduces them.

Most of the groups interviewed are centered in or around Washington, D.C. Limited resources prevented any attempt at developing a representative national sample. Nonetheless, the Washington area provides an interesting variety of groups upon which to draw. Many of those described here differ in purpose and task, in age and denominational affiliation, in style of prayer and form of community life. Some speak expressly of doing theological reflection; some do not use the term at all. All of the groups, however, do some form of reflection and planning together. It is this that offers the starting point or stimulus for the essays that follow.

NETWORK

The first group is called NETWORK. It is a registered Catholic social justice lobby—the only Catholic congressional lobby to address itself to the broad range of social issues as they affect the powerless and poor. Its staff, composed largely of women, researches issues in national legislation, publishes a bi-monthly newsletter oriented to education and action, issues special action alerts to its membership when developments in Congress warrant, offers workshops around the country, and lobbies on Capitol Hill.

The NETWORK membership, with organizations in forty states and two hundred and forty-five congressional districts, selects the issues for attention by the national staff. There are several criteria to guide the selection: the issues should deal with the structures which cause injustice; they must be issues which will empower people to participate in the decisions affecting their lives; they must be issues related to the world vision preferred by NETWORK—a humanizing faith vision rooted in Gospel tradition. Guided by these criteria, NETWORK has supported a wide range of social legislation, including bills on arms limitation, the right to food, full employment, and the Equal Rights Amendment.

When NETWORK was founded in 1971, the staff began by reflecting on Catholic Church documents relating to social justice. This initial theological reflection led to analysis, which led to more analysis. It seemed never to end, nor did it help them to integrate their life-styles with the vision they derived from the documents. Gradually they began searching for forms of personal and communal reflection that could aid in creating a synthesis of faith vision, work, and overall lifestyle.

Sensing that important aspects of their experience would complement the Church documents, the staff shifted the starting point and focus of their reflection. The method they evolved is simple. First, they reflect privately on a common topic—for example, "my preferred world." When the staff gathers, they share their personal visions and experiences and respond to any questions of clarification. Debate or evaluation of the personal views is not allowed; mutual understanding is the first step. They then look for similarities and differences in what has been shared, commenting on what they liked in each other's reflections and suggesting what they would like to include in any consensus statement they might develop. They probe for assumptions, consequences, and questions implied in the individual contributions.

As a shared vision emerges, they explore together its demands for their own organization as well as for social legislation. Finally, they try to express the consensus symbolically—in word and ritual.

Meeting eight times a year for this type of prayerful reflection, the NETWORK staff has been able to formulate their experience of political ministry, articulate a corporate vision, and draw from it the values that guide their working style, their evaluation of legislation, their lobbying efforts, and their personal life-styles. Four central values serve as principles for their political ministry and spirituality: participation, stewardship, integration, and mutuality.[1] It is an important characteristic of the NETWORK spirituality that the staff consciously strive to model in their own structures and processes the values which they promote in the realm of social legislation.

On occasion, professional theologians have contributed articles on political theology to NETWORK publications.[2] Some have been invited to review NETWORK's processes and reflections.[3] The principal participants in NETWORK's theological reflection, however, continue to be the staff members drawing upon their own experience and their knowledge of the Christian Scriptures and theological traditions.

EASTERN MENNONITE COLLEGE
WASHINGTON STUDY-SERVICE YEAR

Each year a small group of Mennonite college students gathers in Washington, D.C. for a work-study internship. The students, drawn principally from Eastern Mennonite College of Harrisonburg, Virginia, are able to pursue academic studies at any one of six colleges and universities in the area while they engage in community-service internships in local agencies. During their stay in Washington, they live together in community.

The urban, secular environment provides a strong contrast to the students' previous college and hometown settings. Traditionally Mennonites have concentrated their communities in rural areas of the United States. The first immersion in urban life causes predictable tensions for the students. It creates a type of culture shock in which significant growth and personal integration become possible— if not essential. The Eastern Mennonite College Washington Study-Service Year attempts to use this context to develop and deepen a sense of Mennonite Christian servanthood for an institutionalized society.

The current program directors, Nelson Good and Ann Tarbell, look to no specific, pre-conceived growth goals. They try to facilitate any development that occurs. They encourage journaling, personal reflection, and group discussion of personal experiences and struggles. In addition, they provide ample opportunities for counseling.

Perhaps the most important educational activity of the program is the weekly Core Seminar. It is an interdisciplinary forum geared to integrate the community, academic, and professional/ministerial dimensions of the students' Washington experience.[4] The students reflect together on their experiences, learning to draw out the theological, sociological, and spiritual issues buried in them. They come to learn that service and social change are not just individual processes but are mediated through institutions. They search for ways to invest institutions with the spirit and forms of Christian servanthood so that the individuals touched by these institutions may experience them as bearers of love. This type of reflection carried on in a community setting helps each of the individuals to develop the analytic skills necessary for discerning interpretation of their experience.

This reflection on internship or practicum or work experience is guided by the program's "Participant/Observer Form." This form is the basis for a number of three-page "monographs" which each student is required to write during the year. Each "monograph" consists of a description and analysis of one or two events in the student's work that bring light to bear on one of the issues under consideration in the Core Seminar—issues such as institutionalization, leadership, secularization, and ministerial methodologies. The analysis of the experience is focused by questions about (1) the external constraints that life and society place on the people being served, (2) the choices facing those people and their ability to choose in the given context, and (3) the feelings of the student while involved in the experience.

The unique aspect of the Eastern Mennonite College program, in my view, is its use of reflection on the theological meaning of experience as a tool for growth as a person, growth in God. The principal emphasis is on *how* one experiences what he or she experiences, not on *what* was experienced. The year is an action/reflection year aimed at deeper appropriation of the Mennonite values of non-violence, simplicity, community, and separation of Church and state. It contributes to building a more just world by helping to develop more just and able Christian servants.

COMMUNITY CREATIVITY INCORPORATED

Community Creativity Incorporated (CCI) is "a consultative organization motivated by Judaeo-Christian principles to bring about life-giving relationships between persons and structures."[5] Its director, Sr. Barbara Valukas, S.S.N.D., points out that structures, such as parishes, can dominate and crush people or they can foster life-giving relationships—that is, structures can be sin-filled or grace-filled. The goal of CCI is to foster life-giving structures so that the men and women in them can have the Christian experience of their worth and meaning as people and parish.

An insight into CCI is available in the variety of images used to describe its role as an "agent of social change." In a memorandum dated March 25, 1981, FCC uses these phrases to describe itself: "catalyst," causing something to happen; "fertilizer," stimulating and supporting growth; "Cana," where Mary was aware of what was happening and intervened; "swimming instructor," supporting others in their learning process; "mirror," reflecting back to groups and persons rather exact pictures of themselves; and, perhaps most important of all, "enabler," not effecting change for groups or individuals, but providing them with the tools to see the changes necessary and decide for themselves both whether they want them and how they propose to bring them about.[6]

These images throw into higher relief the rest of CCI's goals: to aid in freeing people to take responsibility for creating their own lives and building the structures in which they can flourish. Structures can and do change. CCI sees it as pivotal that the people know there are ways to change structures, and that they already have or can find the way to change them for the better. Attention is focused on power relationships and instances of oppression—the structures that need to be changed if the ecclesial vision of Vatican Council II is to be realized in the parish life of the U.S. Catholic Church.

When the CCI staff members go out into the parishes where they are employed, they begin to interview people, to foster the emergence of their "stories." As the stories unfold, the theological issues embedded in them emerge. This is usually a very affirming experience. The people realize they have something to say; something is going on in their lives worth listening to, something worth hearing and repeating.

The staff of CCI thus practices the demanding asceticism of careful listening. They record the stories as they are told and then return them in written form to the people. Seeing their own stories and insights in print fosters in the people a greater sense of pride and self-respect. Grassroots leaders emerge; communication and cooperation are fostered among ordinary parishioners as they begin a new style of relating to one another and to the structures in which they live.

Parish staffs are also generally in need of this ministry of supportive listening. Active staffs rarely take time to reflect on their lives as staffs, as ministers, as persons.

Once both parishioners and parish staff have been enabled to tell and appreciate their own stories, they are brought together to talk about what is happening in their lives. Priests and laity share their faith in ways they have rarely if ever done before. In this process, the goods and evils in the parish life are named. Some problems have arisen consistently: for example, the lack of theological articulation of the local church in the United States which leads to confusion about just what it means to be a Christian here, the lack of unifying vision in collaboration, lack of planning and evaluation, the distance of liturgy and theological formulation from the lived faith of priest and laity, the lack of participation on the part of parishioners in parish planning and decision-making, and the lack of a sense of close and caring community in large impersonal parishes.

There are many levels of woundedness revealed in the enablement process: sexism, paternalism, racism, fear of collaboration with the laity on the part of the priests, and the fact that the pastors are often arbitrarily changed without any dialogue with the parishioners involved. Further, the ordained ministers are themselves oppressed by their seminary training and lack of on-going education, by clericalism, sexism, racism, non-supportive rectory life-styles and a lack of a deep personal spirituality.[7]

Realizing the theological nature of many of these issues, CCI appointed Sr. Anne Marie Gardiner, S.S.N.D. to direct a project on theological reflection. She brought together a small group of professional theologians to ponder the recorded stories and reports from the parish communities that CCI serves. She offered the theologians some sample questions to focus their reflection and then asked them to articulate the theological issues they found embedded in the testimony of the parishioners. This is theology from the grassroots upward, not from the top (hierarchy) down. The project was designed to help narrow the distance between professional theologians and the people of the Church as well as to give clearer theological analysis of the data that had been gathered. Her questions: "What is the Church as experienced in local parishes? What kind of God do parishioners imagine? believe in? speak of? What is the source of ministry in the parish? What in the life of the parish nurtures the spirituality of its members, staff persons, and clergy? How is sin experienced? What hinders the full life of God in the lives of staff, parishioners and clergy? What do the parishes see as their 'mission,' their reason for existence? What are the characteristics of the laity's self-understanding?"[8]

In reflecting on the materials, the theologians have found a great gap between theological theory and the theology embedded in the lives of the people, between the environment in which theoretical theology is worked out and the environment in which that theory is to be lived in the parishes of the United States by priests and their staffs and the people whom they serve.

In actual fact, this project is not the only type of theological reflection undertaken by CCI in its ministry of consultation. Several types can be distinguished. The first is faith-sharing with parishioners or parish staffs. Here they reflect with the people on certain passages of Scripture or on the significance of the liturgical seasons, looking for the meaning of the people's experiences in the light of their own personal faith journey and the faith journey of the people of God. The second is the type of simple discernment method the CCI staff uses for its own decision-making. They gather the information they need and weigh the pros and cons reflectively. They share what comes to them in prayer and reflection and then move toward consensus.

The third type of theological reflection takes place in their interviewing processes as they listen to the theology (implicit in personal stories) that is actually influencing the lives of the people in the parishes. The fourth type is that carried on by the professional theologians engaged in clarifying and stating in more systematic ways the lived theology of this part of the U.S. church.

The term "theological reflection" is, then, applied to several elements of the CCI ministry: reflective prayer together, personal narratives, prayerful decision-making, and reflection upon these experiences by professional theologians. The hope of CCI is that theological reflection undertaken in these ways will free and enable the people they serve to work for the changes necessary to implement their own preferred Church and world.

FRIENDS COMMITTEE ON NATIONAL LEGISLATION

The Friends Committee on National Legislation (FCNL) is a Quaker lobbying group. It was founded in 1943 at Quaker Hill, Richmond Hill, Indiana, at a conference of Friends who sought to oppose universal conscription during the Second World War and to express concern over the pervasive influence of military policy on life in the United States. Its major priorities today have expanded to include disarmament, human rights, the United Nations, world economic development, native Americans, world hunger, and domestic employment.

The Executive Secretary of the FCNL is Edward F. Snyder. He and most of the staff of eighteen belong to Friends' meetings in the United States. The traditional Quaker ideals of love, justice, community, and social concern guide their reflection and action. They see themselves as Christian seekers after truth working to bring about a world in which all people are recognized to be members of one family loved by God and endowed with dignity and personal worth.

FCNL, like Quaker groups in general, makes its major decisions on the basis of consensus rather than majority vote or political compromise. The preparation for the decision-making process includes participation in worship services (which provide opportunities for participants to "wait on the Spirit" for guidance on the issues before them), reading of Scripture and religiously-oriented publications, and careful listening to the insights and proposals of staff colleagues, committee members, and others sharing their values.

The goals of the process are: an appropriate mindset with which to work out solutions to specific problems, insights into decisions to be made, creative ideas, and judgment on the best course of action. The process, which takes place in FCNL meetings, is chaired by a clerk whose basic task is to listen to the discussion to discern when and where a sense of consensus begins to emerge.

The emphasis upon consensus forces the group to listen to dissenters. This is important since Quakers recognize that individuals can have the light of revelation in any particular situation. Those holding a majority position on any issue, therefore, are under a heavy obligation to listen to those with differing views. Those holding minority views have the responsibility to speak out on their perspectives, insights, and convictions. Then the search for a more enlightened consensus can go on. If that consensus still proves elusive, those who disagree with the main direction of the group—if they are not clear enough on the source of their disagreement or do not want to prolong the process—can "step aside" and let the group move ahead. In general, this method is quite time consuming; as a result, it tends to maintain the status quo.

Once the FCNL arrives at clarity on an issue, the lobbyists move into action. Each lobbyist can effectively address only one or two major legislative issues at a time while perhaps keeping tabs on one or two more issues with the assistance of an intern. A realistic assessment of limits has been one of the important lessons of their experience through the years.

"Theological reflection" is not a term used by the FCNL. Prayerful reflection undoubtedly takes place, however. It occurs in worship sessions and in the faith-centered discussions of issues that are an integral part of staff and committee meetings.

NEW JERUSALEM COMMUNITY

The New Jerusalem Community of Cincinnati, Ohio is a Roman Catholic community composed primarily of laity. The members of the community live in a section of Cincinnati which had been decaying until their two hundred members moved in and began renovating their own residences and raising consciousness about such issues as housing, personal responsibility to the poor, political responsibility, and the ability to change situations. Some of the community live a "common life" where a form of Christian socialism is practiced. Throughout the community, there is support for simplifying life-style and education to the dangers of consumerism and liberal capitalism. The community atmosphere does not support upward mobility as that is generally understood and valued in the United States.

The spirit of the community is charismatic; its prayer life is centered on a Wednesday night Eucharistic liturgy which is carefully prepared and enthusiastically celebrated. There is, however, also a heavy emphasis on the place of prayerful solitude and quiet contemplation in the life of each individual. The members of the community are encouraged to take advantage of personal spiritual direction and private times of prayerful retreat.

Scripture serves as a guide for the community's life in a variety of ways. There is individual prayerful reading and pondering of the biblical texts; there are homilies on liturgical texts; and there are weekly meetings of small "circles" of four to twelve members to share faith in response to scriptural texts. The community is concerned to avoid the fundamentalistic use of Scripture found in many charismatic communities in the United States by "incorporating it with more generalized wisdom, while still allowing it a place of authority and preeminence."[9]

The members of the New Jerusalem Community bring their values of openness to the Holy Spirit, vulnerability to one another, accountability, receptiveness, affirmation and sensitivity to one another to a variety of issues. They wish to explore the unique needs of children and their own vocation of Christian parenthood; they wish to become more aware of the ways the poor and weak are oppressed and to develop a compassion for the disenfranchised which manifests itself in action for social justice in the light of the Gospel; they wish to develop a variety of full-time and part-time ministries within the community.[10]

This community is very conscious of being part of the Roman Catholic communion. The pastor and administrator of the community meets regularly with the archbishop of Cincinnati to talk about the community and search for its place in the ministry and planning of the archdiocese as a whole.

Theological reflection takes a number of different forms within the New Jerusalem Community. When the need arises for a specialized analysis of a theological issue, a small group of people trained in different disciplines undertakes the task. This group includes the current coordinator of the community, a Franciscan priest named Richard Rohr, who is the chief teacher of the community and a strong leader. Another form of theological reflection occurs when the members of the small faith-sharing "circles" reflect together on the meaning of their lives in the light of the Scriptures. When a problem or proposal requiring the response of the whole community arises, another, related form of theological reflection is employed. Each member is asked to pray over the issue carefully, weighing the pros and cons. They reflect upon what the Scriptures and the tradition of the Church say on the issue, upon the ways their community has responded to similar issues in the past, and upon what the issue means for the future life of their community. When they gather in a general meeting, they use the general principles of the Management Design Institute (MDI) of Cincinnati to gather the fruits of their individual reflection and discernment. These principles include movement through what is known as the "power cycle" of elements in decision-making: action—evaluation—recommendation—decision.

Underlying their approach to theological reflection and decision-making is the tradition of Christian discernment associated with Ignatian or Jesuit spirituality. They draw upon the literature of that tradition as well as upon the resources and programs offered by the men and women of the Jesuit Renewal Center at Milford, Ohio.

SOJOURNERS COMMUNITY

The Sojourners Community was born at a seminary in Chicago during the Vietnam era. Some of the students wanted to address the question of peace and found little support for their interest among the seminary faculty. They began to meet together to reflect on the issue as a theological concern to be faced by the Church. This reflection led them to the formation of a community to pursue the Christian ideal of peace—a community in which they could live, pray, and support each other. Since 1975 this community has been located in Washington, D.C.

The Sojourners Community presently consists of about forty people—single people, married couples and families with children. Their ages range generally from the mid-twenties to the mid-fifties. It is an ecumenical community, drawing members from about twenty different denominations.

The Sojourners have undertaken a variety of different ministries. Their publication, *SOJOURNERS* magazine, keeps their well-known peace ministry visible to many throughout the country. They have also opened a child development center. Their housing ministry is an attempt to organize tenants in their neighborhood, people of very modest economic means, to empower them to claim their rights as tenants and to take greater control over their own lives. The Sojourners community attempts to live a simple life-style and show a willingness to be "downwardly mobile" in a culture steeped in consumerism. They realize that they must live the vision they hold out to others for it to be credible. They view hospitality as an important ministry as well, receiving many guests with whom they discuss the political and theological issues affecting their work. Finally, in addition to these local and more long-term involvements, the members of the community are increasingly involved in a fairly extensive ministry of lecturing in seminaries, churches, universities, and other communities throughout the United States.

The Sojourners Community hopes that its attempts at living out the Gospel values of peace, simplicity, and community will contribute to systemic change within society in general and the churches in particular. The neighborhood involvements help the community to work out its larger social vision in a realistic way. In their own words, "We want to see our neighborhood be a place where the poor and not-so-poor can each have their place with decent housing and jobs that allow for a dignified existence, rather than the poor being totally at the mercy of people with the wealth in matters of housing, as well as practically every area of their lives. This is simply an example, but is truly at the heart of our hopes and dreams."[11]

Through the years since its founding, Sojourners' self-understanding has grown and changed. In its early history, it was alienated from the mainstream churches and highly critical of their slowness in responding to issues of peace and justice. The members of the Sojourners Community saw it as a remnant—one of the few faithful witnesses to the radical message of Jesus. In recent years its experience has taught it that it is better understood as part of a "broken and often sinful and faithless Church." That experience has called forth deeper commitment of the members to each other and to the Church in the "radical Gospel that (Jesus Christ) preached (as) the basis and very reason of our life together. And that is what we understand Church to be."[12]

There is also present in the community a growing realization of the need for prayer—both individual and communal. No formal regimen of prayer is prescribed, but each member is encouraged to pray and reflect on the Scriptures. A wide range of styles and depth of personal prayer have resulted. Increasingly, the community members are turning to liturgical forms of prayer, especially the Eucharist, to express and celebrate their shared concern for particular issues of social justice.

The Sojourners Community has seen a need for further theological preparation of its members as well. Individuals are encouraged to engage in private theological study, and group projects in theological education are undertaken periodically. In one of these projects, for instance, the whole community studied John Howard Yoder's book *The Politics of Jesus*.[13] They worked through it slowly and methodically, reflecting on it privately and in small groups, evaluating themselves and their community life in the process.

The Sojourners have evolved a process of group reflection for considering the quality of their life together, the integrity of their ministries, and any community issue or problem that might arise. When a proposal or issue arises in a small group, it is presented to the leaders of the whole community. They consider it and may reshape it. They then call a general meeting of the community for preliminary discussion and sharing of information on the issue. This meeting is not intended to bring the issue to a resolution. After the meeting there is time for rest and personal reflection. That is followed by small group discussions. Another period of rest and private reflection then precedes a second general meeting. At that meeting the results of the previous reflection times are shared and the community relies on the Spirit to draw out a consensus on the issue.

While this whole process could be called "theological reflection," the community has noticed that it rarely uses theological language when it is considering past events or evaluating past ministries. Explicitly theological reflection comes strongly to the fore when the members turn their attention to describing the values and vision of the world they look forward to in hope.

THE CHURCH OF THE SAVIOUR

The Church of the Saviour is an ecumenical church in Washington, D.C. whose one hundred and thirty members include Methodists, Presbyterians, Episcopalians, members of the United Church of Christ, Baptists, Mennonites, and Roman Catholics. They range in age from twenty to seventy-five. Ninety percent are white and ten percent are black; just over half are women. The members range in education from those with high school diplomas to those with doctoral degrees. Most live separately, though some of the younger members live together in "loosely structured households."

The church was founded in Washington, D.C. after the Second World War by a former Southern Baptist military chaplain, Gordon Cosby. His war experience forced upon him the pressing question of how to be a pastor; this involved a sharpening of his vision of church. He envisioned a church which would be multi-racial, ecumenical, a church in which ministry would be shared by all because all shared in priesthood.

As the community grew through the years, a committee of eight members was appointed to study the question of church structures. They wanted the reflection process to be rooted in prayer, so they created a lectionary of Scripture readings to guide the year's discussions. An outside consultant was brought in to facilitate the process. He recommended a silent retreat to bring clarity to the group. After an eight month process, a consensus was finally achieved. Six sister communities, called Faith Communities, were created out of the membership. The results of this discernment/reflection process were called the New Land Statement (1976). In essence, it states that the church's faith vision makes demands on the individuals and the group alike: demands for the creation and maintenance of the forms, structures and disciplines necessary for them to remain church. Each faith community, and the church in general, has roles to be filled and gifts to be evoked and used.

The Church of the Saviour emphasizes four important elements: the Journey Inward, the Journey Outward, accountability to one another, and the sharing of personal stories.

Personal prayer and the study of Scripture and theology form the kernel of the interior life of the members. Conrad Hoover, who serves as the Retreat Minister for the church, describes the Journey Inward as one's personal spiritual growth story. Each member of the church is committed to an hour of daily prayer over the Scriptures in the presence of the transcendent God. This prayerful pondering of the Scriptures is to be accompanied by an equally prayerful reflection on what is happening in one's daily life. This reflection is brought to sharper focus by the use of a personal journal. The journal becomes the basis for the personal faith-sharing which takes place in the smaller communities. This accountability to one another for the inner journey has the benefit of promoting the sharing of personal experiences of God (considered contemporary renderings of the good news) and has the effect of building the community.

The Journey Outward includes a commitment to be part of a small mission group sharing a corporate ministry based in the area of Washington, D.C. What happens in the performance of ministry is also shared in the small groups. Ministries performed in the church's Journey Outward include FLOC (For Love of Children), a ministry in which members give aid to abandoned and abused children; Jubilee Housing, in which members purchase and renovate deteriorated housing for the poor and see that such housing is well-managed after it is refurbished; Dayspring, a retreat center outside of Washington; World Peacemakers, the church's ministry for peace; Other Americans, the church's companionship with minority peoples; and Co-sign, a ministry for refugees.

All these ministries have been initiated and performed by members of the community who feel they have a "call" to that work and have attracted others to join them. The Family Place, another of the ministries, is a clear example of this evocation of ministries and their recognition by the church membership. Dr. Ann Barnet felt called to provide post-natal care for unwed mothers. At Potter's House, a bookstore and coffee shop run by the church which also serves as a place of worship, she issued a call for people to join her. Some in the community felt that it was a genuine call; guidelines for the mission were established and gifts were given by members to support the work.

A mission group of this kind will continue as long as people feel called to work in it, as long as that "call" is recognized to be "good news" and is true to the original vision born out of prayer and reflection on Scripture, and as long as there is work to be done there. If it is discerned, however, that the mission has been accomplished or is no longer needed, or that persons in the community are no longer called to it, or that the necessary resources are no longer available, the particular mission group is disbanded. This discernment may be carried on by the group itself, by a committee of the elders of the church, or by the whole community.

Besides the commitment to personal prayer and study (the Journey Inward) and to ministry emanating from one's faith community (the Journey Outward), there are various accountabilities in the Church of the Saviour. These include proportionate giving beginning with a tithe, worship, and the commitment to join another similar community if one moves from the Washington, D.C. area. These accountabilities are known as "disciplines" in the church.

The final element of the four elements emphasized by the church has already been mentioned in passing: each member is required to tell the story of his or her personal faith journey. This forms part of the initiation into the church. The stories are focused around a few simple questions: What has gone on in my life to bring me to this place? What is going on now? How is God calling? What is going on in the world? What does God say about it? What does God want me to do?

These questions provide the basis as well for reflection by the church as a whole or by the six faith communities that comprise it. One striking example of this type of reflection took place during the Vietnam War. Two young members wanted to register as conscientious objectors. They asked the church what stance it took on peace. The church reflected on this for seven or eight months. Discussions became very lively, even heated. Often the discussions would be halted for a fifteen or twenty minute period of silence and prayer. Finally the church reached a general consensus: it took a firm stand against the war. Some of the members who were employees of the Pentagon and the CIA were too uncomfortable with this stand to remain in the community.

Reflection of a religious or theological nature, therefore, takes several different forms in the daily life of the Church of the Saviour. There are the personal daily disciplines of prayer, Scripture reading, and journaling. Each year there are the discipline of recommitment (a review of each member's personal commitment to the life of the community) and the time of retreat. There are group prayer and reflection when areas of prospective ministry are to be discerned. There is a discernment process carried on in the council of elders for many community business issues. There is prayerful discernment by the full membership on issues vital to all such as peace, war, disarmament, church structures and worship.

These forms of theological reflection are different from what might be called "academic" or "scientific" theology. They are a practical theologizing more in the tradition of the Ignatian style of discernment, a form of pastoral reflection aimed at discovering the presence and activity of God in the lives of individuals and of the community.

JULIE COMMUNITY CENTER

The Julie Community Center is a non-profit center founded in 1975 in Baltimore, Maryland to care for the fundamental spiritual and material needs of the people of southeast Baltimore. It serves people of all economic and religious backgrounds, but its services are designed especially to meet the needs of low income persons, those most neglected by other organizations and least able to utilize existing programs.

The purposes of the Julie Community Center include: (1) to bring the message of the Gospel into direct relationship with the lives and shared problems of the people with whom they work; (2) to affirm each person's dignity and worth; (3) to strengthen community bonds; (4) to develop a group consciousness transcending ethnic and social divisions regarding systemic injustices which deprive low income groups and those supported by some form of public assistance of their basic human rights; (5) to develop group action determined by the people victimized by injustices; (6) to enrich the quality of life by fostering more simple ways of living and of providing for basic needs, ways which are alternate to the competitive consumer society and more open to joy, leisure, and celebration.[14]

The center has developed a number of innovative programs. Its social service advocacy program (The People's Rights Office) works to inform the local residents of their rights to public assistance, and offers aid in procuring it. The Health Promotion Program assists the people to assume more responsibility for their own health and that of the community. Information, health skills, and life experiences are shared in weekly meetings between area people and health professionals (volunteers drawn principally from the staff and students of the Johns Hopkins School of Hygiene and Public Health, Department of International Health). In the area of housing, Julie Community Center has worked in collaboration with other local organizations to create Concerned Citizens for Butcher Hill, Inc., a non-profit corporation involved in purchasing and rehabilitating low income housing and developing a participative resident management team. The Human Development Program features art therapy, some individual counseling, and training in management and decision-making skills—all with a view toward fostering community. Through Youth Outreach, the Julie Community Center organizes activities for young people of the area while trying to involve the community at large in responding to the needs of youth.

The staff of the center is composed of women and men from a variety of ethnic and religious traditions. Policy guidance for their work is formulated by a fifteen person Board of Directors, thirteen of whom live within the target area and the majority of whom represent the low to moderate income groups on whom the center focuses its services. The other members bring specific professional and business skills to the board. Although theological reflection has not been carried on in a systematic way at the center, the faith commitment of the board and staff has been consistently nurtured in ways which have changed and developed throughout its history.

From the beginning, the decision-making process has been carried on in a faith context. For the first year, each board meeting opened with a reflection on Dom Helder Camara's *The Desert Is Fertile*. Weekly staff meetings begin with shared reflection on daily liturgical readings, stimulating greater mutual understanding and a deepening sense of their being a community rooted in a faith commitment.

The center has grown and thrived over the past seven years without ever having developed a five-year or even a two-year plan. Planning has taken place within a context of prayer, of reflection on the clear and expressed needs of the neighborhood, and of reflection on the gifts of the staff and area residents. Strategies are not determined by someone's assessment of the most "rational" means to the desired ends—with people then being fit in to execute the plan. The planning of strategies emerges instead from the calling forth of the gifts of the people. Inherent in this process is an understanding of God as one who continues ᵗo create the new and who calls people beyond what they already know and can plan. It also implies a deep trust in God acting in and through each person.[15]

The Health Promotion Program exemplifies many of the characteristics of the center as such—the interaction of local residents and skilled professionals, the emphasis on the skills and gifts of each person and the fostering of an atmosphere which nourishes faith. In the weekly meetings of this program, community residents begin to talk about their own situations either to illustrate the topic being discussed or to ask advice and support from the group. Sometimes they are seeking help for themselves personally; at other times they are consulting the group concerning their outreach into the community.

As an individual describes his or her health problem or life experience, others in the group ask questions or offer comments and attempt to situate the problem in a total life context. Here the health-care professionals have technical expertise as well as experiences of other cultures to offer, while the neighborhood residents understand the social, economic, political and religious realities of the person who is talking. Consequently, there is some analysis of the conditions which impact the situation, although it is not systematic. It is not uncommon for a group discussion to move from (1) the problem of a particular diabetic, to (2) questions about adequate nutrition, to (3) a realization that the person's food stamps have been cut off, to (4) concern over proposed federal and state budget cutbacks. Or, in another sphere, the discussion may move to recognize that (1) a particular person's alcoholism is (2) symptomatic of depression following upon (3) his unemployment related to (4) disability as a result of unhealthy working conditions. Not all of the situations are explored so progressively; however, the group has moved to increasing awareness of systemic injustices. During the meetings, people offer suggestions and solutions and volunteer their own resources and energy to assist with the problems.

The process of the group could not be considered "theological reflection" in any systematic understanding of that term. Yet faith is integral to the experience both implicitly and explicitly. Very often the participants talk about their experience of God, usually describing it as one that gives meaning and is sustaining, particularly in times of crisis. It is not uncommon for the group to turn to prayer, particularly when there is illness or a particular need. Sometimes one person will be asked to pray in the name of the group; at other times the Our Father is recited by all. Most recently the members have moved into a form of spontaneous prayer in which the majority, if not all, participate. It is in the context of prayer, reflection, and action that a few persons have articulated a "new sense of church" while a couple of the students who were more agnostic in their leanings have described a new religious experience facilitated by their relationships with people in the group.[16]

Nonetheless, a desire for a more systematic form of theological reflection is beginning to emerge at the Julie Community Center— one that might help the staff and participating area residents to focus more clearly on the relationship between their activities and their religious vision. Such a process could help to keep them consciously rooted in the religious spirit and living sense of mission that gave birth to the center and was responsible for its initial enthusiasm and energy. It could also provide guidance for their work by sharpening their awareness of the religious significance of their present context and the demands of the Gospel for it.

CONCLUDING OBSERVATION

As we come to the end of this brief, incomplete survey, it seems clear that "listening to story" has been a significant part of the pro cesses of nearly all the groups interviewed. Listening to and valuing the plurality of gifts and religious traditions, attempting to integrate them into work for a more vibrant and just community life—these constitute a spirituality deeply rooted in the U.S. experience. The national motto—E Pluribus Unum—is reflected in the emerging processes of theological reflection as small groups and coalitions work for justice in the U.S. context.

NOTES

1. For more on the process and these values, see the special issue of the NETWORK QUARTERLY on NETWORK spirituality, Vol. 7, No. 3 (Summer 1979).

2. A quick sampling of the NETWORK QUARTERLY reveals articles such as the following: Henri J. M. Nouwen, "Reflections on Political Ministry" (Vol. 4, No. 4, Fall 1976); Jurgen Moltmann, "A Christian Declaration on Human Rights" (Vol. 5, No. 2, Spring 1977); J. Bryan Hehir, "The Ministry for Justice" (Vol. 2, No. 3, Summer 1974).

3. For example, see Francine Cardman and Margaret Farley, R.S.M., "Testing the Vision," in NETWORK (Vol. 9, No. 1, January–February 1981). Feminist liberation theologian Mary Hunt has served as a consultant on the NETWORK method of theological reflection. She has encouraged further development of their process as a praxis-centered feminist spirituality for U.S. residents with a global consciousness.

4. Some of the formative writings used in the seminar include Robert K. Greenleaf, *Servant Leadership: A Journey into the Nature of Legitimate Power and Greatness* (New York: Paulist Press, 1977); J. R. Burkholder and Calvin Redekop (eds.), *Kingdom, Cross and Community Vision* (Scottdale, Pa.: Herald Press, 1944). These are works based largely on Mennonite spirituality. Other texts are Abraham J. Heschel, *The Prophets* (New York: Harper and Row, 1962); H. Richard Niebuhr, *Christ and Culture* (New York: Harper and Row, 1951); and Reinhold Niebuhr, *Man's Nature and His Communities* (New York: Charles Scribner's Sons, 1965). In the Bible they rely heavily on the prophetic literature of the Old Testament. For contemporary issues, they draw upon the magazine *SOJOURNERS.*

5. Taken from the Vision Statement of the CCI published in its "Newsletter" Vol. 1, No. 1 (October 10, 1980).

6. These images were taken from the appendix (p. 6) of this unpublished memorandum.

7. Taken from CCI's "Newsletter" Vol. 1, No. 1.

8. "Newsletter" Vol. 1, No. 3 (February 12, 1981).

9. Taken from a written interview with Rev. Richard Rohr, O.F.M.

10. Taken from a community document entitled "Goals and Objectives, Easter 1981—Easter 1982."

11. Taken from a written interview given by Mildred Bender of the community.

12. *Ibid.*

13. John Howard Yoder, *The Politics of Jesus* (Grand Rapids, Michigan: William B. Eerdmans Publishing Company, 1972).

14. Taken from the "Statement of Purpose" of the Julie Community Center, September 1976.

15. Developed from an interview with Sarah Fahy, S.N.D.

16. Taken from a written interview given by Carol A. Symons, S.N.D.

3

Grassroots Communities: A New Model of Church?

Alfred T. Hennelly, S.J.

One of the most important events in the post-Vatican II Church has been the dramatic emergence of grassroots communities on every continent. In this essay I will focus on this phenomenon in Latin America and the United States, but it is important to situate a discussion of it within a global framework. A flood of recent literature may provide at least a brief survey of what is occurring.

COMMUNITIES IN AFRICA AND ASIA

For example, a missionary reviewing the African scene asserts at the beginning of his article that "the idea of basic Christian communities as a new style of Christian participation in the life of the Church has spread throughout the African continent over the past few years."[1] He then includes episcopal documents supporting the building of BCCs in East Central and West Africa. On a more local level, another missionary has provided a graphic account of the growth of small communities (and of his own version of Church and ministry) in two suburbs of Lusaka, Zambia, concluding that the "secret of success" consisted in the training of lay leaders.[2]

If we turn to the Asian scene, an article on basic communities in Pakistan notes that "almost everywhere in Asia seminars and meetings are being held about the building up of Basic Christian Communities."[3] The author emphasizes the uniqueness of the Asian experience, since it occurs within the context of the great religious cultures of the East and not that of Christian majorities, as in the nations of Latin America. But in the one Catholic nation, the Philippines, the same emphasis on small communities can be clearly seen in a number of recent books on their formation as well as in the widely disseminated writings of the bishop of Malaybalay, Francisco Claver, S.J.[4]

EUROPEAN AND CANADIAN BCCs

Even in the "first world" of Europe, there is evidence that small communities are growing, usually marked by a strong emphasis on social protest. In a review of the situation in Italy, Ed Grace estimates that over three hundred BCCs existed there as of 1981, although "there are only a few dioceses in Italy in which they operate with the blessing or even the toleration of their bishops."[5] In the Netherlands, the first congress of the "Grassroots Movement of Critical Groups and Communities" took place on May 11, 1978 in Amsterdam. At that meeting, a council was formed which succinctly described the origin and goals of the movement and proposed a very interesting ten-point program for the development of Dutch communities on the national level.[6] A much more sweeping survey of BCCs in Europe includes the Latin countries, Northern Europe, and even Eastern Europe and Russia. The greatest growth of BCCs as well as the most open dialogue with the episcopal conference appears to have occurred in Spain; aside from this, however, from the article's own descriptions I remain dubious concerning the assertion that "the hierarchy is increasingly putting its hopes in the BCCs, at least in Western Europe."[7] Finally, still in the first world, Dr. Tony Clarke of the Canadian Catholic Conference of Bishops has presented an excellent description and analysis of communities in Canada, insisting that "one of the striking signs in the life of the Canadian church has been the emergence of small communities of people committed to struggles for social justice" during the past decade.[8]

THE LATIN AMERICAN EXPERIENCE

The BCCs in Latin America deserve greater attention, not only because they are far greater in number than in any other part of the world, but also because their experiences have already informed and inspired many communities in other nations. Along with the description, I will give special attention to the method of theological reflection used in these communities and, where relevant, will include observations from my own experience with base communities in Mexico, Panama, and Nicaragua.[9] Finally, I will present my own judgments concerning the value of the experience of the BCCs in Latin America for Christian communities in the United States.

The Latin American communities consist of a dozen or few dozen members each and emphasize the active participation of each person in prayer, worship, reflection and action, while creating strong community bonds through this relationship of dialogue and sharing. The number of existing BCCs has been estimated at between 100,000 and 150,000; however, it is difficult to obtain exact numbers since many struggle to survive in the context of oppressive regimes which would be glad to identify, and, in some cases, destroy them or their leaders.[10]

It is also difficult to pinpoint the religious and cultural factors that provided the background for the BCCs, especially since the nations of Latin America have very diverse social and religious histories. It seems clear, however, that many of the movements which preceded and contributed to the Second Vatican Council (1962–65), such as Catholic Action, the Young Catholic Students and Workers, the biblical and liturgical renewals, and various organizations for social justice, also provided fertile soil for the BCCs.

Furthermore, there can be no doubt that the Second Council of Latin American Bishops, held in Medellín, Colombia in 1968, was of enormous importance. In this application of Vatican II to their own context, the bishops stated unambiguously that "the Christian ought to find the living of the communion to which he has been called, in his 'base community,' that is to say, in a community, local or environmental, which corresponds to the reality of a homogeneous group and whose size allows for personal fraternal contact among its members."[11] And, although it was one of the most hotly debated issues of the meeting, the bishops provided an even more detailed endorsement of the communities in their gathering at Puebla, Mexico in 1979.[12]

In moving to a more detailed description of the BCCs, two important considerations should be kept in mind. First of all, there is no pre-existing theoretical model which determines the origin or growth of the communities. This point has been stressed by all observers and expressed very succinctly by José Marins: "There will be of necessity a great deal of pluralism in the formation and structure of the BCCs. The more they become part of their social sector and are faithful to the people in their environment, the more they will be distinct with an originality and personality all their own."[13]

A second consideration relates not merely to pluralism but also to the different levels of development and maturity that actually exist in the concrete histories of the communities. To illustrate this, I will refer briefly to three levels or stages in the development of Brazilian BCCs.

The first level may be characterized as a community of prayer and reflection on the Bible. The primary interest here lies in the religious formation of the group and strengthening of religious and sacramental life. The second stage begins when, in addition to the above, the community becomes involved in charitable actions within the group, helping those most in need, building collective facilities like dispensaries and schools, and so forth. This can be termed a community of mutual aid. The final level occurs when the political awareness of the group leads it to demand reforms in society; at this stage it can be designated as a community for social change.[14]

Keeping these precautions in mind, let us turn to a more synthetic description of the BCCs. From the growing recent literature on the topic, I have selected the analysis of José Marins for two reasons.[15] First of all, he and his team are based in São Paulo, Brazil, a country which has experienced both the earliest and by far the most extensive proliferation of BCCs. Second, in addition to publishing a number of books he has presented workshops and courses on the BCCs throughout the rest of Latin America for a number of years and thus has been in intimate contact with these other developments. From his detailed analysis I have selected the elements which appear most important for the purposes of this essay.

POSITIVE ASPECTS OF A BCC

In presenting a positive description, Marins' approach is to analyze the various meanings that are included in the term "basic ecclesial community."[16]

As regards the word "basic," he distinguishes three different levels of meaning. In a *theological* sense, it refers to the level at which the Church truly functions as a salvific event for real, specific people here and now. Such a community is basic because it includes all the essential elements of the Church as people of God. *Sociologically* speaking, basic means popular, grassroots, closely linked with the people. In the situation of Latin America, it thus refers to those who are at the bottom of society, those who are poor and marginalized both in their lives and in their power of decision-making. *Pastorally* speaking, basic refers to the fundamental need of every institution for a network of communication with the grassroots in order to be in touch with the people and to direct change effectively.

The word "ecclesial" signifies that the community's motivating force "is faith in Jesus Christ, the desire to live his commandment of love, to carry out his mission by the power of the Holy Spirit in communion with the local and universal Church."[17] Theologically, ecclesial means the socialization of the mystery of the Trinity within the new pilgrim people of God.

Marins includes more nuances for the meaning of "community" than for the first two terms. These include a stress on primary relationships, solidarity, mutual help, and a deeper, more stable communal life. The term also indicates a conscious personal commitment to a common mission as well as growth in co-responsibility for the group, while at the same time experiencing the affirmation of one's own identity. Furthermore, it implies insertion of the community into its own historical situation, which entails facing real problems together and attempting to solve them in accordance with its Christian mission. As regards organization, it implies minimal emphasis on structures and maximal emphasis on the actual life of the community, while respecting the different talents and ministries of each person. Finally, community means that the group has its own identity, distinct from other groups and from other forms of social structures.

DIFFERENCE FROM OTHER ORGANIZATIONS

Marins is also careful to point out what a BCC is not, and I believe this sheds further light on his positive description.[18]

1. It is not simply a discussion group, prayer group, or service

group, although all these groups have their own proper value and also could develop into BCCs. It differs from these other groups precisely because it exists to be Church, that is, to express all essential ecclesial functions and activities, even though it does not express them all at any given moment.

2. It is not an apostolic movement nor a confraternity nor a pious association such as Catholic Charities, the Legion of Mary, or the Third Order of St. Francis. The reason once again is that the BCC is called to live out the totality of the Church's spirituality and mission, since it is essentially the gathering of the faithful at the grassroots level.

3. The BCC is not a protest group, although it should be prophetic and bring forth prophets. It begins with the aid of the institutional Church and develops in union with it. Though it may criticize persons and institutions at times, it does not center on conflict.

4. The BCC is not an isolated unit, but rather a key element in the pastoral renewal being carried out since Vatican II. Since this renewal is both a grassroots and a universal process and since the BCC is the ecclesial element most integrated into the life of the people, it is precisely the most vital dimension of this process.

5. Lastly, the BCC does not constitute a miraculous cure for all the problems of the Church or society. Difficulties and failures will always be part of the experience of the BCC, since it shares in the limitations and sins of the whole Church. And the community will constantly be re-evaluating its accomplishments and plans in the light of its historical experience.

Whether this description of the BCCs has any applicability to the North American context will be considered later in this essay. At this point I will focus on one element of the life of the communities: their method of theological reflection.

BIBLE, COMMUNITY, REALITY

First of all, I would emphasize the great importance of theological reflection or, as it is often called, faith reflection (*reflexión de fe*) in the functioning of the BCCs. Indeed, one team, considered to be the best interpreters of the Mexican experience, have referred to it as the "keystone" of the entire dynamic of the communities.[19] Also, this

survey will reveal that there are differences of opinion among different authorities regarding the practice of the method.

Speaking from his experience in Brazil, Carlos Mesters distinguishes three different ways in which the communities he has
worked with reflect on the Bible.[20] He summarizes these as follows:

> In the first situation the group involved comes together
> solely for the sake of discussing the Bible; the Bible is the
> only thing that unites them and they stick to it. In the sec-
> ond situation the people focus on the Bible, too, but they
> come together as a community. In the third situation we
> have a community of people meeting around the Bible who
> inject concrete reality and their own situation into the dis-
> cussion. Their struggle as a people enters the picture.[21]

Mesters' conclusion is that all three of these factors—the Bible,
the community, and the real-life situation of the people—are essential elements for Christian theological reflection. If any one of them
is lacking, as in the first two communities mentioned above, he believes that they have no future as a Christian community. He is also
convinced that it is unimportant whether the groups start with the
Bible, or the community, or the real-life situation, as long as all three
factors are included. Mesters also discusses in detail a number of
characteristics of the people's interpretation of the Bible which could
serve as catalysts for discussion in communities in other parts of the
world.[22]

A CHRISTOLOGICAL EMPHASIS

In his discussion of the method of reflection of the BCCs, José
Marins places central emphasis on a Christological perspective that
dominates everything else in the reflection. The following is a good
summary of his approach:

> The person of the Lord Jesus, crucified and resurrected, is
> the center of the life of the BEC (Basic Ecclesial Communi-
> ty). The Christology that is lived comes from a new under-
> standing of the life and mission of Jesus. The meaning and

the immediate consequences of the following of Christ and the contradiction of the cross are better situated and explored within the social and cultural contexts. The life of Jesus is seen as an eloquent expression of fidelity to the Father and of commitment to humanity within a specific historical context. Jesus is the friend who invites us to follow him in community, in a prophetic lifestyle and in a commitment to the service of others.[23]

Since the contact with Jesus occurs through the biblical witness and since Marins also emphasizes the social and cultural contexts, his method contains the same three elements as that of Mesters. His approach, however, seems to imply that contact with Jesus through the Bible is the necessary first step in theological reflection, although later he does note that "in discerning events and reality and by gleaning God's action in these, one discovers *how* to read the Bible."[24]

The Mexican Experience

Arnaldo Zenteno and Rogelio Segundo have produced a very thorough systematic and historical analysis of the growth of the BCCs in Mexico. As already noted, they view the process of "faith reflection" as central to the functioning of the communities. Their method of reflection includes the following four steps:

1. A critical reflection on events and experiences to discover how the word of God and also the reality of sin are already working in contemporary history.

2. Confronting these events with the written word of God, in order to reinterpret them and understand them more profoundly. The reinterpretation does not take place through isolated texts but through the fundamental themes of the plan of God as seen in the Bible.

3. Acceptance and reply to the love of God which leads to conversion and a commitment to action in one's own concrete situation.

4. An evaluation of the action of commitment, which leads back to the first moment of the faith reflection and continues in dialectical fashion, with each element influencing and being influenced by the others.[25]

It should be noted, too, that as regards the content of their method Zenteno and Segundo place a heavy emphasis on Christology. Their study includes detailed outlines of reflections on the identity of Jesus, the absolute centrality of the following of Jesus, and his relationship with the political order.

Actual Use of the Method

My own experience with coordinators and members of BCCs in Mexico, Panama, and Nicaragua generally supports Mesters' conclusion that the three elements of Bible, community, and reality constitute the essential elements in the theological reflection of the communities. But I found sharp disagreements among them with regard to his statement that it makes no difference which of the three elements comes first. Some coordinators believed that reflection on the Bible must come first in order to provide Christian meaning for any subsequent community actions. For others it was essential to begin with a reflection on the situation along with some community action for change. They believed that only in this way could the people be enabled to return to reflection on the Bible and to understand it from the viewpoint of the poor and their struggle for justice. This position reflects the views of several prominent Latin American theologians such as Gustavo Gutiérrez, who asserts that theology (reflection) is the "second step" after action,[26] and Juan Luis Segundo, who sees a specific commitment as a necessary first step in the method of theological reflection that he refers to as the "hermeneutic circle."[27]

My own conclusion from observing the BCCs is similar to that of Mesters. First of all, it would be a very rare event for a group of Christians to engage in common action with no background of Christian symbols and reflection on them at all. Thus it may be a false question to ask whether action or reflection should come first. But more importantly I think that the position of Mesters offers greater freedom to assess the strengths and weaknesses of different communities and to adapt the method in a creative way in accordance with this assessment. The method then would respect the diversity and different levels of development of BCCs mentioned earlier. More profound reflections on the Christian ethical norms for common commitment and action have been proposed by James Hug and Larry Rasmussen in this volume. Also, in her article Jouette Bassler has analyzed the freedom and diversity of Church models in the New Testament itself.

OTHER FEATURES OF THE BCCs

In order to provide more concreteness regarding the BCCs, I will now add some details from my own contacts with clerical, religious, and lay coordinators as well as with actual members of the communities. It should be noted that the three countries I visited—Mexico, Panama, and Nicaragua—have a relatively long history of organizing and developing the communities, and thus may not be typical of other Latin American countries. Also, my experience in the three countries was limited, and thus is not intended as a total picture of the communities.

First of all, it should be stressed that prayer and religious hymns are very important to the life of the BCCs. As Cardinal Paulo Arns has expressed it, "people do not come to the BCCs where there is no praying or singing. They may come four or five times to organize practical things, but nothing further will come of it."[28] Especially impressive are the new popular hymns that express the aspirations and hopes of the common people and are sung with great enthusiasm. Their prayers of petition, too, are startling in the very concrete nature of their appeals: for clean water, a just wage, a primary school, an independent union, police protection, and so forth.

Another important feature is the development of well-organized programs for the training and continuing education of lay "coordinators" or "animators" (the word "leader" is never used). The programs include national and province conferences, workshops, courses, and the publication of popular literature on Scripture reading, religious education, and social analysis. Of particular importance are the weekly meetings among twenty or thirty coordinators from the same area, at which they discuss both past and upcoming meetings of their groups. A key element of the meeting is the distribution and discussion of a typed or xeroxed *morral* (literally a saddlebag that contains food for the people on their journey). These are two-page summaries, sometimes in popular dramatic form, of topics for the next meeting. For example, *morrales* that I encountered in Mexico discussed the causes of unemployment in the barrio, developing more friendly relations with neighboring BCCs, and learning from the situation of other BCCs in Nicaragua. This well-developed system of organization seems to provide an antidote against the temptations to sectarianism or politicization of the BCCs, which were seen as the main dangers to the communities in the Puebla meeting.[29] It also represents an impressive building of lay leadership at the grassroots level, clearly a most pressing need in the Latin American church.

Finally, the most vivid impression I received in talking to BCC members in very poor barrios was the great sense of *dignity* they had gained from their experience in the communities. Those who a few years ago had accepted their designation as "brutes" or "animals" in society now spoke and acted with confidence, honesty, and an awareness of their unique value as persons. Also, in all the meetings I attended, the majority of both coordinators and BCC members were women, a fact which in the long run should have profound consequences in both society and the Church.

The U.S. Experience

In turning to the "reality" of the church in the United States, I want to emphasize that I am not advocating a wholesale import of the Latin American experience. Clearly, any development of small Christian communities must be faithful to our own political, social and cultural history.

It is also important to recall that there are already many forms of small communities existing in the United States. Perhaps the most dramatic example of these are the charismatic communities, but we can include Marriage Encounter, Cursillo, Christian Life Communities, Catholic Worker and allied groups, and others. There are also any number of peace and justice communities, engaged in public education, lobbying, solidarity with oppressed people, research, and caring for the immediate needs of the poor. Whether all these communities have anything to learn from the Latin American experience can only be decided by the members themselves.

Whatever the principle of formation of small communities may be, I will presuppose here that their goals include both development of the faith and spiritual lives of their members as well as some form of commitment to social justice. In this context, I find the distinction made by the Canadian survey of "Communities for Justice" mentioned earlier to be quite helpful. Clarke distinguishes between "popular Christian communities" and "progressive Christian communities." The former include persons who are actually experiencing various forms of poverty and/or oppression—that is to say, they are communities *of* the poor and oppressed. The second category includes those (usually middle class and professional people) who are engaged in actions of support for poor and oppressed peoples; thus, they are communities *for* the poor and oppressed.[30]

All of the action/reflection groups described by William Newell in this volume seem to belong to the second category of progressive communities. This has an obvious advantage, since the middle class comprises the majority of the American church and these groups may provide possible models for reflection and action. However, there is also a disadvantage, because with one exception we did not encounter popular communities composed of the poor and oppressed themselves. The exception refers to the experience of oppression voiced by many women in the action/reflection groups. Their sharing of the pain and anguish they experienced because of sexism in both Church and society has had a profound impact on my own life.

THE HISPANIC CHURCH

At this point I will discuss popular communities in the U.S. church and afterward consider the progressive communities. The most obvious example of popular communities may be found in the Hispanic church in this country. Although it is often ignored, this church has great importance, as may be seen in the statement of Enrique Dussell: "Demographic projections based on birth rate and immigration indicate that by the year 2000 fifty percent of U.S. Catholics will be of Latin American origin."[31]

It is important to emphasize at the outset that the fundamental concepts of the Latin American BCCs are already an essential part of the pastoral strategy of the U.S. Hispanic church. Convincing proof for this assertion can be found in the recent manual for the formation of BCCs published by the Secretariat for Hispanic Affairs of the United States Catholic Conference, where the authors assert that as of 1979 there were already more than twelve thousand BCCs actually functioning in the United States.[32]

A perusal of this manual shows the similarities of its approach with the BCCs of Latin America. In an introduction stressing that the creation of BCCs is a process in which every member must participate creatively, the book places great emphasis on discovering the "reality": "We discover the reality in brotherhood and prayer. Faith sheds light on the reality and they both demand commitment and action."[33] Discerning the reality involves discerning God working in present history in all its aspects and evaluating these signs of the times with a view toward action.

The third chapter provides the theological foundations for God's call to communion and community and discusses at length the selfishness, division and sin, including social sin, that impede the fulfillment of God's plan for true communion. There is also detailed discussion of Jesus as liberator from personal and social sin and as creator of community.

Chapter four emphasizes that "the first community of Jesus was based on interpersonal, fraternal relationships and on Jesus as Messiah and Liberator" and that the BCCs of today are following this model with creative adaptation to different historical circumstances: "This aspect of the incarnation of the ecclesial community is a challenge to our originality and creativity—a challenge met by blending awareness of the here-and-now situation with permanent Christian values."[34] Here and throughout the book much emphasis is given to the Church's preference for the poor: "Any description of the CEB has to include this preference for the poor, since the same preference is one of the characteristics of the Church."[35]

The sixth chapter of the manual is especially interesting because of its description of the process of theological reflection, which is summarized as follows: "It is made up of ACTION—REFLECTION—PRAYER—REFLECTED ACTION—in a spirit of FRATERNITY—and OPEN TO THE HERE-AND-NOW SITUATION."[36] Some action that arises from the real needs of the group is the first step "because action opens up the group and forces the members to reflect on what they are doing and how their actions fit into the liberating work of Jesus." The reflection that follows action stresses a critical consciousness of what is going on, helped by Christian principles that are pertinent and also by the social sciences, at least on a basic level. It also includes evaluation of the action taken to see whether it was truly in line with the liberating work of Jesus. The prayer segment of the method must take place "not in a vacuum or in general or in the past, but within the action and the reflection on the action that we are involved with today."[37] The cycle then concludes with reflected action (action that has previously been reflected upon). The entire process should constantly lead to better and newer ways of acting.

Also of interest is a chapter on ministry, which notes that the BCC should help each member to develop his or her own talents and thus discover his or her personal ministry. It is strongly emphasized that the ministry involved is a *lay* ministry: "It would be fatal to follow the 'clerical' style of ministry. Some deacons have tried copying a clerical style of life with disastrous consequences, and even their own families resent this attitude."[38]

A final chapter discusses the relation of the BCCs to Church structures. On the one hand it insists that the BCCs are the primary level of the Church and are united with the bishops and all that goes to make up the Church. On the other hand it also notes that the present parish structures present difficulties and cause many Hispanics to live on the fringe of parish structures. Despite this, the manual concludes on an upbeat note: "This is an historic moment for the Hispanic and for all who have eyes that see and ears that hear. It is a universal message that comes from the poor to all people of good will."[39]

CONCLUSIONS ON THE HISPANIC CHURCH

The preceding section has made clear that the BCC represents the linchpin in the pastoral strategy of the Hispanic church in the United States. All of the essential characteristics of the Latin American BCC presented in the first part of this essay have clearly been incorporated as the Church model of the Hispanic church. However, it must be emphasized that this strategy is not considered a mere transplant or import from Latin America, since there is constant emphasis in the approach on the need for creative adaptation to the North American situation: "The Christian community of California has to be of California. . . . The communities of Chicanos, Mexican-Americans, South Americans, Cubans, Dominicans, and Central Americans have much in common, but every group has characteristics which the Christian community ought to absorb."[40]

Since Hispanics constitute such a large part of the U.S. church, it seems reasonable to assume that their pastoral strategy will continue to influence the pastoral strategy of the non-Hispanic church. I suggest that this will happen on a number of levels. First, it will challenge the non-Hispanic church to develop its own creative strategies for developing authentic Christian community within the many large, impersonal parishes that exist today. This problem will be referred to again when we consider the applicability of BCCs for the non-Hispanic church.

On another level, the approach could be the providential means for making the voice of the poor heard in the non-Hispanic church and thus making possible its conversion to the cause of the poor. This is especially important since the majority of the U.S. church belong to the middle and upper classes, thus far with little contact or interest in the "base" or marginalized classes. The BCCs in their ever increasing numbers will serve as living reminders that no Christian community today, especially those that form among the middle and upper classes, can consider itself authentic unless it is distinguished by a passion for and commitment to social justice for the poor. Monika Hellwig has analyzed this issue in greater depth elsewhere in this volume.

On a third level, the experience of the BCCs could provide models for other groups that have been marginalized within the U.S. church, such as women, blacks, native Americans, and the urban and rural poor. Again, there is no question of simple translation: rather it involves an openness to learn from fellow Christians in the same national church and creative adaptation to historical and cultural circumstances. Again, such adaptation can only be done by the actual members of marginalized groups.

EVALUATION: THE NON-HISPANIC CHURCH

Are the insights of the BCCs applicable to the middle class and upper class sectors of the U.S. church? That this is a very important question may be seen clearly in the recent social analysis of U.S. society presented by Joe Holland and Peter Henriot. After analyzing the evolution of capitalism into its present phase of "national security state capitalism," they propose a strategy of response by the church to this development which includes the basic Christian communities as an essential element. And, the authors conclude, "the church of the United States can learn much ... from the Latin American church and its strategy of basic Christian communities."[41]

To achieve clarity in this discussion, certain important facts should be kept in mind. As J. B. Libânio has pointed out, "The research on the BCCs shows that they are mainly located in socially deprived rural and urban areas. Few *comunidades* exist among the urban middle and upper classes."[42] Clearly the situation in the United States is quite the opposite, and we will now be concerned with the "progressive" communities mentioned earlier among the middle and upper classes.

Just as in the discussion on the Hispanic church, the first thing to note is that there is already a strong movement underway in the United States for the development of such communities. In their annual meeting of 1979, the National Federation of Priests' Councils selected the formation of small Christian communities as their key pastoral strategy. In a handbook entitled "Developing Basic Christian Communities," the president of the NFPC, James Ratigan, states flatly that "Catholic priests in the 1980's will not be able to accomplish the task of evangelization unless there is a dramatic (radical) restructuring of the parish. The need for smaller faith communities is essential."[43] He also notes that "Basic Christian Communities are by no means an exclusively Hispanic phenomenon. There have been basic communities for over fifteen years in virtually all parts of the U.S."[44] The council has also formed a task force to document models of different types of successful small communities, as well as to create workshops and a speakers' bureau to aid in the formation and growth of new communities. At this point I will offer some reflections on the contents of the handbook published in 1980 by the NFPC.

The contributions of Virgilo Elizondo and Frank Ponce are concerned with Hispanic BCCs in the United States and are not germane to the present discussion. However, Ponce does raise a question in his essay that is never satisfactorily answered: Are the BCCs only for Hispanics in the United States or are they suitable for the whole Church? While emphasizing that the BCCs do indeed work for Hispanics and presenting a wealth of information regarding their formation, he concludes that "whether they will work for the larger U.S. Catholic Church is less clear at this point."[45]

More helpful are the observations of Thomas Peyton, which reflect thirteen years of experience in forming voluntary communities within parish structures in the United States. However, Peyton seems to *presume* that his methods would work in any parish. This argument would be much more effective if he had included some data or concrete examples of the success or failure of small communities in non-Hispanic parishes.

A much more concrete picture is presented by David Killian in "Basic Christian Communities in Boston," where he worked within the structure of the non-territorial parish of the Paulist Center Community. At various times the number of participants in this parish ranged from a thousand to fifteen hundred.

It is interesting to note that the small groups here (called *Koinonia* communities) gradually came into being not because of some previously worked out pastoral plan proceeding from the top but because of the expressed needs and frustrations of some of the more articulate members of the parish. The next key step was to initiate meetings of small groups of parishioners so that they could discuss their experiences of alienation due to the size of the parish (as well as other complaints). Killian observes that "at the end of the session participants concluded that this forum was exactly the type of opportunity for sharing that they wanted."[46] In the beginning, four *Koinonia* communities were formed, all drawing their membership from a cross-section of the city of Boston.

Once again, however, a desire was expressed by some parishioners to relate to others in small groups in the same neighborhood, where they shared common problems and social needs and could cooperate in seeking solutions. Killian concludes: "As a priest I have taken special joy in seeing lay people assume responsibility for their church. I have rejoiced that they have been eager to become partners in ministry. . . . In the coming years, *Koinonia* can be a part of the wider development of Basic Christian Communities in our country."[47]

In another article, Arthur Chavez describes the formation of "little parishes" within the territorial parish of Our Lady of Guadalupe Church in Albuquerque, New Mexico. It is not clear from the article whether this is a Hispanic parish, but Chavez's concluding remarks appear to have relevance for any part of the U.S. church:

> The challenge of the 1980's is that every parish uniquely has to begin a process of not simply understanding their structure, but of building new structures to meet the needs of the people. . . . The Basic Christian Community, the Koinonia experience, or the model of the Little Parish may work for some, and be a special answer for the problems the local church is having in being an effective instrument. For others it may be something else. That which is most necessary is corporate discernment led by the Spirit and action for the Kingdom of God.[48]

CONCLUSIONS ON THE NON-HISPANIC CHURCH

In this essay I have not focused on the significance of the BCCs for a theology of Church or of ministry, although I would note that these topics are important and that there is a growing body of theological reflection in these areas.[49] In line with my approach my concluding reflections are more concerned with pastoral implications than with theological ones.

I have already referred to the great variety of models of small Christian communities that already exist in the non-Hispanic church in the United States. These communities also clearly differ from those in Latin America in that their membership is largely composed of the middle and upper classes. Given all this, it is quite difficult to discern what any particular group here might learn from the experience of the Latin American BCCs. Recognizing, then, that any fruitful borrowing is up to the judgment of the U.S. communities, I here present my own reflections.

One of the key features of the Latin American BCCs has been its emphasis on the importance of discovering and encouraging the growth of genuine lay leadership and genuine lay ministries. This appears to me to have great applicability to the U.S. scene. The U.S. church has a large number of well-educated, talented, and committed laity who are quite capable of assuming leadership roles and developing new forms of ministry. In fact, many of them are doing just that at the present time, both with and without the consent of the hierarchy. Also, the women's movement is very strong in the United States, and it is obvious that feminists are not going to seek out clerical leaders for their communities. Finally, present vocation statistics make it clear that there will be in the near future a serious shortage of priests in the U.S. church, making the question of lay leadership a very urgent issue on the U.S. agenda.

But what will be the role of bishops and priests vis-à-vis this lay leadership? Again, the Latin American experience has been instructive. The clergy (or many of them) have aimed at a new collegial type of relationship, based on genuine dialogue with the people and fraternal response to their real needs. They have put their talents, training, and resources *at the service* of the communities, in order to discover, train, and encourage genuine lay leadership and lay ministries. This is similar to the strategy of the intelligent missionary who aims at putting himself or herself out of a job in favor of indigenous leadership. There is as yet no way of determining whether the U.S. clergy will decide on a similar style of leadership in the future; that decision, however, may be crucial for linking future communities to the official Church.

I also believe that the method of faith reflection has important lessons for the United States. The Christological emphasis obviously has universal and not merely regional implications for authentic Christian spirituality and community. But it is the reflection on "the reality" that I think is most needed in middle class and upper class BCCs, which are often insulated from poverty and situations of injustice. Fortunately, the article on social analysis of Holland and Henriot mentioned earlier provides an excellent vehicle for achieving this type of reflection in the United States. Both elements, then, would ensure that the BCCs developing in the United States would not only be faith communities but also justice communities, aware of and committed to the cause of the poor or oppressed. The formation of such communities will be the great challenge to all members of the U.S. church in the decade ahead.[50]

NOTES

1. Harry Hoeben, "Basic Christian Communities in Africa," *Pro Mundi Vita Bulletin* 81 (April 1980), p. 19. Throughout this article, I use the abbreviation BCC for these communities. In direct quotation of other sources, I have retained their abbreviations, e.g., CEB (*comunidades eclesiales de base*), BEC (basic ecclesial communities), etc.

2. A. Edele, "Establishing Basic Christian Communities in Lusaka, Zambia," *Pro Mundi Vita Bulletin* 81 (April 1980), pp. 21–25.

3. Louis Mascarenhas, "Basic Christian Communities in an Islamic Setting in Pakistan," *Pro Mundi Vita Bulletin* 81 (April 1980), p. 26.

4. Cf. Ted Gresh, *Basic Christian Communities in the Church* (Manila, 1976) and *Basic Christian Communities in the Philippines* (Manila, 1977); John Rich, *Life Together in Small Christian Communities* (Davao, 1977); Francisco Claver, *The Stones Will Cry Out: Grassroots Pastorals* (Orbis Books: Maryknoll, N.Y., 1978).

5. Ed Grace, "Italy: Disobedience as Witness," *Christianity and Crisis* (September 21, 1981), p. 245. Cf. also Marcello Vigli, "Le mouvement des communautés chrétiennes de base en Italie," *Concilium 104: Les communautés de base* (Paris: Editions Beauchesne, 1975).

6. "The Netherlands: Manifesto of a Movement," *Christianity and Crisis* (September 21, 1981), pp. 246–50.

7. "Basic Christian Communities in Europe," *Pro Mundi Vita Bulletin* 81 (April 1980), p. 30.

8. Tony Clarke, "Communities for Justice," *The Ecumenist* 19 (January–February 1981), p. 17. Clarke quotes with approval the statement of the Canadian Bishops, "A Society To Be Transformed," *Origins* 7 (December 29, 1977), pp. 436–40.

9. I am very grateful to Fr. Gerard Campbell, S.J. and the Woodstock Theological Center for the grant that enables me to complete this research.

10. Recent books focusing on base communities in Brazil, which has by far the largest number of them, include: A. Barreiro, *Comunidades Eclesiales de Base e Evangelização dos Pobres* (São Paulo: Edições Loyola, 1977); C. Boff, *Comunidade Eclesial/Comunidade Política* (Petrópolis: Editora Vozes,

1979); R. Caramuru de Barros, *Comunidade Eclesial de Base: Uma Opção Pastoral Decisiva* (Petrópolis: Editora Vozes, 1967); and P. Demo, *Comunidade: Igreja na Base* (São Paulo: Edições Paulinas, 1974).

11. *The Church in the Present-Day Transformation of Latin America II: Conclusions,* 2nd ed. (Washington: Division for Latin America, U.S.C.C., n.d.), p. 201.

12. For the Puebla documents, along with analyses and commentaries, cf. John Eagleson and Philip Scharper, eds., *Puebla and Beyond* (Maryknoll, N.Y.: Orbis Books, 1979); for the teaching of Puebla on the BCCs, cf. Alfred T. Hennelly, "The Grassroots Church," *Catholic Theological Society of America, Proceedings of the Thirty-Fourth Annual Convention* (New York: Manhattan College, 1979), pp. 183–88; a fine history and analysis of the Puebla conference has been provided by Frei Betto, *17 días de la Iglesia Latino-americana: Diario de Puebla* (Mexico: CRT, 1979).

13. José Marins, "Basic Ecclesial Community," *UISG Bulletin* (No. 55, 1981), p. 35. A student of the BCCs in Brazil, Thomas C. Bruneau, reaches similar conclusions: "It must be recognized that CEBs are not all of one piece; they vary tremendously from one country or even from one diocese to another . . . and what is being presented here is a general statement reflecting the higher or more defined level of the CEBs": "Basic Christian Communities in Latin America: Their Nature and Significance (especially in Brazil)," in Daniel H. Levine, ed., *Churches and Politics in Latin America* (Beverly Hills: Sage Publications, 1979), p. 226. Also helpful is Thomas C. Bruneau, *Religiosity and Politicization in Brazil* (São Paulo: Edições Loyola, 1979). Very concrete descriptions and evaluations of how BCCs actually function in different national contexts may be found in *LADOC: Basic Christian Communities* (United States Catholic Conference, Washington, D.C.: Latin America Documentation, 1976).

14. Gottfried Deelen, "The Church on Its Way to the People: Basic Christian Communities in Brazil," *Pro Mundi Vita Bulletin* 81 (April 1980), p. 5; cf. also J. B. Libânio, "Experiences with the Base Ecclesial Communities in Brazil," *Missiology: An International Review* (July 1980), pp. 319–38.

15. José Marins, "Basic Ecclesial Community." Many of Marins' conclusions are supported in the more condensed article of Leonardo Boff and Clodovis Boff, "Povo, Comunidade Eclesial de Base, Libertação," *Convergência* 14 (March 1981), pp. 78–83.

16. Marins, "Community," pp. 30–32.

17. *Ibid.,* p. 31.

18. *Ibid.,* pp. 32–35.

19. Rogelio Segundo and Arnaldo Zenteno, "Un itinerario de la fe del

Pueblo: El proceso de las Comunidades Cristianas de Base (CCB) en México," in *Cruz y resurrección: Presencia y anuncio de una iglesia nueva* (Mexico City: Servir, 1978), p. 270.

20. Carlos Mesters, "The Use of the Bible in Christian Communities of the Common People," in Sergio Torres and John Eagleson, eds., *The Challenge of Basic Christian Communities* (Maryknoll, N.Y.: Orbis Books, 1981), pp. 197–210.

21. *Ibid.,* p. 199.

22. *Ibid.,* pp. 204–10.

23. Marins, "Community," pp. 36–37.

24. *Ibid.,* p. 46.

25. Segundo and Zenteno, "Itinerario," pp. 270–71.

26. Gustavo Gutiérrez, *A Theology of Liberation: History, Politics and Salvation* (Maryknoll, N.Y.: Orbis Books, 1972), p. 11.

27. Juan Luis Segundo, *The Liberation of Theology* (Maryknoll, N.Y.: Orbis Books, 1976), pp. 7–38. For a discussion of the hermeneutic circle, cf. Alfred T. Hennelly, *Theologies in Conflict: The Challenge of Juan Luis Segundo* (Maryknoll, N.Y.: Orbis Books, 1979), pp. 107–22.

28. Quoted in Deelen, "The Church on Its Way," p. 8.

29. The process has resemblances to that described by the article of Avery Dulles in this volume.

30. Clarke, "Communities for Justice," p. 19.

31. Enrique Dussel, *History and the Theology of Liberation* (Maryknoll, N.Y.: Orbis Books, 1976), p. 171.

32. *Comunidades Eclesiales de Base: Experiencia en los Estados Unidos* (Liguori, Mo.: Liguori Publications, 1980), pp. 112–13. Cf. also the endorsement of base communities in *Pueblo de Dios en Marcha: Il Encuentro Nacional Hispano de Pastoral* (Washington: Secretariat for Hispanic Affairs, 1978).

33. *Comunidades,* p. 116.

34. *Ibid.,* p. 137.

35. *Ibid.,* p. 142.

36. *Ibid.,* p. 147.

37. *Ibid.,* p. 148.

38. *Ibid.,* p. 153.

39. *Ibid.,* p. 160.

40. *Ibid.,* p. 137.

41. Joe Holland and Peter Henriot, *Social Analysis: Linking Faith and Justice* (Washington, D.C.: Center of Concern, 1980), p. 38. See also the article by Joe Holland in this volume.

42. Libânio, "Experiences," p. 324.

43. *Developing Basic Christian Communities—A Handbook* (National Federation of Priests' Councils, 1979), p. 1.

44. *Ibid.,* p. 4.

45. *Ibid.,* p. 25.

46. *Ibid.,* p. 46.

47. *Ibid.,* pp. 49–50.

48. *Ibid.,* p. 59.

49. As characteristic examples, see Leonardo Boff, "Theological Characteristics of a Grassroots Church," in *The Challenge of Basic Christian Communities,* pp. 124–44 and Jon Sobrino, "Resurrección de una iglesia popular," in *Cruz y Resurrección,* pp. 83–159.

50. As a possible pastoral aid in meeting this challenge, I include here the address of the task force that is collecting and distributing information on BCCs in the U.S.: BCC Task Force, NFPC, 1307 South Wabash Avenue, Chicago, IL 60605. A recent very helpful analysis of BCCs has been provided by Kate Pravera in "The United States: Realities and Responses," *Christianity and Crisis* (September 21, 1981), pp. 251–55. On the theological level, Avery Dulles has analyzed the model of Church for the 1980's as "a community of disciples" in "Imaging the Church for the 1980's," *The Catholic Mind* (November 1981), pp. 9–26. In my judgment, that is exactly what the many BCCs around the world are attempting to initiate and to foster.

4
Theological Reflection in Ministry Preparation

Robert L. Kinast

Action/reflection groups have a problem with theology. They can't get at it in a usable way. In its customary form theology deals with generalized themes, focuses on classic, authoritative teachings, aims at the articulation of meaning and truth, and relies on disciplined, scientific inquiry. By contrast action/reflection groups tend to deal with concrete experiences, focus on personal decisions and interpersonal relationships, aim at specific actions, and rely on spontaneity and intuition.

These differences are not absolute, of course, but they describe the problem of relating to theology in its typical form. One instance of this problem occurs in preparation for ministry, specifically in field education, practicum, or supervised ministry experiences. Theological reflection in these settings is similar to theological reflection in other types of action/reflection groups.

For example, theological reflection in ministry preparation is based upon concrete, immediate, personal experiences like a hospital visit or a counseling session or a homily. The actual reflection is usually done in a group setting, called the theological reflection seminar. The primary purpose of theological reflection is to illuminate and enrich the person's growth and facility as a minister. Hence it has a direct, practical goal. There is a desire to relate the ministerial experience and theological reflection upon it to the larger theological tradition.

There are also some differences. Ordinarily theological reflection is based upon individual experiences rather than group experiences of ministering. The group itself (the theological reflection seminar) is somewhat artificial or at least temporary. It meets as part of a school program, not as an intentional community. The theological reflection is not necessarily part of other shared experiences of faith within the group such as prayer, joint decision-making, common action, or even common identity.

Nonetheless, theological reflection in ministry preparation is an important example of the general issue under discussion in this volume. In this essay I intend to review briefly the origin of theological reflection in ministry preparation and to situate it in a wider current of developments in theology and Church life. This will help to sharpen the distinction between this type of theological reflection and the dominant mode of theological education. Then I want to review some models for getting at the theological tradition and from this review draw out some general implications for the practice of theological reflection in ministry preparation. Hopefully these implications will also have some benefit for the theological reflection of other action/reflection groups.

Origin of Theological Reflection in Ministry Preparation

The main impetus for theological reflection in the United States came from Protestant educators. A launching pad of sorts was the Study of Theological Education in the U.S. and Canada sponsored by the American Association of Theological Schools and conducted by H. Richard Niebuhr in collaboration with Daniel Day Williams and James Gustafson.[1] A year later Seward Hiltner published his influential work, *Preface to Pastoral Theology,* which argued for the legitimacy of a theological discipline that would begin with the chief functions of pastoral care or shepherding and relate these to the classic, logic-centered fields of theological inquiry.[2]

For the next decade or so, Protestant seminaries pursued this direction, establishing field education programs as a fixture of the curriculum. By the end of the 1960's the Association for Clinical Pastoral Education emerged which gave the movement a more autonomous structure and professional legitimacy. At about the same time the Doctor of Ministry degree appeared. This program aimed to enhance the professional nature of ministerial practice and sought to integrate pastoral experience with theological study and personal growth more effectively.[3]

Roman Catholics joined this movement full force after Vatican II directed that seminaries give more attention to the pastoral formation of priests. This general call was specified in the Program for Priestly Formation drawn up and approved by the National Conference of Catholic Bishops.[4] Many of the techniques and programs already used in Protestant seminaries found their way into Roman Catholic schools, a development aided by the fact that a large number of Roman Catholics had already acquired C.P.E. training.

Roman Catholic emphasis on doctrine reinforced the need for integration of theological reflection with academic theology while certain theological issues received more prominence among Roman Catholics: sacramental ministry, the tension between official Church teaching/discipline and local pastoral authority, the role of women in ministry, and the demands of post-conciliar renewal.

Trends in Theology

This movement within theological field education parallels certain general trends in theology and culture. It is useful to cite a few of these in order to situate theological reflection in a larger context.

1. *Shift to the Subject.* No doubt the chief influence has been the shift to the subject. In modern European theology this was given major impetus by Friedrich Schleiermacher with his attention to personal experience as the starting point for religion and theological reflection.[5] Emphasis on personal feeling became a hallmark of liberal Protestantism and was paralleled somewhat in the United States by the development of empirical theology.[6] Although there are differences between experiential and empirical theology, both trends moved theological reflection away from disembodied ideas and treatises and toward the living context of human persons and their environment.

2. *Locus of Theologizing.* As part of the shift to the subject, the primary locus of theological reflection began to change. Personal witness, conversion experience, formation of Christian communities, mission efforts, especially evangelization, were taken as the starting

point of theological reflection rather than biblical texts, doctrinal or confessional statements, theological classics, or manuals.

As a result another fundamental shift has occurred. Personal faith experience appeared as a *source* of theological reflection generating both questions and insights. Efforts were made on the one hand to integrate theology into these experiences and on the other to discover theological meaning inherent in the experiences. This twofold inquiry has continued to the present time.

3. *Role of the Church and Ministry.* The new locus of theologizing has led to a new interpretation of the Church and its ministry. The meaning of Church has been concentrated much more on the local community and even on specific events within the life of that community. This is especially evident where Basic Christian Communities are the dominant form of organization.

The precise role of the local church ranges from being a supportive community to providing an environment for personal growth to offering a helpful corrective for privatizing tendencies. The local church is a concrete representation and mediation of what is expressed in general in treatises on ecclesiology.

Likewise, the role of the minister has shifted. As a representative of the larger Church, the minister claims greater pastoral freedom in responding to the needs of parishioners in concrete situations.[7] Thus the minister acts primarily as a catalyst, an enabler, a skilled helper who shares life with the other members of the community. The themes of mutual ministry and shared responsibility appear more prominently.

Accompanying these shifts are some special challenges which ministers face. One of these is identifying the distinctly pastoral nature of their ministry. This arises as a problem especially when other professional disciplines are used, more or less intact, in the exercise of ministry. What is distinctly pastoral about one's counseling or administering, for example, may not be immediately evident.

On the other hand, some ministers may not pose such questions at all and thus run the risk of neglecting or avoiding the theological-ministerial aspect of their work.[8] At the same time ministers may individualize pastoral care to such an extent that the crucial social dimension is omitted.[9]

At the present time, theological reflection as part of ministry preparation in the United States is firmly established. But the problem of relating theology to ministerial experience remains. The major task is to develop models for doing this. Before looking at some recent suggestions on how this may be done, it will be helpful to sharpen the contrast between theological reflection and standard theological education.

Distinctiveness of Theological Reflection

Theological reflection as part of preparation for ministry differs from standard theological education in several important ways. These differences are for the most part shared with other action/reflection groups and help to indicate why there is a problem relating theology to ministerial experience.

1. *Starting Point.* In theological reflection the starting point is a specific instance of pastoral encounter. This is usually recorded in verbatim accounts, case studies, critical incidents, personal journals. Reflection is centered on the persons involved—their feelings, needs, attitudes, questions. The "text" is the actual dialogue or interaction that takes place. The controlling factor is the initiating experience and especially the feelings generated by that experience. These determine what is relevant theologically and therefore the scope of theological reflection.

By contrast the starting point for theological education is a general theme, question or thesis. This is investigated from various points of view but always at a general level of discussion. The controlling factor is the self-imposed limits of the investigation. Theology in this mode is abstract and theoretical, but it is also comprehensive, and that is one of its chief contributions to pastoral ministry—it broadens and enriches the concrete context of theological reflection.

2. *Learning Mode.* The way that members of a theological reflection seminar learn is decidedly different from the way students in traditional forms of theological education usually learn. First of all there is no pre-established syllabus. The issues to be discussed arise in the course of the field experience. It is true that certain issues are

predictable. For example, if a student is visiting a cancer ward, the question of death and suffering will surely arise. If a student is placed in a social agency, questions of justice and structural oppression come up. However, the exact questions, their relative importance compared with other concerns in the same situation, and their impact on the student are all unknown until the experience occurs. For this reason a learning *process* is set up, but the learning content depends on what happens during the process. It should be stated explicitly that there is content in this type of learning but it is not pre-determined.

A second important difference is that the learning occasion is initiated by the student rather than the instructor or supervisor. The student presents to the group an account of ministerial experience and usually indicates what the group is to focus on. The group is free to raise other issues, of course, but the presenter begins the learning process and is responsible for what may be learned.

From this comes a third distinctive feature. It is a thoroughly collaborative effort. Members of the group respond to what the presenter offers. This may take various forms: suggestions for further reflection, reinforcement of the ministry performed, confrontation and challenge to certain actions or their underlying theology, questions about the student's assumptions, techniques, effectiveness, motivation, interest, etc.

This learning mode differs sharply from the usual mode of theological education which is related to a syllabus constructed mainly, if not exclusively, by the instructor. Moreover, in traditional theological education extensive reading and research papers hold a prominent place. Personal experience is kept to a minimum in favor of a more disciplined investigation of the opinions of others (authors) and critical analyses of them.

3. *Role of the Teacher.* The role of the teacher also differs. In theological reflection groups the teacher is primarily a facilitator who integrates theology and pastoral input into the discussion as it proceeds. Teaching in this way requires continual listening, relating, and building on the comments of the participants. The instructor in a theological reflection process possesses theological competence but communicates it through personal interaction and dialogue.[10]

In most theological education, the instructor is an expert who shares that expertise primarily by the organization of course material, the selection of readings, the presentation of material in class, the handling of questions, and the evaluation of a student's demonstrated knowledge.

4. *Outcome.* Theological reflection is aimed primarily at enhancing the personal and professional growth of the minister. This may also include spiritual growth, but that is not usually an explicit goal in a theological reflection seminar. Personal growth is gauged mostly by the way a student interacts with group members, the kind of ministerial identity that is developed, and the degree of honesty with which one's limitations and risks are faced. Professional growth is gauged mostly by the way a student learns and uses accepted ministerial techniques, communicates with others (patients, parishioners, and peers), and reflects theologically on ministry experiences. Descriptive evaluations are the prime record of this growth even if a grade is also required.

In theological education the outcome is primarily growth in knowledge, including insight and critical awareness. Sometimes the practical or personal implications of such growth arise, but these are usually not the chief objective. Grades are a standard way of indicating the student's intellectual growth as assessed by the instructor.

5. *Uses of Theology.* In preparation for ministry, theological reflection makes various uses of the theological tradition. The prime objective is to help each student *construct* a living or operational theology. This is the actual set of theological positions the person affirms and bases ministerial practice upon. To construct such a theology presupposes that a student is also engaged in questioning and clarifying both ministerial experience and established theological positions.

Thus a second objective is to use theology in a *critical* way. Here theological reflection and theological education are perhaps most similar. Conventional theological wisdom and confessional positions are tested in order to determine the extent of their claim to truth. This determination is an ongoing inquiry as new ministerial experiences and new theological insights influence each other. In contrast to previous pastoral theology, theological reflection does not merely

apply theology to ministerial situations but examines theology to determine its applicability and influence on ministerial situations.

At this point a major deficiency of both traditional theological
education and current theological reflection in ministry preparation
should be noted. Neither ordinarily takes the factor of social analysis
sufficiently into account. Too often a pastoral encounter is presented
only at an interpersonal level. The wider social context is not included. For example, a parish meeting in which parishioners argue about
the use of church facilities for a civic meeting to discuss social welfare cutbacks may not broach the economic or racial prejudices that
are operative in the debate, focusing instead on conflict resolution
techniques or personal feelings about being a minister of reconciliation.

Similarly the theological tradition is often drawn into a ministerial experience without accounting for the social conditioning of theology. For example, a reflection on the Church's sacramental life
may never take into account how sacramental worship can convey
an a-historical view of God and Christian commitment, thus projecting a separation between worship and social life.

The introduction of social analysis into both ministerial experience and theological reflection intensifies the critical nature of the
process because both ministerial experience and theological reflection are subject to social analysis. It also complicates the process because social analysis calls for a wider set of questions and concerns
than ministerial preparation usually addresses. A social-analytic perspective broadens the discussion and especially the implications for
ministry, urging action that often goes beyond the customary range
of pastoral practice. With this, some new risks arise and a further
challenge to one's ministerial identity is felt.

It is unlikely that social analysis will be initiated by standard
theological education.[11] If it enters the process at all, it will have to
come from the theological reflection side. If it enters neither, theology as such will continue to be problematic for action/reflection
groups. On the other hand, an explicit social dimension in theological reflection would help make the necessary connections and render
theology more communicable and usable for action/reflection
groups as well as for ministry preparation.

How this dimension might be worked into theological reflection in ministry preparation may be seen a little more fully by examining some recent suggestions about how to do theological reflection.

Models of Theological Reflection

The primary goal of theological reflection in ministry preparation over the last several years has been described as integration.[12] Ordinarily this means making relevant connections between academic theology (as represented in a school curriculum) and pastoral training. In the process, a focal issue is one's ministerial identity and development as a person. The result of this effort seems to be more of a juxtaposition than an integration of these primary elements. There is still a long way to go.

Much of what has been learned so far has been gathered together in a valuable study conducted by James and Evelyn Eaton Whitehead entitled *Method in Ministry.*[13] A closer look at this work will focus the accomplishments and remaining tasks of theological reflection in ministry preparation.

In their scheme the Whiteheads first offer a model of reflection, then describe a method and illustrate the method with three examples. The model consists of "three sources of religiously relevant information—Christian Tradition, experience of the community of faith, and resources of culture."

The information from these sources is processed through a three step sequence. The first stage is attending. This means listening, absorbing the information from the three sources mentioned above. This leads to the second stage, asserting. Here the theological reflectors are expected to claim their positions, to affirm where they are, to own their theology. Out of such a committed and informed stance, decisions can then be made for pastoral action (step 3).

The approach which the Whiteheads present reflects a basic three step pattern which many authors have described: experience, theology, action.[14] The Whiteheads' presentation of them makes several helpful contributions.

(1) It recognizes that the integration of pastoral experience and academic theology is a complex task with many elements. It requires

a method; it is not automatic. Here many models appear incomplete. They include theological reflection as one explicit step in the process but don't really indicate how one theologizes at this point, why one selects this or that theme, position, author, or even what form of theologizing is most appropriate: biblical, historical, systematic, narrative, etc.[15]

(2) The Whiteheads broaden the experiential base to include cultural information. This is not yet a social analysis of theological tradition and pastoral experience but it is a step on the way. What is still needed is not just an awareness and identification of cultural factors but a critical analysis of cultural influences.[16]

(3) The Whiteheads' method anticipates an open dialogue among the sources so that theology enters the process and is partially shaped by it rather than maintaining a disengaged and superior, judgmental position, as often happens in academic settings where theology is the dominant discipline.

(4) The Whiteheads expect that the reflectors will claim a theological position rather than just survey the field and offer commentary. It is engaged theology and calls for a personal commitment with the accompanying risks.

(5) The method is decision-oriented and action-oriented from the beginning; thus theological reflection may not remain only an intellectual exercise and still be consistent with this method.

There are some questions which this approach raises.

(1) In what sense is ministerial experience the starting point of the process? Is ministerial experience the starting point only in the sense of triggering the process, or does it have a guiding, and perhaps even a normative, role to play in developing the course of theological reflection?

(2) If the latter is the case, then how does ministerial experience actually guide a group into the theological tradition? How is ministerial experience to function as a criterion for selecting and evaluating what the tradition has to offer, especially if the typical experience is an individual one without its social dimension?

(3) A fair amount of theological knowledge seems already presupposed. Does this method generate theological inquiry and development or does it clarify and organize what one already knows from academic courses and books?

(4) Finally how does the community enter the process and what effect does it have? The Whiteheads make frequent reference to the community, but it is not clear whether the community is providing data for theological reflection which is actually carried on privately or whether the theological reflection is being done in a group setting by the very people who share the experience being reflected upon.

These questions arise because the Whiteheads have done a great service in putting forth a method for integrating ministerial experience and theological reflection. What they have said is valuable, but the further questions are more valuable. In brief, what role and influence does ministerial experience have as the starting point and guide of theological reflection? How much theology is presupposed and how viable is it for a group to do this kind of reflection?

A partial answer to these questions is found in another recent book which wrestles with a similar issue. Edward Braxton's *The Wisdom Community* begins with the problematic of a "decline of common meaning" among Roman Catholics since Vatican II.[17] After listing the contributing factors to this decline and describing the general reaction as a turn to interiority, Braxton proposes a way to recover a new sense of common meaning. The mediating agent in the process is theology.

Relying on Bernard Lonergan's view of theology, Braxton sets forth a comprehensive theological schema which highlights conversion and locates it at any one of six levels: intellectual, moral, ecclesial, Christian, theistic, or religious. This continuum of conversion moments offers a new framework for common meaning.

In order to effect the experience of conversion and mediate it theologically, Braxton proposes the wisdom community. This is not just a metaphor to focus the intended outcome, but is a program including a suggested schedule of activities to help bring about the desired change. Braxton's program takes into account the main features of the Whiteheads' model and also responds to some of the questions listed above.

The initiating experience, analyzed rather thoroughly, seems to act as a criterion for selecting the theological response which in this case is conversion. By attending carefully to the decline of common meaning (and by doing so with others in the wisdom community), Braxton is able to identify some general characteristics of this situation. These become criteria for the adequacy of any theological response that may be asserted.

If a community attends to their experience carefully and thoroughly, the experience can lead them into the theological tradition with some sense of what to look for and some criteria for discerning what seems useful and what does not seem useful in regard to the initiating experience. In this way experience serves as a guide for theological reflection.[18]

In order to make this selection, however, some familiarity is needed with the range of the theological tradition and the possibilities it contains. Perhaps the Whiteheads' exhortation to "befriend" the tradition is all that is initially needed: a familiarity with the main history and systematic outline of theology. This is greatly enhanced when theological reflection is done in a group because the shared resources enrich each person's familiarity with the general tradition. Of course the exercise of investigating the theological tradition makes the resources of that tradition more familiar also. In any event, it would not be necessary to be professional theologians in order to be led into the tradition and to develop in this way a more detailed and useful knowledge of it.

On this point it is clear that Braxton envisions this task being carried out in a community setting. To be effective the members must be committed, prayerful, willing to analyze and share their life experience, keep a record of their reflections, be open to dialogue, do some common reading, and be faithful to gatherings and participation. The shared experience of attending together and helping each other assert their positions more clearly (and perhaps more comfortably) is the goal of the process.

Alongside these contributions, Braxton's work raises a couple of cautions for theological reflection. The identification of the general experience as "a decline of common meaning" is already a description which uses terminology from Lonergan. This can imply that the hearing and interpreting of the experience is channeled too quickly into one particular theological context, in this case Lonergan's treatment of conversion and the role of theology.

Further there is not much indication that the originating experience or reflection on it in the wisdom community might perhaps reshape Lonergan's schema, at least for the members of the wisdom community who use it. The mutually challenging and clarifying dynamic which the Whiteheads call for is not so evident. This warns against putting a pre-determined theological view in place rather than in dialogue with experience.

The point is not to claim that Braxton has done this but only to caution that if the originating experience is to be the guide into the theological tradition, the experience should determine the theological selection and set in motion the dialogue. Otherwise experience is being used only as an occasion for laying out a pre-determined theology or is being made to fit a theological construct which may or may not be helpful in a given case. In either event the connection is more accidental than methodological.

A final contribution to this discussion comes from the Bairnwick Center at the School of Theology, University of the South.[19] The model of theological reflection developed at the Center closely resembles the Whiteheads'. There are three sources of reflection: tradition (salvation history), experience (one's own actions and story), and positions. The last refers to personal values, beliefs, philosophy. The presence of socio-cultural input is not so immediately evident here as in the Whiteheads' model.

The method used to reflect on these sources is more detailed than the Whiteheads' and more clearly involves a group process. Although the reflection ordinarily begins with one person presenting an example of ministry, the group members share similar experiences from their ministry which enriches the presenting experience and identifies the group with the presenter. This collection of experiences is then symbolized in a metaphor or image which becomes the context for reflecting on input from the perspectives of tradition, culture, and personal positions.

Out of this reflective process come new insights for theological meaning and new directions for ministerial action. The same method is used, with slight modifications, for reflecting on general issues (like ministry to the elderly, Church leadership, social action) or texts.

The distinctiveness of this approach is the structured identification of group members with the presenter's experience and the use of a metaphor/image to explore together the meaning and action of the initiating experience.

Implications for Theological Reflection

Any method should encourage and ease creativity. Otherwise it becomes mechanical. The methods described above clearly aim at creativity, at personal growth, and at adequacy to the task of theological reflection. The following summary description may not be a full scale method to be implemented in step-wise fashion, but it does represent some implications for any group trying to get at theology in its theological reflection.

1. The starting point is concrete ministerial experience. This may be an individual's or a group's experience; it may be a single event or a series of events. If it is an individual's experience, time should be given for the group to identify with it. This may be done by asking clarifying questions, sharing similar experiences, affirming the feelings of the individual, etc. If it is a group experience, the same kind of process is needed until a focus emerges for the group's reflection.

2. The focus which emerges from the group reflection provides the key for attending to the theological tradition. If the focus is a decision-point in ministry, then the group would initially reflect on similar decision-points in the tradition, asking how decisions were made, who made them, what motivated the final choices, and what resulted. If the focus is an interpretation or statement of meaning, then the group would initially review similar interpretations, asking again how this particular meaning occurred, who expressed it, how it was received, and what effect it had.

In this step the contribution of social analysis is especially important. A really adequate theological reflection on decisions made or interpretations given or movements endorsed or structures erected has to take account of the social factors influencing those events precisely because the social factors did (and do) influence such events and help shape the theological tradition. To make this explicit is to attend more adequately to what is really there in the theological tradition.

There is a social context to theological developments but it is not usually highlighted or even acknowledged in standard theological studies. If it were introduced explicitly, it would help disclose an important formative aspect of theology and suggest more readily the applicability of theology to contemporary social situations.

Of course, this would also require persons trained in theology (like theological faculties and mentors in theological reflection processes) to become more acquainted with the social disciplines, their language, concerns, methods, etc. This could reinforce the impression that *real* theology isn't being done in theological reflection seminars. Moreover, it would keep calling insulated theological positions into question—which is a risky venture in an academic, theological environment.

On the other hand, introduction of a social-analytic element in theological reflection energizes the process for ministry because the integration of theology and action is addressed jointly all through the reflective process and not just as a final step of applying insights gained from reflection.

3. The third step is to symbolize the focus of the experience. This may occur through a projection based on "what would happen if . . ." we followed our social-theological reflection through. How would we feel? What would we do? Where would we look for support? Who would be with us and who against us? What surprises might we expect? And so on. Answers to these questions may be drawn up into an action plan, although the freedom and openness of the process should not be stifled by such a plan. Symbolization here is a way of inhabiting the reflection, of befriending the outcome, of heading toward the praxis which appears as the group reflects.

4. The final step is to implement what has been symbolized. The implementation serves as a closure to one phase of the theological reflection process and an opening to the next phase, namely, a new ministerial experience which is to be focused, symbolized, and enacted. In this way the process itself becomes the evaluation of both the theological reflection and the action that is inherent in it. If the theological reflection is successful, its inherent action will prompt further theological reflection and additional action will emerge. If the theological reflection is not successful, the action will become

self-contained and the process will either terminate or continue arti-
ficially. In either case participants will know something isn't working.

Theological reflection in ministry preparation faces most of the
challenges of theological reflection in other types of action/reflection
groups. There are no guaranteed methods for meeting the challenges
but there are sincere, intelligent, creative attempts being made. Ultimately such attempts are an affirmation that theology has something
important to contribute to ministry and Christian living. Getting at
theology in a usable way is worth the effort. Getting at it together is
worth even more.

NOTES

1. The first part of this study is found in H. Richard Niebuhr, *The
Purpose of the Church and Its Ministry* (New York: Harper and Row, 1977)
(reprint).

2. Seward Hiltner, *Preface to Pastoral Theology* (Nashville, TN: Abingdon Press, 1958).

3. For a summary of the development of Clinical Pastoral Education
leading to the formation of the Association of Clinical Pastoral Education,
see Paul E. Johnson, "Fifty Years of CPE," *Journal of Pastoral Care* XXII
(December 1968), pp. 221–231. For an assessment of the D. Min. degree, see
the special issue "The D. Min. in ATS," *Theological Education* XII (Summer 1976), p. 4.

4. Vatican II called for seminary revisions in its Decree on Priestly
Formation, especially Chapter V. The National Conference of Catholic Bishops drew up guidelines to implement this directive. The Program of Priestly
Formation in its revised forms is available from the USCC Publications Office, Washington, D.C. 20005.

5. Schleiermacher's best known work is *The Christian Faith* (New
York: Harper and Row, 1963). His collected writings on practical theology
(Bd. 13 Sammtliche Werke, 1850) have been very influential in European
universities but remain untranslated.

6. For a fuller discussion of the relationship between experiential and
empirical theology and the role of experiential theology in theological reflection, see the essay of Thomas E. Clarke in this volume.

7. For a recent discussion of this point see Mary Durkin, Andrew
Greeley, *et al., Parish, Priest and People* (Chicago: The Thomas More Press,
1981) especially part 2, "Leadership in the Local Church," pp. 119–217.

8. See, e.g., Don Browning, *The Moral Context of Pastoral Care* (Phil-

adelphia: Westminster Press, 1976); Paul Pruyser, *The Minister as Diagnostician* (Philadelphia: Westminister Press, 1976).

9. For some suggestions in this area, see Speed Leas and Paul Kittlaus, *The Pastoral Counselor in Social Action* (Philadelphia: Fortress Press, 1981) as well as my "Pastoral Care of Society as Liberation," *Journal of Pastoral Care* XXXIV (June 1980), pp. 125–130.

10. On the role of the supervisor/practitioner as a theologian, see Tjaard Hommes, "Supervision as Theological Method," *Journal of Pastoral Care* XXXI (September 1977), pp. 150–157; Quentin Hand, "Pastoral Counseling as Theological Practice," *Journal of Pastoral Care*, XXXII (June 1978), pp. 100–110.

11. One fortunate exception to this general rule is appearing in recent trends in biblical studies. For reference to those developments and a good example of the use of social analysis in a traditional theological discipline, see Jouette Bassler's essay in this volume. For a fuller discussion of the relationship of social analysis and theological reflection, see the essay by Joe Holland.

12. John Ford, "Discrimination, Desegregation, or Integration: Academic and Pastoral Theology," *Review for Religious* 37 (May 1978), pp. 414–432; Robert L. Kinast, "How Pastoral Theology Functions," *Theology Today* XXXVII (January 1981), pp. 425–439.

13. James and Evelyn Eaton Whitehead, *Method in Ministry* (New York: The Seabury Press, 1980).

13a. *Ibid.,* p. 13.

14. See, for example, John Shea, "An Approach to Pastoral Theology," *Chicago Studies* 12 (Spring 1973), pp. 15–29.

15. On the last point see Eugene King, "Religious Experience and Theological Reflection," *Theological Field Education: A Collection of Key Resources,* III (Association for Theological Field Education, 1981), pp. 63–73.

16. The type of social analysis intended here is represented, for example, in the booklet *Social Analysis* by Peter Henriot and Joe Holland published by the Center of Concern in Washington, D.C. or the general "hermeneutics of suspicion" developed by Juan Luis Segundo.

17. Edward K. Braxton, *The Wisdom Community* (New York: Paulist Press, 1980).

18. For a related but somewhat different approach to the problem of selection from the theological tradition, see the essay of James Hug in this volume.

19. The Bairnwick Center, School of Theology, University of the South, Sewanee, TN. The Manager of Training is John de Beer.

Part II

Analysis

The serious dangers involved in basing social policy on anecdote have become painfully clear in the United States of the early 1980s. To say that is not to contradict the claims for the importance of experience developed in Part I. But it is to recognize some of the difficulties that arise when one group's experience conflicts with another's. There is need for analyses of the stories of experience that can situate them in wider contexts of meaning, contexts capable of revealing more faithfully their true significance for Christian life and action. In Part II we offer a small sampling of theological and philosophical analyses of the action/reflection groups which attempt that task.

John Haughey assesses the interplay of prayer and social analysis in the groups' efforts at theological reflection. He reminds us that Christians involved in spirituality and those committed to social action have long been suspicious of each other and have found communication difficult. Whose experience shall we listen to in such a situation? Can the emergence of these new forms of theological reflection which bring together prayer and social analysis help reconcile these two groups? Haughey asks whether theological reflection as it is being developed in small communities may be "a forerunner of a deep sea change which will change our understandings of theology and prayer and social analysis and, therefore, of Church." He explores the roles of prayer, social analysis, and conversion in the reconciliation that would liberate God's revelation to both the "devout" and the "activists" and allow them to enrich each other.

In Chapter 6, Monika Hellwig carries on the dialogue with third world theology begun by Al Hennelly in Part I. Theological reflection in the small communities of Latin America has evolved an important claim: that the poor have an advantage in understanding the

101

good news. This, too, is a claim about whose experience we should listen to. Hellwig's theological analysis of that claim has important implications for community-based theological reflection in the United States.

In Chapter 7, John Langan brings the perspective of a political philosopher to bear on the action/reflection groups. He analyzes their place among ecclesiastical groups and situates them in the larger political and social context of U.S. society, and he explores the formative effects of four aspects of the U.S. political context on their ideals: its democratic and egalitarian character, its openness and mobility, its respect for the rule of law, and the place of protest movements in the shaping of its history and political awareness. After surveying the images by which the groups understand themselves and the values they profess, Langan suggests that they "should accept liberal society as their natural home and protector. . . ."

Joe Holland reads the situation quite differently. He supports the suggestion that a major social change is in process which is moving us beyond liberal society. He sees some of its earliest signs visible in the theological reflection of action/reflection groups and base communities of all types. Chapter 8 presents his historical and socio-cultural analysis of the emergence of a new root metaphor in humanity's collective unconscious. He describes ways in which he sees this metaphor—which he terms "the artistic metaphor"—subtly transforming the ways we perceive society, social analysis, time, God, theologizing, spirituality, evangelization, the poor, and our very selves.

Holland suggests that a deep human hunger for meaning and for peace and justice is bringing this new governing metaphor to birth. The metaphor, in turn, as it affects our perceptions and values, is the source of the creative energy reflected in the small community movements and the new forms of theological reflection which are integrating prayer and social analysis, faith and the pursuit of justice.

These analyses, with their provocative probing of key hidden forces shaping our responses to the world and to life, invite careful reflection. They are meant to stimulate our own analytical reflection on our experience, not replace it.

5
The Role of Prayer in Action/Reflection Groups

John C. Haughey, S.J.

A feeling of mutual suspicion has stalked two different populations of Christians for a long time. The one group, which we will call the activists, feel that the other group, which we will call the devout, has tended to spiritualize their Christian faith. The indictment reads:

> You devout have been blind to the social transformation that is meant to come about by faith lived out in the world. Your main concern about the world seems to be that you not be tainted by it. You are unaware of the fact that your view of faith has been distorted by the individualism that marks the world. Your spiritualization of the faith has you concentrate on personal piety, create circles of piety, participate in liturgies in which you seek your own union with God. As a result you have created a network of institutions that embody vertical emphases which have missed affecting the world the way Christ intended it.

The other population, the devout, has its own indictment to hand up to activist Christians:

> We can't help feeling that you are undertaking the impossible and that you are pursuing it in ways that are inconsistent with Christian faith, with the result that your faith, if not the faith of all of us, suffers. You assign too great a weight to human activity in general and your own efforts in particular. You make social impact the bottom line test of

103

the efficacy of Christianity and tend to get trapped within the walls of the world which you are out to change. Your view of faith has been distorted by those faithless theorists and activists who in their atheism have taken the world too seriously.

Rather than resolve their contrary views of faith, world, social action and prayer, adherents of these two understandings have tended to go in opposite directions retaining their own different senses of faith and what constitutes fidelity to Christ. The resulting fissure which every Christian denomination experiences lies deeper than any of the pastoral or doctrinal disputes that exist between denominations. Every so often an opportunity arises for these two different camps, so to speak, within the churches to re-examine themselves anew. The phenomenon of the action/reflection groups which we are examining in this volume is such an opportunity. It invites us to seek and examine the deep linkage between faith and the transformation of the world. Rather than dealing with this vast subject, I would like to do three things in this essay. First of all, I would like to examine the religious character of the theological reflection in these groups. Second, I would like to raise some issues for these groups about the role of prayer as that has ordinarily been understood in Christian history. Third, I would like to point out some of the promise that action/reflection groups hold for the future of both of the above mentioned camps.

THEOLOGICAL REFLECTION: A RELIGIOUS ACTIVITY?

I have examined the information which the action/reflection groups have furnished us. I approached this information with some obscurities operating in my mind which I hoped these groups would diminish. The first area of obscurity I had was: where to locate the so-called activity of theological reflection. In what genre of activity is it accurately seen? Is it a religious activity and process? Or is it closer to a socio-analytic activity and hence something that has to pass muster at the bar of social analysis? Or is it a theological activity as it is called, and hence something that is more appropriately located in the area of theology? Although my questions were clear enough, the answers furnished by these groups of the processes employed by them were not at all clear. It seems, in general, that the processes they are undertaking are a combination of all three activities. If this is so, could it be that theological reflection as it is done by these groups is a forerunner of a deep sea change which will change our understandings of theology and prayer and social analysis and, therefore, of Church? If this proved to be the case, it would make theological reflection a very important activity to analyze. If there is something changing in the way theology is done, the way prayer is done, and the way social analysis is done, it warrants our attention.

More specifically, one can ask whether a group's process is religious if it makes use of theological reflection? In order for the activity of reflection employed by these groups to be religious as I am using it here, their reflection would have to be done explicitly within an active-belief-in-God kind of horizon. When a group says that it is undertaking "reflection within a faith context," I am not sure whether faith is being assumed and operating implicitly or whether faith is really affecting the sense of the group. For the reflection to be religious, I would require that their active belief in God include a belief that God has a will—and not only that God has a will, but that this will is not kept secret. This will is not only general, but is a will with particulars for the individuals and for the group. Difficult as it might be to discover what that will is, they actively seek to know what it is.

The methods the group devises concretely indicate how it sees itself. In order to undertake an action or to come to decisions, each group has to create methods for reflection. How they look upon these methods is important for determining whether the activity of the group would qualify as religious or not. Their methods can be self-enclosed or have a transcendental expectation built into them. Unless it is the latter, it is unlikely that the group's reflections would qualify as religious as I am using that term here. By transcendental expectation I mean that the specific processes employed by the group are open to discovering a direction that does not come about merely through reasoning immanently conceived. The group can be spoken to through their processes. Or the group can have a sense of direction come to it from unforeseen circumstances and from outside of their processes. The group's methods would not qualify as religious if they were seen as employing autonomous reason operating within an immanent universe, a universe over which the Enlightenment had placed a ceiling.

Most of the groups which are about theological reflection employ socio-analytical methods and mediations. This is as it should be, of course. There is no contradiction between learning in any of the formal or informal ways in which this is pursued by the methods inspired by the social sciences and the ways persons or groups seek to discover God's will or word for them. There is rather a complementarity between these two different sets of means. An action/reflection group presumably exists to come to understand what action it might take in the world in order that the designs of God might be accomplished. One set of means such groups can employ is analytical/academic/rational. The other is religious. If the group is aware of the complementarity of these means, it augurs well for its religious depth. The increasingly complex levels of analysis, all of which can be insight-producing, can distract a group from its religious purposes. And religion can become an excuse for not doing sound analysis or doing it poorly. We will come back to this issue of social analysis later in the article.

In general, from the information we have from the groups we have inquired into, it is difficult to understand how some groups see themselves in terms of God since their descriptions of themselves lead one to believe that faith is more implicit than explicit and their reflection is more reason-centered. By contrast it is easy to see that some groups are religious. They consciously seek God or seek to experience the divine presence. They implore God's light, strength, will. The prayer of these groups obviously comes in many forms and shapes. There might be liturgy as we ordinarily know it. There is group-sharing *alias* group reflection or faith sharing. There is Scripture study. (It is not always easy to know when Scripture study is itself done in a context of prayer or when it is simply study. Obviously it can be either.) There can be group reflection on a social problem or question or conundrum "done in the light of faith." This seems to be prayer when it is consciously dialogical—the dialogue operating between the participants and God. It is less clearly prayer when the dialogical factor is not in evidence.

THE ROLES OF PRAYER

Prayer has many functions in these groups. To see their prayer as performing functions might appear to be too behavioralist a rendering of this kind of human activity. But saying that their prayer performs functions is not to imply that God can be used by human beings to play certain roles for them. Rather, I mean that, howsoever we understand prayer, it also does in fact perform different functions in our lives—many, in fact. Its many functions correspond to the many aspects of God's action in us. If we are obedient to the commandment that we are to "pray always" and all who pray have different needs, then prayer itself must perform different functions.

It would seem for these groups that there are three different functions that prayer plays in them. They would be a disposing, a disclosing, and finally a confirming function.

When prayer functions in a way that disposes the members of the group it would seem accurate to say that it does this in two different ways. It either transcendentalizes their perspective or it centers them in a deeper place. With respect to the first: the worship of a group can have the effect of freeing God to be God and the worshipers to be God's creatures. Although this may seem synonymous with the meaning of prayer itself, it does not appear all that frequently in the information we have, nor in the experience, I might add, that most of us have of God. It is no small thing for a group to let God be God. By this I mean that a sense of Otherness or Presence so impacts the group that it can hold its own sense of itself loosely enough to be continually reshaped by God.

One example will suffice here. A group had gone through a process of discernment about the purchase of a rather large building. They were aware of the enormous financial risk involved. Immediately before the final decision about the purchase—"I remember the moment very well. We realized how momentous a crossroads we had come to as a group. We all immediately stopped and prayed and had a sense of God bringing us to the choice we made." Their prayer at this moment was not disclosive in the sense that they came to see something different from what they had previously discerned. It was rather a moment in which the group could come to be in awe both of the step it was about to take and the one in whose name they were taking it. They did not domesticate the God they follow and obey. This somewhat spontaneous prayer enabled the group to hear God anew and allow God to be the Lord of the group. For a moment God was clearly Lord and Creator and sovereign, and they had a sense of their creatureliness and dependency. Prayer functioned at this moment in a transcendentalizing way. They were disposed to follow their decision.

Another way in which prayer functions to dispose the members of the group is less drastic and more frequent. Their prayer enables the group to be more centered. Three of the groups begin their meetings together with a fairly extensive period of centering prayer, frequently in silence. "This predisposes us to hear one another and to come from a deeper place in our sharing with one another. The silence enables us to get more in touch with ourselves. The result of being more centered in ourselves is that our subsequent deliberations involve better communication with one another." Their subsequent deliberations are not determined intrinsically by anything that goes on in the centering process since the centering process is notable for its lack of content. The centering prayer, however, disposes the parties to be about the process of deliberation and reflection from a base of greater peace and unanimity or harmony. Each of the three groups is clear that this centering process is more than a psychological process, although it also is psychologically helpful.

The second overall function that prayer performs in some of these action/reflection groups can be described as a disclosive one. By this I mean that the prayer of the group serves to reveal the direction or action the group is to take. For example, one of the groups which delights in the metaphor "journey inward/journey outward" sees its whole identity built and constituted from a number of different ministries that were generated within the hearts and minds of individual community members by "God calling those persons to different works." Once the person felt called to a unique mission in the city, he or she had recourse to the whole community to see whether their communal discernment reinforced the individual's sense that this was indeed a disclosure of God's will. If it did, others in the community were then invited to collaborate, if they felt called to this particular undertaking. The community is constituted, therefore, by mission groups which set about responding to the call which comes to the group through individuals.

Other groups underscored the disclosive function of prayer. One from the Friends' tradition contends that, with regularity, the Spirit operates within the group bringing it to the decisions that it takes, the policies it follows, and the priorities it sets. The group actively believes in "the immediate availability of the Spirit to the true seeker, the concept of continuing revelation, and a sense of the rightness of relying heavily on a sense of the Spirit directing individuals and the group."

A number of the groups in our survey seem to have devised a method which is open to God's disclosive will but one that is much more inextricably mixed in with human processes than the two previously cited examples. Hence, they are predisposed to delve into their own "guts" and carefully weigh what is going on in themselves personally and in their group. Feelings and reasonings would be a large part of this process of weighing. They expect to arrive at the disclosure in this way. The best single word for this family of processes, which is unlimited in its variations, is discernment. The participants actively pursue discernment either informally or through techniques because of their conviction that God's workings can be discerned if the group is sensitive enough to their own human workings.

An example of an informal approach comes from one group:

> We discuss together the life we are living, the sense of things we are called to do and not to do. In that setting we do not come to a sense of resolution but after sharing with one another we depart and allow the input that has taken place to rest in us and be that which we reflect on. Later we come back together from our individual prayer and we feel that the movement of God's spirit among us is not a rhetorical thing but it has drawn us each from where we were toward a sense of consensus, a sense of being one mind.

Another group uses the "Ignatian Principles for Discernment" as a more formal process for reflecting on where they are, where they

have been, and where they are going. From these principles they
have developed a process whereby they weigh the social consequences and implications of the matter about which they are attempting to make choices. Communal discernment takes place after
personal prayer and personal discernment of the matter. Because of
this process "we are coming to trust more in the Spirit's movement
in us. We feel that the community of faith that we are when we gather together is the primary locus of God's word to us. The scriptural
word is secondary even to that." One of the practices of this same
group is to encourage each member in the course of Lent to undergo
a period of personal discernment with regard to the meaning of the
community and the presence of each of them within it. After Easter
this then develops into a communal process whereby "we formally
discern the goals and objectives of the group."

But there is an even more important dimension to this whole
disclosure function of prayer in these groups. While they all would
have set out to do something for God and Christ in the world, what
is frequently disclosed to them is not what God would have them do
in the world but what it is in them that makes them part of the problem rather than part of the solution. Prayer in this sense, whether
they intend it or not, gets them in touch with their biases, addictions,
disordered affects, pre-Gospel mindsets, or conditioned responses.
God can then begin to heal them and purify them and forgive them
and call them beyond where they are. The occasion for this kind of
disclosure is frequently that a strong "prophetic voice" has been
heard by the community. This can be from an author who is studied
or via a conviction which dawns on the community in their prayer
together. The hearers are convicted of the disparity between their ha-
bitual attitudes and the Gospel.

The third overall function which prayer plays in these groups is
one of confirmation. I mean this in several senses. The prayer of the
group can serve as a confirmation of the tradition or spiritual heritage or denominational spirituality which the group has as its heritage. While a few of the groups we have surveyed are consciously
eclectic, several have strong ties to their denominations or religious
traditions and therefore to the spirituality within those traditions.
They note that their prayer confirms their traditions and is a renewal

of them. They are, therefore, retrieving aspects of their traditions and enfleshing them anew in and through their groups.

But prayer also functions to confirm people's experiences, personal or collective. In addition the confirmation which comes from prayer can also be of one's sense of oneself or of what one has experienced with others. It enables people to own their own unique experiences more deeply. Several groups mentioned they experienced, as a result of their prayer together, their common pain—pain, for example, that had been caused them by sexism. God is experienced as confirming them and being present as vindicator or healer or the One who hears their hurt. Prayer in this sense then serves the function of consoling them and convincing them that God is with them and for them.

In brief then, the confirmatory function of prayer has a number of different ways in which it can be viewed: the confirmation of a tradition, of a group's identity, of a personal or group experience, or of a course of action. The confirmatory function reinforces the group or persons after the actions are decided upon or the decisions made. The dispositional function, on the other hand, looks to affect a group or person before its decisions or actions are undertaken. And the disclosive function, finally, affects the group in the actual decisions or actions undertaken.

FUNCTIONLESS PRAYER

Classifying the prayer of these groups in terms of functions can be misleading, for several reasons. First of all it analyzes an act that is usually less than susceptible of analysis and always more unitary in practice. Second, prayer to be authentic must also be functionless. With respect to the first point, an example taken from the June 1981 issue of *Sojourners* puts back together things that, in real life, are virtually inextricable. One can also see from this example the close connection between the different functions prayer plays in a group's decision. More importantly we can see that the action would not have been undertaken if this Jonah House group's prayer had not disposed, disclosed, and confirmed them. The narrator is Father Dan Berrigan. He described what preceded the decision to wreak symbolic havoc on the Mark 12A project at the G.E. plant in King of Prussia, Pennsylvania.

> We have never taken actions such as these, perilous, crucial, difficult as they are, without the most careful preparation of our hearts, our motivation, our common sense, our sense of one another. This is simply a rule of our lives; we don't go from the street to do something like the King of Prussia action. We go from prayer. We go from reflection. We go from worship, always. And since we realized that this action was perhaps the most difficult of our lives, we spent more time in prayer this time than before. We passed three days together in a country place, we prayed, and read the Bible and shared our fears, shared our second and third thoughts. In time we grew closer. We were able to say, "Yes. We can do this. We can take the consequences. We can undergo whatever is required." All of that. I talked openly with Jesuit friends and superiors. They respected my conscience and said, "Do what you are called to." That was the immediate preparation. And what it issued in was a sense that, with great peacefulness, with calm of spirit, even though with a butterfly in our being, we could go ahead. And so we did.

After the action was decided, prayer was employed to confirm a decision already made. The testimony continues:

> I had to continue to ask myself at prayer, with my friends, with my family, with all kinds of people, with my soul, "Do you have anything to say today?" I mean, beyond a lot of prattling religious talk. "Do you have anything to say about life today, about the lives of people today?" I am not at all sure that I do have something to offer. But I did want to say this. I am quite certain that I had September 9, 1980 to say.

Much time was spent by Berrigan and his friends on the question of the action, its relationship to the law, their relationship to law. Notwithstanding all the doubts, he kept posing for himself the question: What helps people?

This was a haunting question for me. Will this action be helpful? Will people understand that this lesser evil done to this so-called "property" was helping turn things around in the Church, in the nation? Will the action help us to be more reflective about life and death and children?

He decided to go through with it. "Our act is all I have to say. I have nothing else to say in the world. At other times one could talk about family life and divorce and birth control and abortion and many other questions. But this Mark 12A is here and it renders all other questions null and void."

The second point I have made is that there is another way of viewing prayer than the ways in which it has been analyzed above. It can be looked at not as having functions to perform but as an activity which is intentionally use-less. For the person or the group, prayer in the second sense doesn't have any end in view other than being done for its own sake. When looked at in this second way, it is not performance-oriented, achieving something in the world, goal-oriented. There is no necessary linkage between prayer and action-in-the-world or prayer and world-improvement or even self-improvement. It is its own reason for being done. It is done because God is God.

This other way of viewing prayer does not cancel out the first way. In fact prayer should have both of these contraries operating in a person who is spiritually healthy or a group which is spiritually healthy. Not only can we have it both ways, we should have it both ways. If prayer is only as valid as the functions it performs, it will almost certainly be perverted to having to prove itself. It will be subjected to some kind of cost/benefit analysis. Prayer should be as far beyond cost/benefit analysis as love is. It should be as use-less as love. It can become so essential to a group's understanding of itself that for the group not to be praying would be for the group to cease knowing who it is. It can undergird a group's sense of itself independent of the tasks which it performs together.

One of the social indicators of the depth of a group's prayer is whether its prayer is equally capable of drawing the members of the group to activity as to non-activity or rest or a simple "being-with" God. The continuation of the prayer and action group will become problematic if it is not capable of being drawn in both of these directions. It does not augur well for the freedom God is accorded in a group if its prayer cannot lead it either to activity in and on the world or withdrawal from activity.

There is a dialectic here as well as an order which must be kept. Prayer, because it is a human activity, has functions which it plays in a group's life, whether they see and intend these or not. However, by the same token, because its object is God, it must also be beyond functionality. But of the two aspects of this dialectic, not having a function is more basic to prayer than any of the ways in which it might function in a group's operational life. Otherwise there is always the possibility that God is employed by the group. There is also the possibility that activity undertaken in the name of Christ can, in fact, be used as a shield against union with him and surrender to him.

The most traditional way within Judaeo-Christian history for this order to be observed was for the believing group to constantly celebrate the saving actions of God. These celebrations generated its liturgical life. When our personal and group actions are undertaken within a framework of active awareness of the saving acts of God, then our actions are more likely to be seen in their actual significance. If our actions are not seen within the framework of God's saving actions, it is almost certain that they will be taken overly seriously. By rooting its celebrants in the activity of God, liturgical prayer acts as a corrective against an exaggerated sense of the importance of ourselves and of our actions. It also creates a frame of reference within which frustrations, failures, persecutions, a sense of insignificance, all of which accompany human activity, can not only be tolerated but given positive meaning. Christians glory in the failure of the ministry of Christ. "By his stripes we were healed."

The sabbath in Israel and Sunday in the Christian liturgical week, if observed, teach these things effectively. Both were days of rest. Both were days within which people came to full-stop with respect to their own activities so that they could marvel at the action of God in their lives and in their world. They learned they were being taken care of by God. They learned to take a correct measure of themselves laboring. They learned the prayer of praise, the prayer of adoration, the prayer of surrender. They learned the functionless prayer of love. They learned to trust. This was formative of both the old Israel and the new Israel. It located the role of activity in their sense of themselves and in their responsibilities in the world. A modern group would pay a high price for its modernity if it ignored liturgy, its traditional values and formative power.

FAITH AND SOCIAL ANALYSIS

As I mentioned before, most of the groups surveyed by our project use social analysis. I am not always sure what social analysis is in these groups, and it certainly is not always the same method that is being employed. What is constant in all of them is that the group is using social analysis to see more deeply into the social situation they are involved in or have chosen to labor in. Since I see no way of classifying the data that we have on this, I will simply limit myself to four observations on the relationship between faith and social analysis or the religious dimension of this activity of social analysis.

First, for social analysis to be connected with religion as I am using that term in this essay, there would have to be some conversion undergone on the part of those employing this method. The social analysis might be the means to the person's conversion. Or the person's conversion might result in involvement in an action/reflection group which employs such a method. By conversion I mean a change of one's mind and heart toward God. But in this context I am also referring to conversion in a social sense. At a minimum this would mean that people and their needs, the neighbor in other words, become an internal part of the person's commitment to God—not merely an intellectual conviction that love of God and love of neighbor are two halves of a whole, but a change of heart that sees persons newly and sees how they must always be part of the enfleshment of one's commitment to and love of God.

Such a conversion admits of many degrees. Any believer of any depth reverences persons. But believers can undergo so profound a conversion in their self-understanding, God-awareness, and neighbor-consciousness that the latter can become Christ himself. In brief, then, for theological reflection groups to be religious as I understand that term, their social analysis would be linked in some way with a process of conversion of their members. And for religious groups to qualify as theological reflection groups, their conversion process would have to be social. Social conversion involves persons in a compassionate involvement with others or in a virtual mystical identification of neighbor as Christ.

Second, I wonder how a deepening religious conversion affects a person's or a group's need for social analysis. My own suspicion is that it lessens the need. One doesn't think of Dorothy Day doing social analysis. The social and religious sensitivity of some people seems to become so heightened that both the existence of humanly deplorable conditions and the indignity to which people are being subjected make social analysis superfluous. Or at least some less formal or more intuitive form of this seems sufficient.

I realize at the same time that it would be false to contrast too sharply the enlightenment which faith can provide and the light which social analysis can cast upon it. In fact it would be a strange love of Christ in the poor which had at hand a way of seeing more deeply into the structural causes of the poverty that individuals are undergoing and chose to forego the use of this instrument. The more enlightened our understanding, the more beneficial the action undertaken.

This leads to a third observation. Enlightenment, whether religious or social, can become an addiction if it loses its relationship to praxis. The group can become so enamored of social analysis that it loses touch with the instrumental purposes for which it employs such a method. Or it can come to an awareness of so many of the complex levels of a social reality that it is incapable of choosing at what level its action should be undertaken. Social analysis often reveals more than one option. The choice between options can be made on the basis of a number of factors relating to resources, time, competence, cost, etc. But methods of social analysis do not of themselves lead to a discernment of what would be right for the group itself to do. Here is another place where religious discernment becomes necessary. In fact, social analysis can heighten the need for religious discernment.

The insight arrived at by social analysis, furthermore, will not of itself stir those employing this method to undertake the necessary action to ameliorate the situation. Methods which inform need to be complemented by methods which stir the heart, galvanize the affect, and put members in touch with the story that will lead them to undertake collective action on the situation. Once again, this is the place at which religious means and analytic means intersect.

A final observation has to do with the relationship between conscientization and conversion. In the past Christians tended to be naive about the amount of social conditioning we unsuspectingly brought to prayer. When our conditioning isn't even suspected it is unlikely that our prayer will pierce it or that our prayer will bring us beyond our conditioning. The conscientization which social analysis can produce helps one supersede one's conditioning. But social analysis may also have only a superficial effect on a person, not a change of mindset or a real transformation at the level of attitudes. Social analysis can change a person's perception about a particular situation or social condition. A deep experience of God, on the other hand, can change people's mindsets, their sense of who they are, who God is, and who the neighbor is. One can begin to see the close relationship between religious means and analytical means. Either of them can effect a conscientization of the person. Each may be necessary in order for a conscientization to be brought to conversion or a conversion to be sufficiently social.

Reconciling "The Devout" and "The Activists"

The phenomenon of action/reflection groups reintroduces in a substantial way the dualities that are peculiar to Christian faith. They reintroduce the issues of the relationship of Church to world, reason to revelation, theological reasoning to listening to God, societal transformation to union with God. These have been with Christianity from the beginning. Thus religion is at its healthiest when it keeps dualities together in a healthy tension. It is at its unhealthiest when it falls into one of the many forms of dualism or reductionism that have plagued the Church throughout the centuries. To avoid this something more foundational must be kept in mind. Dualities become dualisms when there is an inadequate grasp of the necessary tension between immanence and transcendence which is at the core of Christian faith. When this tension is disregarded we get the indictments of one another that were noted at the beginning of this article.

In particular, if the emphasis on transcendence is overstated, God can become all in all and the living out of one's faith can begin to exclude what God includes in saving intentions, namely, people, humankind, the world itself. The more likely temptation within action/reflection groups, however, is to overemphasize the importance of immanence to the neglect of transcendence. A resolution of the tension in favor of immanence develops a kind of Christianity that knows too much about God's intentions for the world and too little about God. Salvation becomes continuous with and linear to the world as we know it. This is only a hair's breadth away from a faith which is reduced to functionality or from a justice vision that is reduced to laws and an eschatological vision which is reduced to politics. A reductionism that errs on the side of immanence is prone to instrumentalize people and separate the world into those who are good and those who are bad—a judgment based on whether they agree or disagree with my vision. A healthy reachievement of the tension is aware of the fact that our need to transform this world is always under the measure of a transcendence—"As high as the heavens are above the earth, so high are my ways above your ways and my thoughts above your thoughts" (Is 55:9). No sooner do we say this than we must realize at the same time that a transcendentalization of our faith has been the more frequent form of error. This error deprives the world of followers of Christ who are intent upon the enfleshment of the salvation which God intends for this world—reconciliation, shalom, forgiveness, and justice.

It is all very well and good to get these tensions in perfect balance theologically and in one's mind. It is more important for the heart to be attuned to them. Attunement of the heart comes about by conversion. Unconverted hearts are comfortable living in one side of dualism and taking it to be the mystery of faith. The heart that follows the Lord into the mystery we are called to live in lives happily within the tension between immanence and transcendence. Bernard Lonergan's definition of conversion is germane here. It is the movement from inauthenticity to authenticity. Inauthenticity for Lonergan is found in a person who is innocent of self-transcendence; the person is still in some form of self-absorption. Authenticity by contrast is achieved through self-transcendence.[1] There are a number of ways in which a person moves from self-absorption to self-transcendence, and a number of levels within which this takes place. One of them is intellectual. When a person is concerned to move beyond sentiment or opinion or an it-seems-to-me attitude toward truth, seeking to make use of the means whereby he or she can come into knowledge of "what is so," this is an indication that a conversion of intellect is taking place. The employment of social analysis could be one form which this would take. A moral conversion, furthermore, is the movement beyond seeking one's own advantage or acting on one's own preferences to the movement toward value and good for others or the good for the whole. Unless there is contrary evidence it would seem that membership in an action/reflection group would be a movement in this direction, a move toward self-transcendence into concern for the good of others.

Lonergan goes on to analyze the kind of conversion which is an even more profound conversion. This happens when self-transcendence moves from "capacity to actuality when one falls in love. Then one's being becomes being-in-love." It is as if a person moves from one life support system on to another, for being-in-love now becomes a "first principle. From it flows one's desires and fears, one's joys and sorrows, one's discernment of values, one's decisions and deeds."[2] ". . . Once it has happened and as long as it lasts being-in-love takes over."[3] One now knows and chooses and acts toward and within a new horizon. If the beloved is God then "being in love [is] without limits or qualifications, conditions or reservations."[4] Having migrated to being in love, one's values are now transvalued, one's knowing transformed. Being in love with God is self-transcendence with a vengeance, is conversion full-throttle.

One can immediately see how errors they might incline toward intellectually are less likely to be made by Christians if they practice their faith. There is no recorded case of a Christian having achieved authentic self-transcendence or conversion or a state of being in love with God without that love being expressed in deeds. In a word,

transcendence and immanence are always self-correcting and reciprocal. The more fully converted people are, the further they will
move from dualism and one side of the dialectic toward the center.
There was something of a caricature in the indictments of the activists and the devout toward one another at the beginning of this article. It should be obvious that anyone or any group which conceives
of the meaning of the faith in the way the indictment reads is a person or a group still in deep need of conversion. The experience of
conversion will move a person or a group to the rich duality at the
center, a duality that keeps immanence and transcendence in a
healthy tension with one another.

One could go mad trying to keep these two aspects of Christianity together if the only way of doing that was abstract or theological.
Happily, their resolution is achieved not *cogitando* but *ambulando*—
not by thinking it out but by living it. Christian faith is in the person
of Christ who is both "the perfect reflection of God" and "a man like
us in all things save sin." To be in Christ relieves one of having to
solve the relationship between the immanence and the transcendence
of God in the Christian life—valuable as such an attempt might be in
itself. That mystery can be lived, so to speak, experienced, resolved
in the living out of the love one has been given for God in Christ
through the Spirit. In short, Jesus is the shape of the mystery we
have been dealing with in this article. The action/reflection group
phenomenon is itself a symptom of a widespread dissatisfaction with
emphasis on only one side of the mystery of his person—Jesus as
transcendent spirit. Equally unacceptable is a Jesus who is sent—
spirit reduced to ideology. An action/reflection group which has
combined a love of Christ actively shown within its own ranks and
outside itself can be an important witness to dualisms overcome in
modern Christianity.

I always thought that the symbol of the resolution of these tensions has been well depicted in the 21st chapter of John where the
risen Jesus questions Peter three different times: "Simon Peter, do
you love me?" With each confession on Peter's part of his love, Jesus
calls him to "feed my lambs" (Jn 21:15). This vignette shows the order within the dialectic. From within a life of communion with Jesus,
Peter could proceed to an activist manifestation of love all the way to
the point of the loss of his own life.

NOTES

1. Bernard Lonergan, *Method in Theology* (New York: Herder and Herder, 1972), p. 104.

2. *Ibid.,* p. 105.

3. *Ibid.,* p. 106.

4. *Ibid.,* p. 106.

6
Good News to the Poor: Do They Understand It Better?

Monika K. Hellwig

One of the most interesting and controversial aspects of the contemporary flowering of theological reflection among groups of Christians who are not professional theologians is the way that such groups invoke experience. This is examined at length in the essay by Thomas E. Clarke in this volume. The analysis of the role of experience in that essay is both relevant and helpful for the question proposed in this one. The claim of an "hermeneutic privilege of the poor" which is so widely made in our times[1] is perhaps the most controversial example of the controversial question concerning the role of experience in theological reflection. It is, on the one hand, a source of great inspiration to many devoted persons who work for and among the poor and see a need for "evangelization of the Church *by* the poor."[2] On the other hand, it is seen as a source of scandal and confusion by others who feel personally or professionally threatened by the claim.

The claim of "an hermeneutic privilege of the poor" is evidently a claim that being poor gives one an advantage in understanding the good news of salvation. It does not deny or supplant claims for other sorts of advantage in understanding the Gospel, such as the advantage that may be claimed for the prayerful, the studious, the detached, the more thoroughly and correctly instructed, the generous, the humble, and so forth. It does not say that only the poor understand the Gospel. It simply suggests that being poor is an advantage. If the claim is well founded, it has implications that are of utmost importance for us all, and it deserves close attention and sober reflection.

It is the purpose of this essay: first, to consider what the claim might mean in more detail; second, to present a selection of the more persuasive contemporary authors making such a claim; third, to attempt an analysis of the claims they are actually making; fourth, to present and evaluate the foundation in Scripture and tradition alleged by these authors; fifth, to draw some conclusions that may be of help to groups engaged in theological reflection.

WHO ARE THESE POOR AND WHAT IS THIS PRIVILEGE?

Just as Clement of Alexandria found it necessary in his time and social context to ask the question who that rich person is who *can* be saved, so in the present context it seems necessary to ask the question who the poor person might be who has privileged access to the meaning of the good news of salvation. The question, of course, is at least as old as the difference in the Beatitudes as reported by Matthew and Luke respectively (Mt 5:3; Lk 6:20, 24), and it seems, indeed, to be an issue even in the Hebrew Scriptures. If one replies that the poor intended are the "poor in spirit," the humble who seek their security in God alone, this answer is undeniably right in what it covers but surely inadequate in the texts which it ignores, in which actual deprivation is expressed.

If we extend the meaning, then, to those actually deprived, there remains the question as to how the category is defined. Are we speaking, as the Scriptures often seem to do, of those who live in simple sufficiency but not in luxury, or of the destitute? Further, there is the question: Is it material deprivation that is primary or is it powerlessness in society? In the contemporary context one may also need to ask: Are we speaking only of those who are poor because of injustice and oppression, or do we include those who are poor from causes that cannot be directly attributed to sin? Finally, are we really speaking of all who experience their powerlessness in face of suffering? Clearly all these possible definitions of the poor might be used in considering the claim of privileged access to the meaning of the Gospel. However, the claim itself varies significantly according to which definition of poverty is used.

The other half of the phrase, the "hermeneutic privilege," also lends itself to differences in meaning. There is a claim to privileged access to understanding. It could be a claim of greater openness to the Gospel as a call to conversion or it could be a claim to better understanding of the concrete demands of such conversion, whether personal or societal. In terms of the societal demands, it could apply to technical, structural aspects or attitudinal aspects. Actually, the privileged access of the poor to understanding could be considered seriously at any of these levels but the questions would be different and the answers might be different.

Clearly, the further the discussion moves into technical and structural implications of the acceptance of the Gospel, the more one relies upon what Clarke calls "empirical" rather than personal and existential experience,[3] and the complex configurations of this tend to be in the possession of those who are not poor. For example, the Gospel certainly calls for a conversion to trust in God and concern for others. The disadvantaged urban poor might be expected to be particularly ready and disposed to grasp the need for trust in God and to know from their own experience of deprivation the need of others. They might also be expected to understand readily that needs can be met by the sharing of the community. But one would not ordinarily expect such poor persons spontaneously to grasp the possibilities of community cooperatives or to negotiate capital loans, rental of space and all the other things necessary for implementation.

The same is of course true in the theoretical realm. A claim for privileged access to the meaning of the Gospel on the part of the poor does not compete with the claim to special competence of the biblical exegete, for example. There can be no question of poverty having any relevance to the technical aspects of textual analysis. Whatever is claimed for the poor in special means of understanding texts could only be in complementarity with the technical expertise of the exegete. It might consist in the tendency to ask quite different questions of the text, or in the likelihood of setting imagination to work on the text more concretely and simply.

With this range of possibilities in mind, it will be helpful to look at some of the authors and at the claims they are in fact making. The next section will simply describe these claims, and the third will attempt an analysis of them.

THE AUTHORS AND THEIR CLAIMS

The claim that the poor have privileged access to the meaning of the Gospel is not the same as the claim that Christians are committed by their faith to an "option for the poor," but the two are certainly related.[4] The option for the poor is described by Alejandro Cussianovich in this way: "to identify with the poor and the oppressed, to accept their standard of living, their justifiable aspirations, and their efforts to attain them as our own."[5] The same author writes, "Our solidarity with the poor and the oppressed, with sinners and the suffering, with the persecuted and humiliated, has real historical import because it is a truly evangelical option and the fulfillment of the good news."[6]

This in itself is a powerful and exigent claim. Yet it does not amount to the claim of an hermeneutic privilege of the poor. It could be understood as an appeal to more privileged Christians (in Cussianovich's writing, an appeal to religious congregations professing the evangelical counsels) to bring the good news, which they supposedly understand, to the poor of the world who are in need of it. The claim that this is a demand intrinsic to the Christian faith and not a matter of personal preference, temperament or special vocation is a claim so exigent that it is frequently disputed because it puts us all in the wrong. But this is not the concern of this essay. The claim of the hermeneutic privilege goes beyond this by claiming that we who are privileged must identify with the poor and the oppressed not only because they need us but also because, from their experience of poverty and oppression, they are in a better position to understand the Gospel. Therefore we need to have them teach us that meaning.

It seems at first sight as though this contention is not well thought out. It seems as though those who have had more opportunity to study Scripture and theology must understand the Gospel better and should bring it to the poor who have had less opportunity because lack of education and of human culture almost invariably is an important element of poverty and oppression. Even if personal conversion plays a role in understanding that goes beyond book learning, it still seems as though those who from their positions of privilege have made voluntary renunciations for the sake of the Gos-

pel must necessarily understand it better than the poor and oppressed who are so from necessity. So one might be tempted to
interpret the claim for the hermeneutic privilege of the poor as referring to the "poor in spirit" or to those who "have left all things" in
order to follow Jesus. But the claims that are made so persuasively
by contemporary authors cannot be reduced to this.

Julio de Santa Ana, writing for and to the World Council of
Churches, makes a plea that not only should that body concern itself
with what he calls the scandal of poverty in today's world, but that it
should adopt as its own the theology of the "underdogs" of history.[7]
He denies the position described in the last paragraph, which would
suppose the poor in the material sense to be poor also in theological
insight and reflection. Thus:

> It would be wrong to believe that the poor have no theolo-
> gy, that they do not reflect on the experience of being
> Christian, that their reflection includes no protest of their
> condition of poverty. Much of their theological thinking
> takes place in community; it is not individualistic. Much of
> their reflection is geared to the particular and concrete; it is
> seldom systematized or expressed in abstractions. Much of
> their thinking bears on their pressing situation and prob-
> lems; it is seldom ahistorical.[8]

Noting that the theology of the poor has "a different starting
point, a different agenda, a different raison d'être," de Santa Ana
points out that the primitive Church was poor in the sense in which
he has defined the poor, namely, as the oppressed, the marginalized,
those struggling for their most basic rights, the exploited and plun-
dered and those whose country is struggling for its liberation.[9] It is
by such communities that the Gospel of Jesus Christ was formulated
and transmitted to us in the Bible and (though Santa Ana who writes
from a Protestant perspective does not make this explicit) at the earliest stages of tradition. He concludes that the message formulated by
the primitive Church of the poor has "an immediacy, concreteness
and historical character" which "makes it particularly accessible to
the Church of the poor today."[10] He points out further that with the
hierarchic structuring of the Church in the course of time, and par-

ticularly since the Constantinian establishment of the Church in society, there has been a continuous ambivalence in attitudes toward the poor and poverty because the voices of the poor have in the main been silenced in the forum of theological reflection.

Julio de Santa Ana pleads for a Church that listens to the voice of the poor precisely in their interpretation of the good news—that is, in their theological reflection. He sees this as an urgently needed corrective to prevailing theologies that "legitimize oppression" because their concept of revelation is static (placing the event of revelation in the past and ignoring the present action of the Holy Spirit in the community). As a result, they do not expect structural change in society within a continuing salvation history. He sees the theological reflection of the poor as corrective also of a theology that has captured discipleship in a closed system, the slavery of the law applied on an *a priori* basis. The poor, like Jesus, begin where they must, namely from the demands of the real human situation in the particular and concrete circumstances of their lives. Finally, the voice of the poor in theological reflection is a corrective because theology done by the relatively privileged, frequently under the practical patronage of the very wealthy and powerful, has been "used and manipulated in order to communicate the ideals and expectations of dominant sectors of society. . . . It has helped to legitimize unjust structures and mechanisms of oppression, calming the people and leading them to accept with resignation the status quo in society."[11] Thus certain societal expectations and values of more powerful interest groups have subtly been identified with the Gospel.

Gustavo Gutiérrez makes the link between the "option for the poor" and the "hermeneutic privilege of the poor" as follows.

> Within a society where social classes clash, we are true to God when we side with the poor, the working classes, the despised races, the marginal cultures. . . .
>
> The Gospel read from the point of view of the poor and the exploited . . . requires . . . a Church which arises from the people, a people who wrest the Gospel from the hands of the great ones of this world and thus prevent it from being used to justify a situation against the will of the liberating God. . . .

Perhaps we should go further and say that the preaching of the Gospel will be truly liberating when the poor themselves are the preachers.[12]

What Gutiérrez means by this is further spelled out as follows:

... if the Church wants to be faithful to the God of Jesus Christ, it has to rethink itself *from below*, from the position of the poor of the world, the exploited classes, the despised races, the marginal cultures. ... In the last resort it is not a question of the Church being poor, but of the poor of this world being the people of God, the disturbing witness to the God who sets free. ...

... history (in which God reveals himself and we proclaim him) must be re-read from the viewpoint of the poor. ...

Great efforts have been made to blot out the memory of the oppressed. ... The memory of Christ is present in every hungry, thirsty, oppressed and humiliated person. ...

Remaking history means subverting it, that is to say, "turning it upside down," and seeing it from below instead of from above. ...

This subversive history involves a new experience of faith, a new spirituality and a new proclamation of the Gospel.[13]

This statement by Gutiérrez dates from 1979. In a statement of his position first published in 1971, when liberation theology was in a very early stage of formulation, the notion that liberating theology must in some sense come from the poor themselves was not so clearly expressed. Yet it was certainly implicit. In that earlier statement on poverty and the poor, Gutiérrez was at pains to repudiate any romantic idea of a Church of the poor in terms of an aesthetic or bucolic return to simplicity of life-style. Poverty in our times means oppression and struggle, and solidarity with the oppressed is not separable from protest against their condition. The implication of this seems to be that the demands of the redemption are perceived from the perspective of those involved in the crushing reality of oppression and not from the perspective of those flirting with some romantic fantasy of poverty constructed to fit *a priori* expectations.[14]

Julio de Santa Ana, also in an earlier study, one which dealt with the biblical and patristic basis for the special claims of the poor, argued for the link between the "option for the poor" and the "hermeneutic privilege of the poor," though without using the latter term. His argument is that "since the poor live in hope of justice, poverty becomes a condition for true piety—the quality of those who suffer but nevertheless continue to hope in the Lord and remain humble before God."[15] He sees Jesus as the poor man who is not resigned to his poverty "but practices the hope which kindles hope in others too." The profile is sharpened by contrast with the rich, seen as "those who base their existence on the accumulation of wealth," a definition that is extended to all who will not part with their wealth in response to the dire need of others:

> The road to the kingdom, at least for the rich, is signposted by the search for justice, in whose service they must offer their possessions as a sign of charity and solidarity with the less privileged, with those in the lowest rank of the pyramid.[16]

There is a negative argument here. His interpretation puts all of us who are wealthy in comparison with the destitute and the oppressed masses of the human race more or less in bad faith as long as we maintain a standard of living higher than theirs at their expense. If we are in bad faith, we are bound to interpret the Gospel for our times in less than the fullness of its promise of redemption. Conversely, those who are not guilty of oppressing others, because they themselves are powerless, are by that very fact better disposed to hear a Gospel of hope and community for all. Yet de Santa Ana also admits that there is a need for an awakening of the hope of the poor, a hope which seldom springs forth spontaneously but is most often "encouraged by the tenacious, dedicated and persistent work of people who, although not originally poor, have decided to join forces with the poor to fight against oppression and social inequality."[17]

Helder Camara, also admitting the tendency to fatalism in the unaided poor, nevertheless puts the same negative argument even more bluntly. While selfishness is universal, he writes, it operates differently in the rich and in the poor. In the rich it obscures the solution which is community, sharing of resources and goods out of unconditional love of God and love of neighbor as oneself. The poor are also likely to be selfish, but that will not interfere with their ability to grasp the solution that goods and resources must be shared. Rather it should lead them into a quest for some grounds of hope that this will happen, and it is at this point that they are attuned to hear the promise of the reign of God among human persons and human societies.[18] "The more we have to lose, the more weighty becomes our decision to respond to God's call, and the more fiercely and subtly we resist."[19]

In his suggestion that even the selfishness of the poor tends to open them to God's promise, Helder Camara turns the negative argument into a positive one. Julio de Santa Ana does something similar when he writes: "But what do the poor want? What are they expecting? Basically, the manifestation of the kingdom."[20] Linking the idea of the year of Jubilee in Leviticus 25, as John H. Yoder also does,[21] to the proclamation of the mission of Jesus given in Luke 4, de Santa Ana explains good news to the poor in terms of their ability to perceive it better than others. Referring to the oppressed who live in dependency because they are weak and powerless, he writes, "Because their hope was not in themselves but in the powerful arm of God . . . the poor, according to the Scriptures, were united in the expectations of the kingdom that comes, when prevailing oppressive structures will be reversed." He sees the immediate outcome of this in the community of goods in the early Church described in the Acts of the Apostles.[22]

Leonardo Boff reasons somewhat differently to an hermeneutical privilege of the poor, also without actually using that term. Present action in response to the Gospel cannot simply be deduced from an evangelical model, as by doing exactly what Jesus did in the concrete. Rather the understanding of the way of Jesus must continually emerge from the historical praxis in which Christians engage in the spirit and with the attitudes of Jesus and thereby keep learning what the new concrete demands are in the new situations. These are largely discovered in terms of suffering and the suffering is largely that of the poor and oppressed. Therefore it is out of the experience of the poor and the oppressed that an authentic interpretation is, in the last analysis, drawn.[23] Boff does, however, envisage a mediating function for those who by voluntary renunciation and commitment involve themselves in the suffering and struggle of the poor.

A similar case is made by José Miguez Bonino. He argues that the special position of the poor in the interpretation of the Gospel and its demands for our times is a direct function of the relationship between truth and praxis. That relationship is expressed concretely in fruitful tension between love and reconciliation on the one hand and class struggle on the other.[24]

In all of the positions mentioned so far, the basis of the claim for special access to the meaning of the Gospel seems to be that the poor and oppressed suffer the consequences of sin and sinfulness in the world in the most obvious and immediately painful way. For this reason their whole existence disposes them to look for redemption and attunes them to listening for any message of hope. For this reason also, they are in the best position to discern whether the hope held out is an authentic answer to the human dilemma or not. Enrique Düssel expands this claim by pointing out that if poor is to be equated with oppressed, then it is a category that includes all who suffer from the sins of others and the sinfulness of the world. Thus it includes discrimination against and repression of women, as well as oppression by education to false values and expectations, and so forth.[25] Alex Morelli is further willing to extend the category of the poor and oppressed almost universally, seeing those who are more obviously in the oppressor class as themselves trapped in suffering and frustration by the false values and expectations and relationships into which the structures have maneuvered them.[26] This somewhat weakens the claim on behalf of the more blatantly oppressed of the world, but it offers a less controversial variant in which access to the meaning of the Gospel is for each and every person first and foremost through personal participation in the suffering caused by sin.

The more controversial, narrower form of the claim seems to find its theoretical formulation in the thesis of J.B. Metz. He states that the future is realized in the memory of suffering. Seeing the dynamic of history in "dangerous memories," the memories of suffering which keep the political imagination alive, Metz interprets it theologically in terms of the eucharistic *anamnesis* (the calling to mind or bringing into full awareness) of the cross of Jesus. Metz, a German Catholic fundamental theologian, sees both the cross and the Eucharist as standing at the heart of the Christian proclamation of the good news of salvation. His concern as a fundamental theologian is to ask whether they offer any answer to the questions that people are really asking in our times, namely questions about the viability of the whole human project within the current social and political situation.

In this frame of reference, Metz sees the action of the Eucharist and the symbol of the cross as making a startling statement in the contemporary world. What we are asked by these symbols to call to mind, to bring into the center of our awareness, is the identification of the divine with the crucified—that is, with the marginated or rejected, the powerless, the suffering and the poor. He sees this as radically challenging the order of things in the world of our human affairs, because the saving intervention of God does not come from those respectable and "trustworthy" authoritative sources from whom we would expect it. It comes from below, from the suffering and outcast. Because the cross stands at the center of Christian history, and because Jesus presents himself to us in the Eucharist as the crucified, Metz sees the divine Word in the world irrevocably identified with the outcast, lending them new vision and revolutionary hope. He sees the cross of Jesus as an invitation to a more dynamic, creative appropriation of history by looking at it "upside down" from the viewpoint of the vanquished, the excluded, the repressed. It is in this perspective that the unfinished agenda of history can emerge into view. It is in this perspective that political domination and social power must continually justify themselves in the face of actual suffering—and are continually found wanting.[27]

This is certainly the basis for the claim made by Carlo Carretto, Alejandro Cussianovich and others that the bias of the poor and oppressed is the bias of Jesus himself and therefore inclines the followers of Jesus to a more authentic understanding of his message.[28] In other words, they acknowledge that any Christian theology, any interpretation of the good news of our Lord Jesus Christ, is caught in an "hermeneutic circle." That is to say, any interpretation is conditioned by the social, economic, political and cultural experience of those who propose it. Their experience is, of course, likewise conditioned by their reading of the Gospel. However, while acknowledging this, these authors claim that when this bias or cultural conditioning of experience comes out of the situation of poverty and oppression it is a help rather than a hindrance to authentic interpretation.

WHAT, THEN, IS THE ISSUE?

It seems clear that these authors are not all claiming the same thing. Yet there is common ground to their assertions. First of all, those who are designated "the poor" are an "ideal type." That means that there is no attempt to identify them concretely with certain particular people. The circulation of a preliminary draft of this essay evoked some very angry responses from people who asked, "Don't these dreamers know how ghetto dwellers oppress one another and how street crime by the poor is turned against their fellow poor?" This response, while making an important and obviously true observation, seems to miss the target. Whenever anyone gains power over others, that person is in that respect not of the poor but of the powerful. Whenever anyone uses power to oppress others, that person is, in that respect, not one of the oppressed but one of the oppressors. There is nothing in the positions cited which denies the untidy interpenetration of the categories of rich and poor, oppressors and oppressed in practice. As already pointed out above, Enrique Düssel and Alex Morelli, for instance, make a special and quite explicit point of this. It does not weaken the claim but rather makes it more subtle and more easily subject to evaluation by any of us, inasmuch as all of us are at some times and in some relationships poor and oppressed and helpless, though we may avoid facing it as long as we can.

Second, not only are the poor an "ideal type" but the category is rather broadly drawn to include the materially deprived, the oppressed, the marginated and the despised. Because these writers are for the most part concerned with the "third world" of our own days, material poverty in extreme forms looms large in their thought, and colonial dependency patterns are frequently described as part of the situation that defines poverty. Because most of the writers are of Latin American origin or experience, material poverty, oppression, margination, cultural deprivation and contempt are often presented as intrinsically linked. However, the central factor at issue appears to be powerlessness and suffering. This is why these authors do, in fact, admit that the categories are broad and may be diverse. One could, for instance, include wealthy Jews in Nazi Germany, Japanese Americans interned during World War II, Christians persecuted for their faith in Communist countries, battered wives, all prisoners, and so forth.

Third, however, while the categories are acknowledged as very broad, there is also a certain consensus among the authors that the concrete poverty of material deprivation is prototypical or paradigmatic for all kinds of deprivation, helplessness, oppression and suffering. Therefore there is an undeniable common thread running through the claims for the hermeneutic privilege of the poor. That common thread is a plea to the churches and to individual Christians to listen to the voices of the masses of the socially underprivileged, to mingle with them, to identify with them by sharing their plight in some practical way, trying to discover their felt need of redemption and thereby trying to experience and understand their sense of what constitutes salvation.

In all of this, it should be noted, the advantage or privilege that is claimed for the poor is not seen as a consequence or reward of virtue in them. One of the reasons for the angry responses frequently evoked by this claim is that some readers seemed to feel threatened by what they took to be an assertion that the poor are more virtuous than the rich. "Don't these starry-eyed idealists know about violence and greed among slum-dwellers?" This objection is tilting at windmills, for even a casual reading of the claims made by the various authors as outlined above will show that they do not base the "hermeneutic privilege of the poor" on virtue but on vulnerability. The poor may indeed be more virtuous than the rich, but there is no way in which that could possibly be ascertained. And it is, in any case, quite irrelevant to the case. The objection that lists the vices of the poor and the virtues of the rich is curiously inept. It assumes that God speaks to people because they are deserving, whereas the biblical and Christian position is quite consistently that God speaks to people because they are needy and that those who are able to hear the word of God are simply those who know they are needy. The claim of the authors cited really amounts to this: that the poor are more likely to own their need because they cannot so easily escape it or hide it from themselves and others. This seems to be in keeping with the Gospel testimony that Jesus kept company with the poor, the disreputable and outcast, and the known sinners who were generally despised.

A final common point in the positions taken by these authors is the possibility of entering into the experience of the poor and learning from them. One has some possibilities of entry through direct experience by sharing their deprivation, as by living in a slum, observing a fast, making do on a welfare budget, identifying publicly with members of a despised minority, doing menial or backbreaking work, using broken equipment or doing without the conveniences which the poor (any particular group of poor persons) cannot afford. It is true that this never really reproduces the experience of the poor person who is not poor by choice and cannot escape from poverty at will. It never really reproduces the poverty of the poor person who has always been poor and is therefore also culturally and educationally deprived. But besides such a move into direct experience of the poverty of the poor, there is also some possibility of entry by empathy. We all have some fund of analogous experiences of frustration, deprivation, humiliation, fear and so forth from which we can build bridges of empathy into the experience of other people. Without this, social life, friendship, community and communication, education, the arts, science, government, the economy and much else would all be impossible. We can build bridges of empathy when we really want to do so. If we do not build them to the poor but claim that their experience is either inaccessible to us or not worth entering into, that may be because we are afraid to acknowledge our own vulnerability and deprivation.

Beyond these common points there lies also some diversity in the claim made of an hermeneutic privilege of the poor. Some authors write of the uprooted, socially disorganized, culturally destitute urban, migrant or displaced poor. One might say that these people most effectively embody the "pure type" of the poor person. Their dominant characteristic is the inescapable and desperate nature of their need. It is in this that they most poignantly manifest the true situation of the human person before God, and it is for that reason that their situation predisposes them to recognize the human situation as sinful, in need of redemption. Moreover, it is for that reason that they are predisposed to grasp the utter gratuity of redemption, seeing the good news of salvation for what it really is.

Other authors write of the poor in the sense of those who struggle close to subsistence level materially but who are securely integrated in their traditional peasant culture—a culture which is wholesome and has not been disturbed. These authors tend to invoke not only the sense of dependency which the poor have, but also some natural virtues that seem to be integral to their austere and simple and often necessarily communal lives. Such virtues are honesty, dependability, hospitality, pervasive piety, modesty in personal wants, and similar qualities. It is among these authors that one meets some of the more lyrical statements about the lives of the poor. In their writings there is little or no acknowledgement of the brutalizing, crushing, deforming effects of poverty, nor of the need to come to the help of the poor. There is more emphasis on the suggestion that we would all be better if we were poor like the populations among whom these authors live. The authors are writing from their own experience of this. There is surely no need to deny their conclusion from experience that this is a good life, one in which people are happy and inclined to acknowledge their dependence and need and to welcome the redeeming God into their midst.

These are, of course, two quite different kinds of poverty and that accounts for the different responses they inspire. There seem to be two ways of calling the poor blessed. The destitute and desperate are called blessed only inasmuch as their need is manifest and inescapable and predisposes them to reach out for help and accept it. They are certainly not blessed in such a way that it would be better for them to remain in their present condition. On the other hand, the modestly situated are blessed because theirs is (or can be) a life both predisposed to acknowledge total dependence on God and close interdependence with one another, and also somewhat resistant to the destructive, trivializing and corrupting forces in human society. This latter claim should not, of course, be exaggerated, but it is this poverty of simplicity of life that is held out to Christians as desirable and blessed, not the poverty of destitution and desperation. When this

distinction is accepted, the positions taken by the authors cited in
this essay do not contradict one another.

APPEALS TO SCRIPTURE AND TRADITION

There are basically two claims made by the authors cited so far
concerning the foundation in Scripture for the positions which they
present. The first of these is that the whole Bible is a story of the liberation of the poor and oppressed by God, a story evolving in the
concrete circumstances of political and economic and social history,
a story which makes the people of Israel prototypical for the whole
human race, and a story whose direction is not essentially altered by
Jesus, though it is given a certain depth, immediacy and intensity by
him.[29]

The second claim is that Jesus, the incarnation of the Word and
presence of God, comes into the world as a poor man and makes it
his business to enter progressively deeper and deeper into poverty
among the despised and oppressed of every category (those considered as sinners and outcasts, the economically poor, the culturally
despised, political prisoners, condemned criminals). Jesus is seen as a
member of an oppressed people suffering military and economic imperialism, and as one who identifies himself with the suffering and
the struggle of his people for human dignity and freedom. He does it,
however, in a radical way that envisages liberation as far more than
attempting to drive the Romans out by armed rebellion.[30] Jesus is
perceived as a poor man preaching to the poor a message of hope for
the poor, and therefore it follows that those most likely to understand him are those who are in a very similar life situation. They will
tend to catch the message concretely rather than through a process
of abstraction into universal categories and reapplication to particular circumstances.

This position is further substantiated by these authors in detailed exegetical studies of biblical references to the poor, to Yahweh's preferential care for the poor, and (especially with reference to
the New Testament) to the greater receptivity of the poor toward the
kingdom. Such, with appropriate footnote references, is found in Julio de Santa Ana's *Good News to the Poor* in the first two chapters.[31]

Other authors offer a wealth of biblical quotations; a good example is found in Chapter 7 of Albert Gelin's *The Poor of Yahweh.*[32] It would not be possible to reproduce that wealth of quotations here. The pertinent thesis is that because wealth is an obstacle (as set out, for example, in Mt 19:24), poverty is to be seen as an advantage. Gelin does not hesitate to write, "... the Gospel repeats and deepens an Old Testament idea, namely, Yahweh's preference for the poor, whom he practically identifies as his own people...."[33]

The argument, in fact, implies that there have been many distorted interpretations in the process of abstraction and reapplication. Two clear examples are a spiritualization of the message that was not intended in the apostolic Church and an individualization that cannot be reconciled with the New Testament or the earlier history of the Church.[34] Considerable support for this is adduced in studies such as that of Richard J. Cassidy on Luke's Gospel[35] and that of John H. Yoder on the political implications of the New Testament[36]—and even indirectly by the arguments of Cullmann,[37] Hengel,[38] and others over the relationship of Jesus and his disciples to the Zealot party.

Concerning the foundation in tradition of the claim for an hermeneutic privilege of the poor, the authors cited all find it necessary to distinguish true and false developments in Christian piety, moral teaching, Church practice and organization. They use the model of a history and counter-history of Church and redemption, and Catholic and Protestant authors use it differently, as might be expected.[39] Yet the common element is the discernment of a prophetic tradition which again and again summons the Church to be a Church of the poor and which, though bitterly disputed at the time of each protest, is consistently canonized in retrospect and can be seen as a corrective factor when one looks over the history of the Church across the span of the centuries.[40] Julio de Santa Ana works this out in very persuasive detail.[41]

Yet perhaps a more convincing reconciliation of the claim with our more conventional expectations comes from quite another quarter, namely the contemporary spiritual testimonies of the followers of Charles de Foucauld—more particularly in the writings of Arturo Paoli and of Carlo Carretto. They stand, of course, in a long tradition in Christian history which has interpreted the Beatitudes of the

Gospels as an invitation to become poor in the most literal sense with the really poor and to identify with the powerless and despised. It is a tradition that read the Gospel as promising salvation on the grounds of need, not of moral rectitude or virtuous achievements. It therefore saw a double reason for identification with the poor and despised and oppressed: on the one hand compassion and love for the neighbor and on the other hand humility and trust in relation to God. It was a double reason for a single response, and it has come down to our own days in ever new expressions. The reason for selecting the expression of the followers of Charles de Foucauld here is that in their contemplative and suffering identification with the poor they present a certain contrast to the militant identification with the poor that characterizes the liberation movements and the liberation theologians. For this reason the testimony of the Little Brothers seems particularly persuasive.

Out of the pilgrimage of their own lives, both Charles de Foucauld[42] and Carlo Carretto[43] offer eloquent testimony that riches are an obstacle to true understanding of the Gospel, because one cannot relate so deeply to Jesus who chose to be poor and live among the poor and talk to them in terms of their own daily experience. Thus, for instance, De Foucauld in a meditation on poverty which he wrote out at length, having spelled out his reasons for wanting to imitate the poverty of Jesus in various ways, adds the observation:

> My Lord Jesus, how quickly he becomes poor who, remembering that whatever is done for one of your little ones is done for you and whatever is not done for them is not done for you, relieves all the sufferers who come to his gate.[44]

And Carlo Carretto writes in a similar vein from the Sahara (where he had withdrawn in his forties from a frantically busy life in Italian Catholic Action):

> Let us not deceive ourselves and let us not dilute the most precious things Jesus said.
> ... If I love, if I really love, how can I tolerate the fact that a third of humanity is menaced with starvation while I enjoy the security of economic stability? ...

I know that what I have said about poverty is challenging, and I also know that when in the world I did not really put it into practice. . . .

Riches are a slow poison. . . . What a number of men and women, religious people, let themselves get caught up in their later lives by the spirit of middle-class tastes.

Now that solitude and prayer have helped me to see things more clearly, I understand why contemplation and poverty are inseparable. It is impossible to have a deep relationship with Jesus in Bethlehem, with Jesus in exile, with Jesus the workman of Nazareth, with Jesus the Apostle who has nowhere to lay his head, with the crucified Jesus, without having achieved within ourselves that detachment from things, proclaimed with such authority and lived by him.[45]

Besides this personal testimony, however, these authors also reflect extensively on what they have learned from the poor among whom they live, those who are poor and sometimes destitute and bitterly oppressed by necessity and not by choice in voluntary response to God's call. They point out that the poor are closer to God inasmuch as poverty is the truth of our relationship to God and the poor know it, while for the rest of us this is quite a difficult discovery.[46] The poor know that of their own efforts they are powerless to change the world; they cannot think of themselves as important, but do see themselves as dependent on power beyond themselves and on one another. Yet Carretto, like Camara, acknowledges the need for persons who have made voluntary renunciations to bring to the poor the good news that puts this inability in the context of love and hope.[47] The poor know about sin and the need of redemption because it is revealed in their suffering; yet they have continually an experience analogous to the burning bush because life goes on and they are not consumed and utterly destroyed by their sufferings.[48]

Moreover, the poor are aware of their own vulnerability. They are not in a position to despise anyone. Their asceticism is one of reality, not fashion or fancy. It is imposed by God's providence expressed in the needs and situation of the community; it is not chosen according to personal inclination. This is especially true of manual labor, and Carretto describes the backbreaking, heartbreaking labor of people trying to wrest a living out of the expanding and merciless desert.[49] To these reflections, Arturo Paoli adds that the poor must live in the present and trust God for the future, while the relatively rich may fool themselves into thinking they have secured the future. Capitalism is based on a frantic effort to secure the future.[50]

Similar moving and persuasive testimonies come from those who have worked intimately with basic Christian communities among the very poor. Thus Carlos Gaspar, economist and full-time Church worker in the Philippine Islands, testifies that the poor always have time—time to listen, to reflect, to pray, time to be genuinely present to others, time for community. The reference is especially to the rural poor. The poor have little to lose and much to gain by sharing, and they take it for granted that what there is will be shared. The poor tend more to community because they have little or no need to guard their possessions and they have no possibility of guarding their privacy. For them, to be is to be in community with others, a community of life and goods and destiny.[51] Yet Gaspar also testifies to a certain fatalism and passivity among them unless and until someone who has made voluntary renunciations identifies with the poor, challenging and encouraging them to effective hope and therefore to initiatives in response to the Gospel. Once such a challenge is offered and accepted, deep insights may be expected from the poor, and those who brought the good news to them in the first place will find themselves learning a far more concrete and immediate grasp of the Gospel which deepens and transforms it in previously unsuspected ways.

In evaluating these testimonies, of course, the previously mentioned caution is in order, namely that these authors are not all speaking of the same poor. The more lyrical descriptions of the qualities in the poor that predispose them to hear the Gospel refer in the main to the rural poor who have not been uprooted from their culture or their traditional societal structures. Moreover, even in these cases, there is frank admission of a tendency to fatalism and passivity and of the need for proclamation of a Gospel of hope by those not in the culture of poverty.

To evaluate the foundation in Scripture and tradition alleged by these authors for an hermeneutic privilege of the poor is not, of course, a purely intellectual undertaking. These authors make a good case. Those who wish to dispute it will usually point to the vices of the poor they know and the virtues of the rich they know. But, as shown above, this line of argument is not relevant; God's favor is shown to us not on account of merit but on account of need. Those who object will also point to isolated texts from the Hebrew Scriptures calling for no partiality to the rich or the poor. There are two problems with this objection: first, that such texts are so few compared with the many that essays like Gelin's can easily cite,[52] and, second, that the notion of impartiality in this context really begs the question.

If it is understood to be the intent of God, right and just, that some should be rich and some should be poor, then impartiality means accepting this discrepancy as given and judging any given issue within that assumption. This might be justifiable in situations in which some have more and some less but none are deprived of the necessities of a truly human life. But it would be justifiable only as long as it can also be shown that those who have more have not come by it through sin (whether by conquest as with the American Indians, or by kidnaping and enslavement as with the American black ancestors, or by driving sharp and unjust bargains against the stranger and the weak, as with later groups of immigrants in the United States and with migrant farm laborers, or by manipulating international markets to give unfair value for the products of poorer nations who are newcomers to international trade, and so forth). If those who have more have originally come by it through sin, and if those whom they have deprived have been progressively weakened and impoverished to brutalizing levels, one might readily suppose that the impartiality of God would be realized in a judgment that vindicates the poor.

However, as stated above, the real task of evaluation is not a purely intellectual matter. It is a task for Christian discernment involving prayer, an asceticism of detachment, and the Christian formation of imagination and sensibilities as a basis for the judgments of conscience. Academic argument cannot solve an issue like this because the issue itself depends on a radical and pervasive conversion of individuals and communities. It is for this reason that the significant evaluation is the testimony of those who, like the Brothers of Charles de Foucauld, radically share the experience of the very poor. And it includes the testimony of those who, like many of the action/ reflection groups discussed in the essay by William Newell at the beginning of this volume, do their theological reflection on the basis of their experience of Christian community and of action for social justice. The academic contribution to such a question as the hermeneutic privilege of the poor consists really only of a certain expertise in marshaling testimonies from Scripture and tradition, some technical competence in the interpretation of texts, some skill in analyzing arguments and positions taken.[53]

When all such academic exercises are said and done, the real discernment is made along some such lines as the following. We, who claim to know much about the Gospel of salvation from study and reflection, come by the grace of God to proclaim it to people who have not had those opportunities: the deprived, the uncultured, the outcast or despised. At some juncture we begin to understand that we have been mouthing words and formulas carefully domesticated and stripped of their sharp edges and meticulously insulated from those real issues in our lives where we are most vulnerable. We begin to understand this because these official words and orthodox Christian formulas that we have been mouthing have come alive with searing immediacy and concreteness in the response of these people we thought were too stupid and ignorant and depraved to understand. And even as it dawns on us in a self-validating flash of understanding, the pomposity of our learning and our righteousness and our power is "cut down to size" and God is vindicated in the divine justice.

SOME PRACTICAL CONCLUSIONS

Reflection on the foregoing does suggest some conclusions that may be helpful to Christian groups engaged in theological reflection growing from their own community life and from their social action for justice and peace and the betterment of living conditions for the poor and suffering.

1. It seems clear, first of all, that one cannot simply take the at-

titudes and responses of the poor uncritically as the expression of the Gospel of salvation. It is necessary to question to what degree there has been or must yet be what Paolo Freire has named "conscientization"[54] and what J.B. Metz intends in his *memoria* thesis.[55] In other words, there has to be a certain awakening or coming to awareness before the experience of systematic and general deprivation can bear fruit in the recognition of the good news.

2. For this to happen, there must usually be a catalyst or mediator who engages the poor and oppressed in the process of "conscientization." This must be someone, or some community of persons, genuinely sharing the conditions of deprivation of the poor. But such persons seldom arise from among the poor. They more usually identify with the poor by voluntary renunciation of privilege, wealth, power and personal security. The Hebrew Scriptures describe Moses this way, and the New Testament consistently sees Jesus in this light.

3. Such persons, however, come in the first place not to bring answers to the poor but to experience and help them to articulate their questions. They come to enter as deeply as they can into the situation and life and experience of the poor and to listen to the good news with the poor from their vantage point among the poor. The task, as described by Paolo Freire, Julio de Santa Ana, Helder Camara, Arturo Paoli, Elizabeth O'Connor[56] and others, is a delicate one. It is the task of approaching the poor and oppressed with great humility because there is a sense in which the poor are and remain the experts. The experience of poverty, humiliation, oppression and all the pains and penalties that accompany poverty is their experience in a far more profound and pervasive way than it can ever belong to those who have chosen to enter into it and be there with the poor. Moreover, the experience of the burning bush, the experience of surviving and not being consumed or destroyed by suffering and contempt, is also already theirs though they may not have become reflexively aware of it or have learned fully to savor it. The task, then, is really twofold: to help them to articulation by an encouraging and welcoming practice of listening (as Elizabeth O'Connor describes it), by gentle, respectful but relentless questioning (as Paolo Freire describes it), by challenge (as Helder Camara describes it), but, beyond this articulation of the experience of the poor, also to listen to the good news from within that experience.

4. When such mediation is offered, certain characteristic responses and attitudes are often expressed by the poor (as articulated in a particularly moving way by Carlo Carretto and Arturo Paoli among others) which must certainly "ring true" to anyone who has meditated seriously on the Gospels. The following seem to be particularly significant:

(a) The poor know that they are in urgent need of redemption.

(b) The poor know not only their dependence on God and on powerful people but also their interdependence with one another.

(c) The poor rest their security not on things but on people.

(d) The poor have no exaggerated sense of their own importance.

(e) The poor expect little from competition and much from cooperation.

(f) The poor have no exaggerated need of privacy.

(g) The poor can distinguish between necessities and luxuries.

(h) The poor can wait because they have acquired a kind of dogged patience born of acknowledged dependence.

(i) When the poor are exposed to the Gospel, they interpret it very concretely and readily see it as having historical, practical import. An example of this is the ease with which Martin Luther King could invite his followers to identify with the exodus theme and with the non-violent protest of Jesus as seen by John Wesley.

(j) When the poor have the Gospel preached to them, it sounds like good news and not like a threat or a scolding.

(k) The promise of future salvation is truly present joy and therefore present incipient salvation to the poor.

(l) The really (desperately) poor can respond to the call of the Gospel with a certain abandonment and uncomplicated totality because they have so little to lose and are ready for anything.

(m) The fears of the poor are more realistic and less exaggerated, because they already know that one can survive very great suffering and want.

These, it would seem, are all advantages that would give the poor privileged access to the meaning of the Gospel.

NOTES

1. Notably by political theologian J.B. Metz, by liberation theologians Gustavo Gutiérrez and Alejandro Cussianovich, and by contemplative and former activist Carlo Carretto, in works to be cited hereafter.

2. See, e.g., "Pilgrimage" by Peter C. Hinde, O. Carm., in *The Wind Is Rising,* ed. William R. Callahan, S.J. and Francine Cardman (Hyattsville, Md.: Quixote Center, undated), pp. 22–25.

3. See the essay by Clarke in this volume.

4. Alejandro Cussianovich, *Religious Life and the Poor* (N.Y.: Orbis, 1975).

5. *Ibid.,* p. 111.

6. *Ibid.,* p. 112.

7. *Towards a Church of the Poor* (N.Y.: Orbis, 1979) (especially Chapter 9).

8. *Ibid.,* p. 114. His point is well substantiated by Ernesto Cardenal in *Gospel in Solentiname* (N.Y.: Orbis, 1976).

9. de Santa Ana, *op. cit.,* p. 98. Cf. Richard J. Cassidy, *Jesus, Politics and Society: A Study of Luke's Gospel* (N.Y.: Orbis, 1978). Also Jacques Pohier and Dietmar Mieth, eds., *The Dignity of the Despised of the Earth* (N.Y.: Seabury, 1979), Part I.

10. de Santa Ana, *op. cit.,* p. 114.

11. *Ibid.,* pp. 118–121.

12. Appendix in Julio de Santa Ana, *op. cit.,* p. 126. Many people have observed that this liberation coming from the poor as preachers is what happened in some measure in the black civil rights movement under Martin Luther King.

13. *Ibid.,* pp. 124–125. This is developed further later in this essay with reference to J.B. Metz.

14. *A Theology of Liberation* (N.Y.: Orbis, 1973), pp. 299–302.

15. *Good News to the Poor* (Geneva: World Council of Churches, 1977), pp. 95 ff.

16. *Ibid.,* p. 96.

17. *Ibid.,* pp. 106–107; cf. Helder Camara, *The Desert Is Fertile* (N.Y.: Orbis, 1974). Alfred Hennelly makes a similar point in his discussion of Basic Christian Communities in Chapter 3 of this volume.

18. Camara, *op. cit.,* pp. 24–26.

19. *Ibid.,* p. 35.

20. *Good News to the Poor,* p. 118.

21. *The Politics of Jesus* (Grand Rapids: Eerdmans, 1972), Chapter 3.

22. *Good News,* pp. 118–119.

Good News to the Poor: Do They Understand It Better? 147

23. "Salvation in Jesus Christ and the Process of Liberation," in *Mystical and Political Dimensions of the Faith,* ed. C. Geffre and G. Gutiérrez (N.Y.: Herder, 1974), especially pp. 87–90.

24. *Doing Theology in a Revolutionary Situation* (Philadelphia: Fortress, 1975), Chapters 5 and 6. The word "praxis" is used by liberation theologians to designate our engagement with reality by action in which truth reveals itself and from which theory is drawn.

25. "Domination-Liberation: A New Approach," in *Mystical and Political Dimensions of the Faith,* pp. 34–56.

26. "Man Liberated from Sin and Oppression—A Theology of Liberation," in *Freedom and Unfreedom in the Americas,* ed. Thomas E. Quigley (N.Y.: IDOC, 1971), pp. 81–95.

27. "The Future in the Memory of Suffering," in *New Questions on God,* ed. J.B. Metz (N.Y.: Herder, 1972), pp. 9–25.

28. Carlo Carretto, *Letters from the Desert* (N.Y.: Orbis, 1972), pp. 80–81; Alejandro Cussianovich, *op. cit.,* p. 15.

29. E.g., de Santa Ana, *Good News,* Chapters 1–3. Cf. Albert Gelin, *The Poor of Yahweh* (Collegeville: Liturgical Press, 1964), especially Chapter 7.

30. See, e.g., Jon Sobrino, *Christology at the Crossroads* (N.Y.: Orbis, 1978), Chapter 6. Cf. Ignacio Ellacuría, *Freedom Made Flesh* (N.Y.: Orbis, 1976), Part I. Also, Lee Cormie, "The Hermeneutical Privilege of the Oppressed," in *C.T.S.A. Proceedings,* Vol. 33, 1978, pp. 163–167.

31. *Op. cit.*

32. *Op. cit.*

33. *Op. cit.,* p. 101.

34. E.g., de Santa Ana, *Towards a Church of the Poor,* Chapter 9.

35. *Op. cit., passim.*

36. *Op. cit, passim.*

37. *Jesus and the Revolutionaries* (N.Y.: Harper, 1970).

38. *Was Jesus a Revolutionist?* (Philadelphia: Fortress, 1971).

39. For a Protestant perspective see Julio de Santa Ana, *Good News to the Poor,* Chapters 6–8. For a succinct statement of the Catholic perspective see Gelin, *op. cit.* or P.R. Regamey, *Poverty* (London: Sheed & Ward, 1949).

40. See, e.g., Gutiérrez, *op. cit.,* Chapter 13.

41. *Good News to the Poor,* Chapters 6–8. See the footnote references for documentation.

42. *Spiritual Autobiography of Charles de Foucauld,* ed. Jean-Francois Six (N.Y.: Kenedy, 1964).

43. *Op.cit.*

44. *Op. cit.,* p. 63.

45. *Op. cit.,* pp. 80–82.

46. E.g., Arturo Paoli, *Freedom To Be Free* (N.Y.: Orbis, 1973), especially Chapter 10.

47. *Op. cit.,* Chapters 13–15.

48. Jews commonly invoke the symbol of the burning bush for the contemporary experience of the Nazi holocaust. Carretto implies it, *op. cit.,* Chapter 14.

49. *Op. cit.,* Chapter 14.

50. *Op. cit.,* pp. 144–145.

51. Testimony of Caspar is quoted from a lecture he gave in Maryland in the summer of 1981. It is not published.

52. *Op. cit., passim,* but especially Chapter 7.

53. For a splendid marshaling of the academic arguments, however, see Lee Cormie, *op. cit.*

54. See Paolo Freire, *Pedagogy of the Oppressed* (N.Y.: Herder, 1970).

55. Metz, *op. cit.* The thesis is concerned with the importance of recalling, or bringing into sharp awareness, the "dangerous memories" that generate the energies by which social change comes about in history.

56. Elizabeth O'Connor, *Journey Inward, Journey Outward* (N.Y.: Harper & Row, 1968), especially Chapters 3 and 4.

7
Models and Values: The Search for U.S. Christian Community

John Langan, S.J.

THE CHRISTIAN TRADITION

The theological reflection groups described in William Newell's essay all share two central characteristics. They are explicitly Christian in their religious allegiance and they operate within the political and social context of the United States. The dreams that they have for themselves as Christian communities and for their members as Christian individuals are shaped both by the religious tradition or traditions with which they are affiliated and by the ideals and the performance of the pluralistic and secular society to which they and their members belong. This double influence of the religious and political context on the theological reflection groups can be obvious or subtle, requiring conformity or provoking rejection, explicitly acknowledged or regarded with distrust or aversion. But I take it for granted that no one would deny the reality of such influences and their importance for our understanding of Christian groups engaged in theological reflection on social action and experience.

So my interest here is not to establish the existence of such influences or to measure their precise weight, but rather to encourage both members of action/reflection groups and friendly observers to explore and assess some of the different forms that these influences take. We will be looking at the effects of this religious and political context not so much on the performance of action/reflection groups as on the ideals or models or dreams that these groups propose for themselves both in their internal workings and in their relations with the major institutions of society. My intention is not to prescribe any of these possibilities either singly or in combination with others nor to proscribe any of them.

While it is easy to describe the theological reflection groups or communities as U.S. and Christian, these labels actually cover a wide range of experiences and possibilities. For these traditions, while distinctive, are also differentiated and complex. To be a Christian may be to be a Roman Catholic, an Anglican or Episcopalian, a Lutheran, a Greek or Russian Orthodox, a Mennonite, a Presbyterian, a Baptist. It may be to belong to one of many other denominational groups or to none. It may involve being a priest or deacon, an elder or minister, a convert or a dissenter, a layman or laywoman. Belonging to the Christian tradition normally takes the form of affiliation with a specific denominational tradition, which brings with it a certain psychology, a style of worship, a set of expectations about religious community, and a certain role in the community. These exist not merely as abstract possibilities in some religious pattern book, but as real effects of the process of religious socialization even in people who repudiate the specific ecclesial tradition in which they were formed or the Christian tradition in general.

The specific traditions may also include, even within the bounds of one church polity, a considerable variety of forms of religious community—small rural parishes, large urban or suburban congregations, religious orders, parish organizations, fraternal organizations, educational groups and organizations, small prayer groups, ecumenical organizations. Many of these forms of community may shape the reactions and the hopes of a single person. Thus one Catholic may serve on a democratically elected parish council, belong to a purely voluntary and largely anarchic prayer group, deal with a hierarchically appointed pastor, work for a religious order that combines authoritarianism and egalitarianism, and belong to a Catholic professional society which is run by an anticlerical oligarchy.

These considerations may serve to remind us of the wealth of theologically and ecclesially structured social experience that the members of the groups draw upon and react to in fashioning their new communities. What is their general attitude to it?

There are obvious risks in generalizing about the experience of groups of people whom one does not know at all well. But there are three tendencies, which may vary in strength with individuals and groups but which all seem to be present to some extent. First, there is personal acceptance and public affirmation of central Christian doctrines that bear on our understanding of community—the great themes of creation, sin, grace, justification and sanctification, and the vision of salvation history as the work of the triune God reaching fulfillment in the work of Jesus. Parallel with this is a desire for a Christian form of community, a community of faith and love (rather than a community arising from historical circumstances or coercion or interest).

Second, the communities show a strong ecumenical tendency. Sometimes this is a matter of drawing members from a variety of denominational backgrounds. Sometimes it is a matter of drawing inspiration from elements of different ecclesial traditions, e.g., the Catholic, Anglican, and Orthodox emphases on liturgical prayer and on contemplative prayer, the Protestant concern for self-governance, the Quaker strategy for arriving at the sense of the meeting. While the groups generally remain recognizably Catholic or Protestant in their style and allegiance, they often show a frame of mind which thinks nothing Christian alien and a readiness to learn from others whose way of following God may be quite different but is judged to be fruitful. What is common to all Christians, and particularly to all converted or committed Christians, is taken to be more fundamental and more important both for action and for self-understanding than what divides different Christian bodies from each other. The ecumenical aspect of these groups, however, is not a matter of forging institutional connections, but of drawing on resources which are nourishing for the spiritual and communal life of the group. This attitude allows many important doctrinal and disciplinary issues to remain unresolved.

Third, there is often a sense of dissatisfaction or tension with a denominational past and its structures. The search for a deeper and more authentic Christian community arises from commitment to Christ but also takes much of its energy and urgency from the perceived inadequacies of churches and congregations which "are doing business as usual." This tension may take different forms such as rebellion against Catholic authoritarianism or revulsion against the suburban captivity of Protestant congregations, and it may be prominent in certain individuals without setting the tone for entire groups. But there are classic difficulties and dangers built into every search for a deeper Christian community; these involve perceptions and accusations of self-righteousness, elitism, deviation from tradition, alliances with the worldly or the alien, factionalism, disobedience to authority. A great deal depends on the tact, patience, and understanding with which these groups and denominational authorities treat each other. A great deal also depends on whether negative themes such as dissatisfaction with denominational traditions and structures or positive themes such as the search for a deeper commitment to Christ and for new forms of social action prevail in the minds of group members and of interested observers.

The result of these tendencies is that the groups in their search for an appropriate form of Christian community are both able to draw on the resources of the comprehensive Christian tradition and are often at odds with particular elements of it. Their expectations and aspirations are shaped by this tradition and their earlier experiences of it. They share a desire for something new, however, that need not be a rejection of the past but that must be an appropriate adaptation to their own unique situation. They are not inclined to the scholarly or antiquarian revival of earlier styles of ecclesial life, but they do seek inspiration and guidance from the diverse representations of the early Church in the New Testament. Like Christian communities through the ages, they seek for a form of community that will recognize and realize (1) the fundamental religious equality and unity of members of the believing community (Gal 3:28; Ja 2:1–13), (2) the diversity of gifts of the members (1 Cor 12:4–31), (3) the need of the community for leadership capable of reconciling factions and resolving conflict, (4) the need of the community to preserve its sense of distinctiveness from the world, and (5) the need of the community to articulate and carry on its evangelical mission to the world.

THE U.S. EXPERIENCE

But the search for Christian community is not carried on by the groups only in the light of the Christian tradition; it is also worked out in the light of the U.S. experience. This experience is more limited in time, space, and spiritual ambition than is the Christian tradition, but it is, for citizens of the United States, more pervasive and, in many respects, more unquestioned. This is not to deny that some of the groups and many of their members are in varying conditions of opposition to, rejection of, and alienation from what they take to be the policies of the United States government and the dominant attitudes of U.S. society. Nor is it to suggest that there is one coherent set of normative beliefs about justice and community in the United States which the groups and their members accept implicitly or explicitly. But it is to underline two things: first, the massive impact on any Christian community of living in an enormously powerful, diversified, and flexible society which is continental in scale and often cosmic in ambition; second, the diversity of norms and experiences which provide abundant opportunities for both justification and criticism of what the people of the United States and their communities and governments do or aspire to do.

Out of this reality which is both massive and diversified, I will point to four aspects which have figured both in our early history and in our recent past and which are particularly important and valuable for the shaping of authentically U.S. religious communities of action and reflection. I will also mention two themes in U.S. cultural and political history which present special problems for efforts to build such religious communities.

The first of the formative aspects of U.S. experience is its democratic and egalitarian character. The country has long abhorred fixed hierarchies of status (to be distinguished from the functional hierarchies of the military and corporate worlds). It has witnessed surges of populist feeling against political and cultural elites, and it has proclaimed the sovereignty of the people and the superior wisdom and goodness of the people in comparison with government and experts. This democratic tendency can degenerate into anti-intellectualism, can be exclusivist, and can be used to deprive minorities of their rights. But I believe that it is an integral and valued part of the attitudes of most U.S. citizens. It is so strong and central a part of our national experience that endorsing it is beside the point. Groups will exemplify it both in the confidence of their internal operations and in the character of their social concerns.

Second, U.S. society has by and large been an open society. This openness has extended from entry into the country to access to jobs and land, from communications and the availability of information to membership in churches and associations. Two of the great shaping experiences of our society have contributed to the sense of openness—immigration and the frontier. Lincoln was surely right in his claim that the nation could not endure half-slave and half-free, and something analogous holds for most efforts in our country to exclude and to conceal. The sense of openness and mobility in our society is not easily purchased. It probably presupposes affluence (new land, new jobs, new opportunities), and it brings a rootlessness and a lack of stability and a certain lack of compassion for those who fall by the wayside. It also brings a receptivity to understanding life as a pilgrimage, as a movement beyond the fixed boundaries of a static social order to the new and the infinite. People on the left are usually struck by the barriers and exclusions that remain and that limit the opportunities of women, blacks, Hispanics, Jews, Muslims, and others. All this is true, but it should not blind us to the vulnerability of most forms of non-rational exclusion and discrimination in the United States. A consequence of this openness for small Christian communities is that they can expect little stability themselves. Their members will, for economic and professional reasons, be under pressure to move. They cannot expect to draw members because of traditional ties or community expectations. This accords well with the Protestant stress on the connection between individual conversion and Church membership. The mobility of our society also allows for informal contacts among like-minded Christian communities over considerable distances. The value accorded to openness and mobility in the culture generally will also put strains on groups that wish to retain a strong sense of denominational roots, or a form of exclusivity.

Third, U.S. society has a strong respect for the rule of law, a rule which is to apply to the agencies of government itself as much as to private individuals and groups. (This co-exists with acceptance of a remarkably high level of violence, particularly in urban centers.) The centrality and power of respect for the rule of law is manifest in the power and prestige of our judicial system, in our recurring struggles to regulate private activity and to curb governmental discretion, in our stress on the place of procedural norms in carrying on the work of justice, and in our persistent yearning for an order of norms that can be applied universally, consistently, and fairly. This creates abundant possibilities for criticizing the performance of private institutions and corporations, of powerful individuals, and of government agencies and bureaucrats. There is a rich vein of popular indignation, of muckraking journalism, and of independent social criticism which does not work from a comprehensive ideology or theory of society but which takes as its central theme the gap between norm and performance, between lofty ideal and sordid reality. This can provide Christian groups interested in social action with orientations and techniques for social and political action, even in the absence of a comprehensive social analysis or of consensus on a model for a future good society. The discovery of violations of law and of partial and biased enforcement of the laws, when these bring harm to the poor and the disadvantaged, and agreement on the need to seek adequate legal remedies for gross injustice can serve as bases for action for justice in a way which affirms and does not challenge the rule of law.

Fourth, much of U.S. history and political awareness has been shaped by protest movements. These have been operative from colonial time through the abolitionist agitation against slavery and the formative period of organizing U.S. labor down to the civil rights movement and the anti-war movement of the recent past. Protest movements of one sort or another have shaped the experience and awareness of members of the groups and present them with both techniques and challenges for wider action. Members of the groups are likely to participate in or be sympathetic to current protests against nuclear power plants, against nuclear weapons, and against reductions in welfare programs. Contact with and participation in protest movements is likely both to provoke strains and tensions within groups seeking deeper Christian community (some of whose members will resist what they see as the politicization of the group) and to create a new task of preserving Christian distinctiveness in a larger setting. Protest movements are likely to continue to provide both paradigmatic experiences and challenges to small Christian groups.

These four aspects of the U.S. historical experience, while not unmixed blessings, can all be seen as setting conditions for the growth and self-definition of U.S. religious groups that wish to engage in action for justice. There are two further tendencies that are much more likely to be regarded as restraints and obstacles for such groups. These are, first, the strong emphasis on individualism present both in the historic U.S. conception of freedom and in contemporary life-styles and, second, the tendency toward the privatization of religion, which shows up as more or less acute discomfort in many circles when a religious group takes a definite stand on politically significant issues or takes sides in a social conflict.

MODELS

This overview of some of the factors in the U.S. Christian context of the action/reflection groups which shape their search for an appropriate form of community should alert us to the complexity of the social situation in which the groups find themselves and to the broad range of opportunities that it offers to them. I will argue that the fundamental way in which the groups deal with the complexities of this double context is by refraining from commitment to a single pattern or ideal of community and by employing a plurality of models of community.

Before we examine the models and metaphors that different groups employ in thinking about themselves, it may be helpful to reflect on the function of models in our thinking generally. In focusing on dreams and images and models of community, we are operating primarily on the level of perception and insight rather than on the levels of judgment and decision, where one must affirm or deny, choose or reject. Different dreams and images and models can coexist in a pluralistic world or society or consciousness; taking up one need not commit us to rejecting the others. In this respect they are unlike doctrines and theories and law and decisions. There, at least in central cases, the prisoner is innocent or guilty, a given number is or is not a prime, direct creation of species by God excludes evolution, the law forbids or allows certain business practices, one affirms or denies that Jesus is the Messiah or admits that one does not know. But on the levels of perception and insight we are accustomed to living with a plurality of approaches and results. The penny sometimes appears round and sometimes appears elliptical, the sea can look green or grey, light can be thought of as waves or as particles, Jesus can be thought of as God's Word or as God's Son, human beings can be described as information systems or as biological organisms, social unity can be presented in terms of contractual agreement or of organic growth and cohesion, an object of choice can be seen as good and satisfying or as limiting and not good. The possibility of perceiving and conceiving things in a variety of different ways does not imply that all such ways are equally acceptable or that truth cannot be attained by the use of models.

But it is true that we are particularly ready to speak of employing models or images when the reality we are trying to understand or to control impresses us as too complex or too mysterious to be captured by one set of concepts and theories. This also happens when we recognize that different individuals or groups have conceived or presented a complex reality in different terms and along different lines which are not readily reducible to a simple unity. Thus we find ourselves speaking about Luke's image of Jesus (in contrast to Matthew's or Paul's) or about the Catholic understanding of the Eucharist (in contrast to Lutheran and Calvinist views) or about a Marxist conception of history (distinguished, say, from an evolutionary progressivism or a Buddhist view). Here, of course, we are actually coming back to differences of doctrine and theory and to issues that have been highly controversial. But we have the power, at least since the rise of modern historical consciousness, to think of conflicting theories as models or images or partial views of the complex reality which is their object. We can in effect reduce their weight and their hold on us, and we can use them as aids for understanding a reality which eludes capture within the limits of one standard theory. We often treat theories or doctrines as instruments for understanding. We retain a certain freedom to use them at our discretion according to the variety of our needs and purposes. We are then using them as images or models without strictly affirming or denying the conclusions which they ordinarily include or imply.

Our intention in doing this may be either to facilitate action by building up a picture of an unfamiliar reality from what we already know or to extend our understanding in areas that are particularly resistant to direct or literal patterns of conceptualization. It is not the move that we make when we want to achieve a systematic unity of

understanding. But elements of an intellectual system (the philosophical theology of Aquinas, the dialectical materialism of Marx,
the metapsychology of Freud) can serve as sources for images and
models. Intellectual systems, like automobiles, can be cannibalized
for their parts. Of course, in doing this we give up much of our concern for the completeness and consistency which good intellectual
systems aim to provide. But we do not give up all of this concern, for
we are troubled if the models we employ lead to contradictory conclusions about action or if they seem so discordant that we feel we
are not getting a coherent picture of our objective or if we feel we are
splitting our attention and our intellectual processes in a schizo-
phrenic fashion. There are psychological as well as logical limits to
the diversity of models and images we can employ in a given period
of time. Conversely, it is possible for images or models to become associated in our minds in ways that lead us to neglect or suppress the
contradictory implications they may have. Thus, we can think of
God as father, lover, judge, shepherd, and rock without a sharp sense
of discontinuity, though these are quite different models, precisely
because all of these are customary ways of speaking about God in
our religious tradition. So we look for some order (logical, psychological or historical) in our use of images and models, but we are also
satisfied with a vital and stimulating plurality of models and images.

Now it seems to me that this double craving for order and plurality figures in a special way in our awareness of and reflection on
society and community. Here we are confronted by our need for and
our reliance on models and images for both the purposes mentioned
previously, namely, to facilitate action and to extend our understanding. It is safe to say that most citizens in advanced industrial societies
such as the United States do not feel that there is one coherent picture of their social experiences or one clear direction in which their
society is moving. Nor is there one theory or one scientific body of
theories which most people are prepared to accept as the central in-
terpretative framework for their social lives. The struggle with experiences of social discontinuity, of rootlessness, and of alienation
grows broader and more intense in our society with its high degree of
social and physical mobility, its shifting political agenda, its increasing awareness of the diversity and interconnectedness of the elements
that comprise it. In this situation people feel both an intense need to

fashion more satisfying forms of community and a need for maps, schemata, symbols, models, and images. They need these latter to locate themselves and the social groups to which they belong and to energize themselves to action. Our social reality is too complex and its destiny is too mysterious for us to be able to dispense with the plurality of models and images that are available to us in favor of some unique theory or normative system, whether this be the free market or the Constitution, the Code of Canon Law or the Sermon on the Mount, the socialist revolution or the predictions of the Club of Rome. This point can be grasped both in a theoretical way by those who affirm the insufficiency of various ideologies and also as a theme in our ordinary experience of the complexity and unpredictability of social life with its range of ironic and even perverse outcomes.

THE GROUPS

The religious groups that have cooperated in the Woodstock project do not show any strong tendency or desire to pass beyond the stage of orienting themselves by the use of a plurality of social models and ideals, which they feel free to employ for understanding their own communities, the larger society, and their relationships with both the Church and the political order. In this regard they differ from the separatist utopian and religious communities of the American past and from the religious orders of Roman Catholicism which normally sought clear lines of distinction from and integration with larger social and religious units and which often operated with definite and comprehensive systems of norms for regulating the various forms of society (though these systems were only partially applicable at best).

I would suggest several reasons for the flexibility and pluralism in the use of social models and images among these contemporary groups. First, there is the general tendency to ideological disillusionment characteristic of our age. This tendency has affected at different times and in different ways the socialist left (after both Stalinization and de-Stalinization), Roman Catholicism (after Vatican II), and U.S. society generally (after Vietnam). The groups and their members may be more or less aware of these tendencies and more or less in agreement with them, but they cannot avoid trying to function in a world where to a large extent "whirl is king." The distrust of institutional power (be it ecclesiastical, corporate or political), the relativistic attitude taken to many social and moral claims, the popular diffusion of ideas deriving from "the masters of suspicion" (Marx, Nietzsche, Freud)—all of which have been prominent in recent American culture and education—shape the minds even of those who seek to build new forms of Christian community.

Second, and a point that more specifically bears on the experience and the aspirations of the religious groups we have been looking at, their members generally have a sense of something amiss in contemporary U.S. society. This sense inevitably puts them at a distance from prevalent patterns of practice and justification in large areas of that society. But, on the other hand, since these groups are explicitly Christian, they and their members do not embrace a comprehensive radicalism which would put them in opposition to all the major traditional values of our society. Their stance toward the larger society, then, is bound to be complex and divided, even when groups on particular issues are in radical opposition to centers of institutional power or to prevalent attitudes in the culture. Neither the groups themselves nor their members, neither critics nor sympathizers should expect univocal radicalism or a comprehensive ideology to develop from within these groups.

Third, the groups themselves are voluntary and experiential. They report some departures and schisms provoked by previous decisions of the group, but their general style and their sense of values is not compatible with employing coercive techniques against either their own members or outsiders. Most of them implicitly accept a principle of respect for experience both in the lives of others and in the stages of the life of the individual, particularly when this experience is explicitly religious. Different kinds of experience in response to the hearing of God's word might lead people in different directions and might shatter the unity of the group, but the principle of respect for experience precludes relying on traditional structures of discipline and modes of legislation to maintain unity. Rather, what is called for is a renewal of commitment, a deepening of the choice originally made in founding or joining the group. Groups of this type will tend to be more homogeneous because they take their life from commitments freely made by people with similar or comparable experiences.

Thus, if one may venture a general sketch of these groups, their members are above average in education without being professional academics or intellectuals; they belong to the post-1945 suburban phase of U.S. church history rather than to immigrant nationality groups. They are predominantly white and middle-class, inclined to frugality and generosity rather than to conspicuous consumption. They are disinclined to violence but prize order and security. They are democratic and egalitarian but not rebellious or anarchist by disposition. The central members of these groups, who may or may not be in positions of leadership at any given time, are articulate and are accustomed to stating and resolving the issues of their lives on their own terms. Most of the groups describe themselves and their members as ranging from center and slightly left of center to the far left on the contemporary spectrum of political ideology. As a consequence, issues of power are often central for these groups. The groups and their members are anxious to preserve their autonomy in the face of larger religious and social units. They are likely to be uneasy about the unequal distribution of power within the group, and they are drawn to conceive of the empowerment of people (both their own members and their clients) as a characteristic contribution of the group.

The result of this set of attitudes combined with the principle of respect for experience is likely to be a community that is more like a floating island losing disparate members at its edges than like a bridge linking together opposing masses in a stable bond. For the principle of respect for experience, when taken together with the voluntary character of the group and the group's need to maintain internal cohesion and a sense of direction, puts effective limits on a group's ability to assimilate people with very divergent experience or people who stand in a continuing situation of conflict with each other. Of course, it is also possible for a group to avoid areas where differences in experience threaten to become unbridgeable or where conflicts destructive of the unity and cohesion of the group are imminent; this usually involves some suppression or restriction of the principle of respect for experience. There may also be restrictions of this principle or of preferences manifested in the internal life of the group for the sake of the group's mission to the larger society or to clients. Alternatively, the group may come to believe that its own value and its mission consist precisely in the articulation and embodiment of its own sense of Christian community.

METAPHORS OF SELF-UNDERSTANDING

Elements of these different possibilities can be seen in a number of the metaphors which the groups employ for presenting their relationship to other forms of society. Thus they speak of themselves as model, mirror, servant, critic, midwife, intervener (on the side of the poor), laboratory. They speak of their work as walking with, listening actively, testing, providing therapy. This variety of images and models should, I suggest, be thought of as an example of the pluralism in ways of perceiving and conceiving social reality which we ought to expect in religious groups that attempt to proceed on a basis of experience rather than from a pre-determined religious or social doctrine. We should not be in a particular hurry to reduce this plurality of metaphors and models to a systematic unity.

But we should note the divergent implications of these models for three key options in the working out of relations between religious groups and larger units of society. These are also important issues in the formation of the group's own consciousness. The three options are: (1) Is the group active or reactive, initiating or responsive? (2) Is the group ready to enter into conflictual or adversarial relationships with larger or more comprehensive social units (the state, the Church, a consensus of civil society)? (3) Does the group claim to have a higher, deeper insight into social reality, at least in its religious aspects, than is prevalent in the larger social units or in society at large?

If we look at the metaphors which the groups offer to describe themselves, the responses to these key options which the metaphors imply are mixed, except for the first question. Here the metaphors are overwhelmingly on the reactive and responsive side. This may be seen as an instance where the world sets the agenda for the Church. It may be a consequence of the recognition by religious groups that the fundamental forces propelling and altering our society do not originate in religious interests and do not move under religious auspices and that therefore religious groups may at most aspire to redirect or correct or clean up after forces that are already present and effective.

The denial of activity envisioned in these metaphors is not total; but activity is reactive or responsive to problems or needs that have already arisen (critic, intervener, midwife, therapist) or it is instrumental (servant, mirror, laboratory). But even if the activity of the group is responsive or instrumental, some of the metaphors imply a willingness to enter into conflictual relationships (critic, intervener, testing); others do not (listening, mirror, servant). The preferred metaphors are not strongly or ultimately conflictual; rather, they suggest an overarching common realm of interests and standards to which an appeal can be made even as conflict is expressed.

However, these common interests and standards are not available to all in the same way. Responsive or reactive activity by the groups depends on some higher or deeper or clearer insight or consciousness. This is what justifies the activity of the critic, the intervenor, the midwife, the therapist. The metaphors that go against this line of thought are the mirror, walking, and listening. The elitist implications of a claim to superior insight are troubling for people living in an ecumenical and pluralistic age and raised in an ethos of democratic egalitarianism. They can also set up barriers between the group and the people it is trying to serve or to heal or to persuade. But this can be mitigated in a number of ways: by dwelling on metaphors with contrary implications (servant, listener), by interpreting the difference in insight or consciousness not as a contrast between knowledge and error or ignorance but as a contrast between the explicit and the implicit (critic, midwife), or by stressing the gift character of the insight or awareness. It is also possible to cast the difference in less intellectualist terms, namely, in terms of a greater sensitivity to certain types of values or groups of persons (e.g., a preferential option for the poor). The general shape of the problem and of the range of possible solutions can be seen on a larger scale if one examines the rhetoric of Vatican II's Constitution on the Church in the Modern World, *Gaudium et spes.*

I would argue that members of religious action groups should not be unduly troubled by the claim to a higher or deeper awareness or insight. The fundamental reason for this claim has to be the group's appropriation of the central symbols of the Christian faith and its use of these symbols to interpret the perplexities and needs that arise within our common social experience. The claim has to be qualified because the group's application of the symbols may be faulty in a number of ways. But it has to be made because the members of the group as believing Christians, even while they acknowledge their imperfect grasp of the complexities of the social sciences and the free and unpredictable character of social reality, affirm that the ultimate issues of meaning and value in our life together as human persons are illumined by the mystery of Christ.

This illumination may be partial and indirect; it has to be striven and prayed for and is not available as a fixed asset for Christian communities. As a consequence, these communities work from an appropriation process rather than from a political or ideological program. The group loses its point and its claim to a distinctive and better or deeper insight or awareness when this appropriation process is not the central nourishing and directing element in its life and work.

VALUES OF THE GROUPS

Here I will look at an alternative approach to understanding and structuring Christian communities in the U.S. context. I will briefly list some of the major social values mentioned by the action/reflection groups with which we have been in contact. Then I will try to locate current groups in relation to current ideological possibilities and to indicate some sources of tension and uncertainty in the groups themselves.

Among the major social values mentioned by the groups themselves are participation, equality, accountability, mutuality, integrity, stewardship, sharing of scarce resources, concern for the poor, recognition of the human dignity of all, non-violence, openness, tolerance, and sense of community among low-income groups. Prominent among the disvalues that were mentioned are competition, domination, and centralization. Such a list of values and disvalues can be seen as a first specification of what these groups have in mind when they speak of "a just society" or a "commitment to social justice."

We should remember that generic language about justice in society both is available in very different religious and intellectual traditions and is used by people who have varying degrees of altruism and different interests to protect and advance. While some of the values (such as mutuality) might take us beyond the strict limits of a conception of justice, most of them deal with matters that have been the concern of political philosophers and theorists and that are demonstrably affected by both politics and legislation.

On the other hand, this listing of values and disvalues does not give us either a definite program or a picture of what a just society might look like. The values listed are too general and indefinite to do that, though they are not so indefinite or abstract that we cannot tell when they are being violated. It is a further question to what extent these values are compatible with each other and to what extent they should yield to other values in case of conflict. The social conscience portrayed in this listing of values and disvalues is not riven by obvious contradictions; the values it espouses may be in tension with each other, but this would have to become apparent at deeper levels of theory and practice.

While the list may not give us a definite program or a detailed picture of a just society, it nonetheless does show a certain profile which comes both from selectivity and incompleteness. This profile shows an interesting similarity to the conclusions that I proposed earlier about the models and metaphors that these groups offered to describe themselves and their relationship to larger societies.

I suggest that the choice of these values as a first specification of the demands of justice in society makes sense primarily when it is seen as corrective and reactive to two characteristic themes in contemporary U.S. political life. These are the insistence on restricting the power of the state in order to protect the freedom of the individual and the acceptance of great inequalities in power and access to resources so long as these do not involve violations of law. The social action of the groups we have been studying originates mainly (though not exclusively) in a concern for those who have been excluded from the opportunities of U.S. society because of patterns of discrimination or who have been deprived of the exercise of their rights and the meeting of their basic needs because of economic circumstances and their inability to compete in the marketplace.

Thus these groups are inclined to be skeptical about the beneficence of the private sector of the economy. They tend to question the value of competition and to yearn for a more collaborative organization of society. This puts them in harmony with standard themes in Catholic social thought and in opposition to the laissez-faire economic liberalism which shapes current U.S. conservatism. On the other hand, they are uncomfortable with the secularism, moral agnosticism, and permissiveness which mark a great deal of U.S. political liberalism and radicalism. They stress the importance of including more people both in the benefits of social programs and in the decision-making process. This sets them in opposition to those forms of conservatism which reject the demands of outside or alien groups and which preserve the dominance of established elites, and it puts them on the side of the poor and minority groups.

It also puts them in an opportunistic relationship with the public bureaucracy, which can function at times as the protector of the poor and at times as the instrument of powerful interest groups and local elites, depending on the way in which issues are formulated and on the political pressures and directions of the moment. The distrust of centralized power and the desire for greater accountability and participation put the action/reflection groups at a critical distance from bureaucratic organizations, whether these function in the public or the private sector.

In general, the social values espoused by the groups separate them from doctrinaire proponents of either capitalism or socialism, though the critical edge of these values with respect to existing institutions and practices generally causes the members of these groups to be and to be perceived as people on the left.

Thus, the social values endorsed by the groups provide a moral basis for criticism of government actions, of political movements, and of social and economic conditions, even though they do not constitute a program. The desire of the groups is to extend values of mutual respect, participation, openness and generosity which are effective and vibrant in the lives of the groups into the larger society. With the important exception of nuclear arms and the possibility of nuclear war, the groups generally avoid the issues of justice among the powerful institutions of modern society, the clash of interests among economic and political forces that determines the general direction of society.

There is a certain temptation to describe the social situation and the social vision of these Christian groups as parasitic on the liberal society of which they are so often critical. In one sense this is right, for liberal democracy in its U.S. form does provide both the legal and political space for these groups to form, to express their opinions, and to engage in public criticism and agitation. It provides the economic resources which enable at least some members of these groups to live in relative independence from the major institutions of society and to carry on a social ministry that requires some use of scarce resources. Indeed it is important both for members of the groups and for observers not to lose sight of the social context in which the groups function and not to overlook the often complex and ambivalent relations they and their members have to the larger society and to different elements within it. It is also true that liberal societies provide a more hospitable environment for independent and creative religious groups than do more traditional or more regimented societies.

One need only look at the experience of ecclesial base communities in Latin America (described by Alfred Hennelly in Chapter 3), however, to realize that permissive liberalism is not the only environment in which groups like the ones we are considering can come into being and flourish. Also, if one looks more broadly over the history of Christianity, one can find comparable groups arising in different social and political environments (many of which developed into religious orders in Roman Catholicism or sectarian movements in Protestantism).

Nonetheless, one may still have doubts about whether such groups can long survive pressures to institutionalization or privatization except in a liberal society. The question here is about what kind of larger society can allow and sustain the formation of religious groups that are loosely connected to established religious institutions and that have a politically significant prophetic edge to them. One might suggest that religious action/reflection groups should accept liberal society as their natural home and protector and that they should acknowledge a good thing when they see it.

Indeed, just as there is little in the way of comprehensive political or social ideology in these groups, so also there is very little in the way of revolutionary consciousness. The critical and denunciatory stance that these groups often take to the larger liberal society does not originate from an alien ideology but from concrete experiences of human needs which are neglected in the operations of the larger society and of human dignity which is disregarded in the case of the poor and the powerless. These groups strive to avoid the complacency which a comparison of functioning social and political systems can well induce in a defender of democratic capitalism. They are spurred to action by the contrast between the justice of the kingdom of God and the greed and injustice that mark the actual performance of U.S. society today.

Both the focus on the human needs and the human dignity of the powerless and the desire to shape community in a participatory way put the action/reflection groups in tension with standard patterns of bureaucratic rationality as these are manifested in social service agencies, government departments, and Church organizations. The urgency of meeting the needs of others and the strength of the desire to have and to mold one's own community combined with the importance of mutuality and face-to-face dealings in these groups are likely to produce reactions of suspicion, criticism, and protest when these groups collide with bureaucratic structures either in dealing with cases or in setting general policies. From the standpoint of the larger society, this tension is one of the costs involved in having groups that will take seriously the needs and rights of those who are not protected by the existing distribution of power and property and of those who for whatever reason fall between the cracks of existing systems of social service agencies.

The action/reflection groups stand, I would argue, in a situation where, by reason of their members' educational and work backgrounds, they can feel the pressures on large scale economic and political institutions; at the same time, when they commit themselves to working for justice and to serving the poor and the powerless, they are in contact with some of the most vulnerable and troubled aspects of society. In responding to this double exposure, they can draw on the resources and the visions provided by the political tradition of democracy in the United States and by the religious tradition of the Christian churches—from the Bible through monasticism and the Reformation to the Catholic social encyclicals and the ecumenical movement. Their actual contact with these resources is not very explicit or reflective, but it seems likely that there is a complex circular movement at work. The values which the groups draw from this double tradition and the values which figure in their inner life and their outer work direct, modify, and confirm each other. This is not a process in which particular models or visions of community are likely to have explicit philosophical or theological labels.

8
Linking Social Analysis and Theological Reflection: The Place of Root Metaphors in Social and Religious Experience

Joe Holland

Behind every theology there is an implicit social analysis that is an interpretation of the society within which the theology functions. Behind every social analysis there is also an implicit theology that is an interpretation of the ultimate source, foundation, and goal of society. Hence one task of linking social analysis and theological reflection would be to make explicit what is implicit in each. But behind both theology and social analysis there is something deeper. This is the *root metaphor* on which both draw.

In this essay, I would like to explore the emergence of what could be called a new or *post-modern* root metaphor at the foundation of fresh social and religious praxis from small communities. This may be described as an *artistic* metaphor, for it strives for a society which will be a communal and religious work of art, shaped by the creativity of faith-bearing communities linked in solidarity.

This artistic metaphor contrasts with the *modern mechanistic* metaphor dominant in the scientific ethos of both industrial capitalist and industrial communist societies (and of mixed or social democratic ones as well). The modern metaphor ultimately sees society as a machine. It has risen to dominance out of Enlightenment rationality, but it is now at the root of our social crisis.

The artistic metaphor also contrasts with the *pre-modern organic* metaphor which was dominant in traditional Western societies. This saw society as a biological system, but without a dynamic prin-

ROOT METAPHORS

PRE-MODERN ORGANIC: Space: Integralist (order)
Time: Cyclical (tradition)
Governance: Hierarchical
(authority)
Metaphor: Organic (body)

Theology: Catholic Illuminist
(analogy)
Spirituality: Monastic
Contemplation (mind)
Evangelization: Aristocracy
(imperialism)

MODERN MECHANISTIC: Space: Pluralistic (competition)
Time: Linear (progress)
Governance: Managerial
(competence)
Metaphor: Mechanistic (machine)

Theology: Protestant Fiducial
(opposition)
Spirituality: Individual
Privatization (will)
Evangelization: Middle Classes
(personal experience)

POST-MODERN ARTISTIC: Space: Interdependent
(community)
Time: Wave-like (rhythm)
Governance: Participative
(creativity)
Metaphor: Artistic (work of art)

Theology: Ecumenical Synthesis
(dialectic)
Spirituality: Prophetic
Transformation (praxis)
Evangelization: Poor & Oppressed
(community)

171

ciple of change. This organic metaphor was at the foundation of classical Western social and religious thought and action.

In pursuing the exploration of this post-modern artistic metaphor at the root of a new form of social and religious praxis, I would like to set it in context with an historical overview of the life of the three metaphors (organic, mechanistic, and artistic) and some reflection on how social analysis, theology, spirituality, and evangelization are experienced within each.[1]

This essay is written from a biased perspective (as indeed all essays are). The bias here is, first, that both liberalism and Marxism, despite their mutual antagonism and separate contributions, have entered together into the common crisis of the mechanistic metaphor of Enlightenment rationality and its scientific civilization, and, second, that the Spirit of God is unleashing new religious and social energies of creativity precisely to transform our increasingly oppressive and increasingly destructive modern civilization. Hence the normal liberal academic claim of distinguishing description from evaluation does not apply here. Indeed such an impossible separation (equivalent to the claimed fact/value split in autonomous science) is at the heart of the crisis of our present civilization and of our difficulty in finding both the vision and the energy to carry us beyond it.

THE CRISIS OF MODERN CIVILIZATION

Our civilization has entered upon a profound crisis. This crisis could unleash the most destructive and demonic forces ever felt in human history. Such forces could even destroy the entire human race. But the crisis could alternatively unleash creative or redemptive energies. For that to happen, our religious and social questions need to become radical—that is, to go to the root of our civilization. To go to the root means to go to the foundational metaphor out of which our civilization has been constructed.

Today as Christian communities go to the root of our crisis, we are seeing a new historical form of Christianity being born. This new form relinks the social and the religious in a counter-cultural marriage of faith and justice. It is a prophetic form of Christianity, blending Protestant and Catholic insights, and rooted in networks of small communities across the globe.

These communities are especially centered in the poor and oppressed, or are in dialogue with them. They attempt to read the signs of the times and to hear the word of God in and through this experience of the poor and oppressed. They are in turn pioneering a new model of evangelization, where the Gospel is carried from base to elite, from black to white, from poor to rich, from female to male, from periphery to center, etc. God thus appears for us in the face of the poor, of women, of those without freedom, in those who hunger for peace, in peoples of color, and in the earth itself.

To understand this emergence of a prophetic church rooted in small communities and of the artistic root metaphor which nourishes them, it may be helpful now to review the movement of root metaphors since before the rise of the modern period.

THE PRE-MODERN ORGANIC METAPHOR

The organic metaphor nourished pre-modern or traditional societies, but it had a special form in the life of the Christian West. There the unit of analysis was Christendom, or Christian civilization.

In this metaphor, the society is analogous to the human body. Everything is connected, and each part has its proper place with reciprocal rights and duties. The aristocracy at the top is the head which commands, and the peasantry at the bottom is the feet which obey. But in its best form, the aristocracy has major responsibilities to the peasantry (*noblesse oblige*). Thus we might say that spatially the organic society is viewed as a single whole, and the parts are only functions of the whole.

Historical consciousness is not developed in the classical organic metaphor. Society is seen as static and relatively unchanging. Of course there is change, but it is cyclical—the movement of the life cycle and of the natural seasons. Change is ever present, but the pattern remains constant. Change is thus a stable circle, going round and round, but bringing nothing new. Tradition is the perpetuation of this stable circle.

Since there is nothing new, there is little need for adaptation or flexibility. So the human personality is bound to traditional role models. Authority tends to be lifelong.

But bodies have their cycle of growth and decay, so will not the same apply to civilizations? It was here that the organic metaphor shaping the world of Christendom was strained. For while it was acknowledged that other civilizations rose and fell, there was the hope that the Christian civilization would not decline. Thus the metaphor of the body was supplemented by the metaphor of the rock, which provided a firmer foundation and walls of defense. In this sense, Christian civilization built up permanent institutions which could withstand the ravages of organic or temporal decay. Archaic organic cultures knew that death and decay would invade all, but Christian civilization tried to shut death out from its institutions. It shared in the Eternal Being of God. Individual Christians, even Popes, would die, but the institutions would endure. To defend the institutions was to defend the civilization.

As a result, while in earlier communal organic models the society often was governed by a consensual circle (as in Indian tribes), in Christian civilization the governance was hierarchical, with rigid class lines and a military structure taken over from the Roman Empire. Further, since there was nothing new to be developed, and since change meant subversion, the function of authority was to control the social order and to preserve the tradition. This was supplemented, however, by missionary expansion of the rocklike center, through construction projects of fortresses, monuments, and public buildings, especially religious ones.

The civilization had a religious foundation. Indeed the whole order of Christian civilization was seen as a manifestation of the divine within the world. Sacred and secular were bound together, with the sacred reigning over the secular and the secular witnessing to the pre-eminence of the sacred.

There were many ways the sacred and secular were linked. The rulers of the Church followed the same organizational model as the wider society, and themselves came from the same ruling classes. The Church was the most rock-like institution, providing the innermost core of the civilization's center. In turn, a theological model flowed from the religious institution to reinforce the social structure.

The *theological model* of Christendom was constructed around the primary principle of analogy, as David Tracy has so helpfully explored in regard to the overall Catholic tradition.[2] At the heart of this principle is a vision of being and its emanations. The world, and people within it, are seen in the image of God. The world is an emanation or expression of the Divine, and analogously carries its pattern. Thus the social order is an expression or imitation of the divine order. But there are limits to this principle of analogy.

The analogy is limited to the reigning social order, in this case Christian civilization. Pagan civilizations share less or not at all in the analogy. Sometimes they may be seen as weak anticipations (as for Greece and Rome), while in other cases they may be seen as mortal enemies, even viewed as demonic (Islam). Thus Christian civilization is seen as a privileged place of disclosure of the sacred.

In this theological model, a certain kind of *spirituality* emerges. It is centered in the contemplative vision of being, which climaxes in God. The scholastics referred to this as the beatific vision.

This spirituality focused on the axis of space, to the exclusion of the axis of time. The closer one rose to the source of being, the further one was removed from history. This movement to the height of space was reflected architecturally in the construction of temples at the center of civilization. The temple was analogously the social expression of the spatial centrality of God in being.

The act of rising above the distractions of history to the spatial center and source is called transcendence, and God was seen as transcendent Being.

This sense of transcendence provided an internal check on the pride of Christian civilization. The Church would defend the civilization from all enemies, but it would always remind the civilization that its splendor was but a pale and finite reflection of that which it analogously resembled.

In order not to allow the energies of religious legitimation to surrender totally to the civilization, the monastery (and its analogously weaker expression in later mendicant and activist religious orders) provided the important check. The Church encouraged some people to leave the world, as testimony to its finiteness. Thus the distinction of the two states of life, and the higher role of the "religious" state. The two states of life model provided, on the one hand, a way to channel dissident religious energies away from a potential undermining of the civilization and into a stable and transcendent religious structure, while at the same time diminishing the arrogance of the civilization itself.

The three religious vows—poverty, chastity, and obedience—classically played this same functional role of legitimation and diminishing of arrogance. Poverty (with exceptions like the Franciscan movement) was not so much a commitment to the poor, but more a rejection of the cares of the world to be free for contemplative transcendence. Chastity was not so much the prophetic celibacy of Jeremiah who sacrificed himself in order to change the history of Israel but more the priestly transcendence which rose above the distraction of generative sexuality so bound to earth and time. And, finally, obedience was less an openness to the Gospel's call in history and more a reinforcement of the hierarchy and unity of the religious and social structure to which the personality submits himself or herself.

This model of spatial transcendence plays down the eschatological fears and hopes of a more historically-oriented Christianity. The promise is seen as fulfilled, or at least satisfied to the extent that can be expected within the finite world. There will be an end of history, but there is no historical tension to reach for it. The end of the history simply lurks as an unexpected catastrophe behind the horizon of a stable and balanced Christian civilization. The end reminds us of the finiteness of all the existence and of the overpowering role of transcendence but offers no real critique of present structures or history.

The organic body does not move historically in the evolutionary arrow of progress as in the mechanistic model; rather it moves organically. That is, it reaches out to that which surrounds it and assimilates it like food, digesting it into its own system. Thus Western Christendom and the Western Church grew together by continuing the imperialistic thrust of Greece and Rome.

This imperialistic movement heightened as the check of religious transcendence was weakened by the humanism of the Renaissance and the utilization of early scientific developments, such as navigation and gunpowder. Out of these two tendencies—the weakening of spiritual energies and the development of science—would emerge the modern mechanistic metaphor as the unruly but powerful child of the classical West. But before exploring this second metaphor, let us review the model of evangelization implicit in Christendom.

The model of *evangelization* flowed directly from the implicit perceptions of the social dimensions of sin and grace. In these perceptions the social structure as a whole (the organic body) was seen as grace-bearing—that is, as the mediator or expression of the divine. The social order expressed the divine order of creation and redemption. By contrast, internal or external challenges to the social order were seen as sin-bearing or religiously subversive.

So in this model, evangelization is mediated *through* the social structure. The social structure and its aristocratic authorities are protectors of the Gospel and instruments for bringing it to society. Individual authorities may be corrupt and need to be chastized, but the office itself and the structure behind it have a clear and unchallenged place in the divine plan. The Gospel thus proceeds from elite to base and from center to periphery (e.g., from rich to poor, from powerful to powerless, from man to woman, and from the white West to other cultures).

But now that the gift of the Gospel has been brought to all the globe, and also now that the destructive energies of Western civilization are so clearly triumphing over its creative energies, we are seeing a massive Catholic and Protestant disengagement of theology, spirituality and evangelization from their classical alliance with established power. This is what the new networks of prophetic, counter-cultural communities represent. But let us review the roots of this disengagement further in the trajectory of the next root metaphor.

THE MODERN MECHANISTIC METAPHOR

The medieval synthesis of classical Catholic Christendom, founded on the organic metaphor, was disrupted and eventually displaced by the rise of what we call the modern world. This took place over approximately five centuries. The rise of humanism and the emancipation of science in the Renaissance were an initial sign of the new culture, as the human dimension began to take primacy. The Protestant Reformation further weakened the old culture by heightening the sense of the individual (private conscience), undercutting the power of the institutional Church, and orienting religious energies more toward history. The American and French revolutions, along with the general rise of liberal nation states, began a national centralization of diffused communities, weakening the overarching imperial culture tied to the heritage of the Roman Empire and advancing the modern stress on progress and freedom. Finally, the industrial revolution provided the technological opening, initially through industrial capitalism and later through industrial communism, to unleash the powerful modern engines of production and destruction.

If there is a key word throughout the rise of the modern world, it has been "freedom." This meant historical freedom from the chains of the past for the sake of a better future. Successively it came to mean cultural freedom (humanism), religious freedom (Protestantism), political freedom (democracy), and economic freedom (capitalism and later socialism).

To focus on the freedom from the past for a better future means that the focal axis within the culture has shifted from space to time. Historical freedom replaced spatial transcendence as the galvanizer of cultural energy. Contrast for example the extreme of the two ideals—to leave the world for the sake of a timeless contemplative gaze into eternity (the classical ideal) or to plunge into the world in pursuit of the efficient use of time.

Just as time rose to dominance over space with historical freedom, so in the modern world the part rose to dominance over the whole—or, perhaps better, the liberated parts shattered the organic whole—in spatial freedom or pluralism. This happened most clearly in the case of the liberated individual.

A whole new modern psychology developed in which the personality is so much more than an expression of his or her role within the society. To facilitate the development of a flexible, self-contained, and individuated ego, society eventually created the long process of modern education. As a result, the modern world stresses the freedom of the individual and looks suspiciously upon all institutions, seeing them as constraining freedom.

The same process of fragmentation or differentiation proceeded over centuries in other areas of the social structure. The academy distinguished description from prescription, as science distinguished fact from value. Economics was emancipated from politics, and politics from religion. Church and state, work and family grew separate. Eventually religion was privatized from the rest of society. Personalities, pursuing their intellectual development, turned to even greater specialization. Still today the more one studies, the more distant one usually grows from a view of the whole.

This focus on the part over the whole can be described as the emergence of "analytic rationality." Analytic rationality breaks the whole down into smaller and smaller parts in order to understand how it works. It assumes that the answer is in the parts, not the whole. More and more the modern world perceives disjoined things as existing to be controlled and manipulated.

In this process of "differentiation," we can see clearly the distinction between the organic and mechanistic metaphors. For the organic metaphor, the whole is more than the sum of its parts, and so has a life and purpose beyond the parts. For the mechanistic metaphor, however, the whole is only the sum of the parts, so only the parts are important. The difference of parts in tension or opposition (mutual negation) is its organizing principle, in contrast to the vital or organic unity of the biological organism.

The mechanistic metaphor, however, produces eventually a paradoxical opposite. What began as a culture stressing individual freedom winds up converting itself into a culture of mass society where the individual is powerless. As the social machine becomes more complex, centralized, and powerful, many people become more easily replaceable or even not needed. Powerlessness becomes the broad social experience. The individual has a place only in conformity to the social system—a place, as the expression goes, like a cog in a machine.

It is here in the cultural sphere that the deepest crisis of the modern world emerges. It is not primarily a crisis of politics (though democracy is being replaced by domination), nor of economics (though the poor are being crushed and the middle sectors driven into downward mobility), but primarily a crisis of meaning. The spiritual energies which fueled the emergence of the modern world are now exhausted and even turning demonic.

The two basic thrusts of the modern world were, as mentioned, the freedom of the future from the past (historical freedom) and of the part from the whole (spatial freedom). These have led over time on the one hand to an uprooted, despiritualized, and secularized civilization (the spiritual crisis) and on the other hand to the most powerful and destructive control of elites over majorities ever seen in human history (the social crisis). The secularization is so deep and the domination so destructive precisely because the technological tools for both have been developed to such a colossal degree.

Thus the modern world comes full circle. Born of the desire to liberate humanity from classical domination, it produces a technological domination which makes the classical form pale by contrast. Born of the desire to liberate humanity from its technological limitations, it now produces a militarized technological system stealing resources from the poor and threatening to destroy all the earth. Born of the desire to liberate humanity from the constraints of religion, it now discovers its own god, autonomous technology, destroying foundational values, human community, and the ecological matrix.

The *theology* paralleling the rise of the mechanistic root metaphor is predominantly Protestant, although the modern world quickly broke beyond the weak constraints of Protestantism. (Major sectors of liberal Catholicism also eventually adapted to the Protestant model.) Protestant theology arose precisely as a protest against the organic domination of the late medieval Catholic Church. Because the whole was so oppressive, it had to be shattered. Because the structure was so corrupt, it had to be challenged historically. Protestantism thus arose as a negation of the organic unity and spatial absoluteness of the medieval synthesis.

History entered theology indirectly through the Protestant delegitimation of the medieval synthesis. By projecting the judgment of God's total sovereignty onto the corruption of the classical society, Protestantism set society in historical motion toward a new focus. The contemplation of the temple yielded to the journey of the pilgrim.

As analogy receded from dominance in theology, the sense of sin deepened. Salvation ceased to be understood as the organic integration of grace and nature in a two-tiered universe of sacred and secular, but became instead the linkage of distant divine power and the trusting human will. Human nature was no longer considered simply wounded by sin, but rather totally depraved. Thus so much greater is the redemptive power of God. But it is a redemptive power which now works in spite of human institutions, not through them.

Catholicism of course always saw sin in the world, but sin was viewed in terms of personal deviance from the social structure, which was a presumed reflection of the divine. The Catholic struggle against sin thus shut out history. In the Catholic view there was a basic goodness in the social order—grace and nature, or law and redemption, were more in continuity than discontinuity—so there was no need to change it.

By contrast, the Protestant stress on total depravity led to a distrustful view of human institutions, including the Church as institution, as well as the social order. The individual in turn, redeemed by the sovereign power of God, became the carrier of grace. Thus while classically in the medieval synthesis the whole was grace-bearing and the part suspect, in the new movement there would be a growing shift to distrust the whole and to favor the part.

In a dialectical inversion, this eventually provided the legitimation for what we have come to know as liberal societies built on checks and balances, pluralism, and liberal democracy. If the social structure was evil, the only legitimate social structure could be one which counter-balanced one evil-prone institution against another (checks and balances) and spread the power as broadly as possible (liberal democracy and the free market) to prevent centralized power from emerging. And so, while claiming to hold the sovereignty of God in judgment over every social structure, this theology winds up nonetheless concluding that there is only one social structure which checks evil. Thus it indirectly legitimates the social model of liberalism, a model essentially founded on a vision of human depravity and discontinuity between grace and nature.

In recent years, as American industrial capitalism has come into crisis along with industrial communism, we see neo-conservative expressions of this indirect social legitimation. The legitimation is based on a modern application of Luther's classical division of the two kingdoms. Because the kingdom of God is entirely separate from this world, in Luther's view, all human kingdoms are basically evil. But liberalism at least, in the neo-conservative theory, restrains evil by mutual checks and balances. Hence to try to change liberalism in the name of justice would be to try to build here the kingdom of God, but this is socially dangerous and religiously blasphemous. Hence, as Luther once supported the nobility in a bloody repression of the peasants, the neo-conservatives seek to strengthen the repres-

sive hand of the late modern liberal state. Social welfare functions begin to yield to the primacy of national security in the internal and
external war against communism.

For the neo-conservatives, all attempts to change the society
and directly pursue the common good are either dangerous expressions of communist penetration or else naive utopian attempts which
play into communist hands. For the neo-conservatives, the only real
alternatives are the present form of late capitalism or totalitarian
communism. They do not allow the possibility that utopian social
and religious energies could actually construct something beyond
these two. They deny the possibility of a post-modern society. In so
doing, they reject the on-going creative and redemptive presence of
the Spirit of the living God in history.

This leads to a double standard in terms of social change across
the world. Authoritarianism becomes the defense of "democracy."
As General Pinochet described his military government in Chile, it is
a new form of government called "authoritarian democracy." Presid-
ing over the executive, judicial, and legislative branches and guaran-
teeing their defense is the new, fourth, and newly pre-eminent sector
of government—the national security branch.

As has been mentioned earlier, the *spirituality* which nourishes
this social–theological movement functions primarily by isolating
and compartmentalizing religious energies. Its focus is the individual, but only on the private side of life. Primary relationships such as
family and sexuality are focal concerns, as are private social relationships. But those dimensions of the individual and community which
open positively onto the public realm or structural dimensions of society are neglected. The notion of explicit and positive responsibility
for the common good is downplayed.

Of course individual and communitarian religious energies need
not be cultivated in isolation. They can also be charged with prophetic social energy. So it is not that individual prayer, subjective religious experience, and a focus on primary relationships are wrong
(quite the contrary), but only that they are not followed to their full
social consequence.

By so isolating them, a spirituality emerges which distorts the
living God who is Creator and Redeemer of history. On the one
hand, there is constructed a god of private spirituality who bears no

relation to the wider social arena. For such a god, there would never have been an exodus, never a prophetic debate with Israel's kings, never a captivity of the chosen people. On the other hand, as the social system enters into crisis, spiritual energies are summoned for defense in an opposite distortion. The private god yields to a war god who strengthens the determination of the society through militaristic rituals. Industrial capitalism, seen as protecting Christianity, sets out to destroy industrial communism, seen as the major force of atheism in the world. But in reality, both systems collapse in their global war into common worship of the war god, and both now even persecute Christian communities to further their destructive goals.

The model of *evangelization* which accompanied the emergence of the modern world and its related theologies and spiritualities also focuses on the individual and the private. At the extreme, evangelization is an aggregate of personal conversions ("born again") in which isolated individuals one by one are impacted by grace. Thus evangelization focuses on the part (the individual) to the exclusion of the whole (the society). The carrier of evangelization in this new model is primarily the middle classes. They are the ones around whom the liberal world is centered.

To conclude the review thus far, we have seen the rise and crisis of a second root metaphor in the life of the West. First we saw the organic metaphor—focused on the image of the body, with a rock-like center, absolutizing of its social space, repressing images of time or historical change, legitimated by a theology meditating on the vision of absolute Being and its analogous expressions, nourished by a spirituality of discipline and assimilation, and mediating the evangelization process through consolidated social structures under the patronage of powerful social elites.

Second, we saw the mechanistic metaphor—focused on the image of the machine, stressing the counter-tensions of its many parts, repressing the vision of the whole, legitimated by a theology of the sovereignty of divine will and the depravity of human endeavor, favoring a compartmentalized and privatized spirituality, mediating evangelization through the private life of the individual in the middle classes, and growing into a militaristic crusade against communism.

There are strengths and weaknesses to both metaphors, and a dynamic internal life to both as well. When the weaknesses grow dominant, the social system and its religious legitimation begin to turn idolatrous. This is now happening in our own society.

THE POST-MODERN ARTISTIC METAPHOR

Only in recent times as the modern project turns against humanity has the optimism of the modern movement begun to shift to pessimism and fatalism. We have lived through two major world wars, the emergence of totalitarianism (fascism and communism), the continuing growth of militarism, the threat of nuclear holocaust, the ecological crisis, the persistence of widespread poverty and the spiritual emptiness of modern materialism. As a result, people are increasingly experiencing two great hungers in the "post-modern" world—the hunger for peace and justice and the hunger for meaning. In their responses, a new root metaphor is beginning to take shape.

On the spatial axis, the first theme around which the new root metaphor takes shape is *community*. This is the defining spatial construct. The classical organic metaphor also stressed community, but it was bound to rigid tradition and ruled over by hierarchies of strict domination.

The rise of the modern world shattered this constraint of tradition and domination of hierarchy, but only recently has it become clear that the modern spirit has been profoundly eroding community. The centralization of economic, political, and cultural power into vast elite-dominated bureaucracies (both public and private) has unleashed the dual processes of hyper-individualization and massification ("the lonely crowd").

In this context, the strength of pre-modern communal structures and values is a resource for the post-modern metaphor. By contrast, more deeply modernized societies like the United States have a more severe cultural crisis precisely because the structures and values of community have been so deeply eroded, at least in certain sectors. In the former case, the existing broad residue of community must be tapped in order to defend and transform community in resistance against mechanistic domination. In the latter case, the existing weak residue of community must be strengthened and even recreated for the same purpose.

On the historical axis the post-modern metaphor reaches in two directions at once—back to a *rooted past* and ahead to a *transformed future.* It shares with Marxism the view that the present needs to be fundamentally transformed, but it departs from all modern thought, including Marxism, in that it seeks to tap the tradition and recover roots as part of this movement toward a renewed future. It also differs from Marxism in that this renewed future would not have an eschatological character, but would be simply one more shift in a continuing process of historical challenge. Thus this movement transcends liberalism by being utopian—that is, reaching for a new form of society beyond the present one—but it also transcends Marxism by reaching back to the past for guidance and spiritual energy, and by refusing to grant the new society absolute status.

The post-modern struggle is primarily *cultural* because to tap the tradition and to unleash the imagination is precisely a cultural task. Similarly the defense or building of community is also a cultural task growing out of a redefinition of the relation of the individual and society. While the movement which flows from economic and political strategies can be described in terms of power, force, and control, the movement which flows from cultural strategies is *energy,* indeed even spiritual energy.

The governing task in addressing our present crisis is also quite different from that of the formerly dominant metaphors. The answer of the classical organic metaphor to the post modern crisis is to reassert authority—"law and order." This is what the New Right and neo-conservatives are suggesting in varying degrees. The standard liberal mechanistic response is simply to balance the tensions—a procedural response which fails to address questions of substance in the culture. This is what is behind the collapse of the political center in American society. The standard Marxist mechanistic response is to build a mass bloc with enough strategic force to overpower the opposing class. But then what? Of itself, the theory offers not a radical alternative to, but only a radicalization of the mechanistic model.

This brings us then to the governing virtue of the new paradigm, namely *creativity.* How creatively to tap the tradition? How creatively to imagine a future beyond the logic of the mechanistic model? How creatively to network and empower communities of ordinary people? How creatively to reshape technology and capital, and reintegrate them back within the community matrix? These are the challenging questions of the new path.

In short, the new metaphor suggests what might be called a *communitarian society,* carrying a mixed economy, linking the creativity of rooted communities in solidarity, with the state playing a secondary and facilitating role (its power checked by the autonomous control of rooted communities over capital and technology and by interlays of mediating structures according to the principle of subsidarity), tapping the cultural roots of the past for the sake of a transformed future, employing new creativity in decentralized social and material technology, and recasting its view of the whole and the parts by the ecological principle as well as its view of production and reproduction by what might be termed symbolically a masculine/feminine balance. Small communities are the central agents of this new metaphor.

This brings us then to the religious side of the new metaphor, or to the questions of what theology, what spirituality, and what model of evangelization flow implicitly from the preceding social model in the crisis of the mechanistic root metaphor.

Because of the depth of the social crisis upon us, religious energies are central. At stake are the basic perceptions of the nature of society, its source, its redemption, and its end. It is not surprising then that all across the world religious energies are disrupting standard patterns of secular modernization, whether capitalist or communist.

Confining ourselves to the Christian tradition, however, and focally with the Catholic expression of it, we see two new but relatively separate expressions of religious energy—on the one hand the prayer movement and on the other hand the justice and peace movement. This is not the place to trace extensively the history or nature of each, but they are potentially complementary and converging expressions of the Spirit of God active in the re-creation and redemption of contemporary history, perhaps even planting religious seeds for a post-modern civilization. John Haughey's essay in this volume explores this theme more fully.

The leading expression of *theology* addressing the social side and coming from the new metaphor is, in my judgment, Latin America's "liberation theology," especially what might be called its second stage of engagement with popular culture and popular religion.

Liberation theology has been strongly attacked from some quarters as being Marxist. Indeed it has learned much from the Marxian tradition. But I believe it can best be seen as a "post-modern" theology. This means also that it is "post-Marxist"—that is, transcending the limitations of Marxism even while learning from its insights. Thus, I would argue, by its special stress on communities rather than the state, by its rooting class conflict in the richer framework of the community and popular struggle, by tapping the cultural and religious tradition of the community, and by drawing energy from prayer and worship of the living God, it represents something well beyond Marxism, and much deeper.

It is true, however, that liberation theology looks to the Left rather than to the Right for alliances. That occurs within a framework of societies where the dominant oppression comes from the Right. Yet it seems remarkably similar in effect to the patterns of the Church/worker alliance in Poland, where the struggle is with the dominant oppression of the official Left. If there were more dialogue between these apparently opposite forms of struggle, I believe we would find that both are converging in a post-modern form.

Avery Dulles sensed this new dimension of theology when he described two past historical modes of theologizing but pointed to yet a new third mode taking shape.[3] His description of the classical illuminist mode corresponds to the Catholic principle of analogy and to the organic metaphor. His description of the fiducial mode corresponds to the Protestant principle of opposition and the mechanistic metaphor. Finally, I would suggest, his description of the new performative mode of theology corresponds to the truly dialectic principle of artistic root metaphor.

The *spirituality* coming from the new root metaphor offers fundamental challenge to the present social system. It turns its spiritual energies precisely toward social and personal transformation, even while insisting that the source of these energies is outside the self. Classical Catholic spirituality stabilized the system by rising above it. Modern Protestant spirituality balanced the system by compensating for its harshness. But post-modern spirituality challenges the system by opening itself to prophetic and transformative spiritual energies.

This new spirituality is communal; the small group (basic community) is the mediator of the spiritual dynamics.

The mode of the small group may be described as charismatic. By this I mean something broader than what is termed the "charismatic movement," although that is not excluded. Classical spirituality was dualistic. On the one hand there was the monastic mode (pertaining to those who "left the world"). On the other hand there was the official mode (based on the leadership of consecrated religious rulers who reflected the lifetime office of the hereditary aristocracy). In the modern mode, the stress fell more to competence, to those who were trained in the discipline (e.g., the Ignatian "Exercises"), and in recent times especially the discipline of psychology. In the post-modern mode, however, while office and competence still remain important, priority passes to charism, to the presence of spiritual energy whenever, wherever, and in whomever it appears. The Spirit blows where it will within the world, and often it blows wide of consecration or training. Yet this must not collapse into spiritual anarchy, so what we are actually speaking about is a new balance where office and competence are redefined as servants of charism.

This means finally, then, a new spirituality. The doctrine of the two states of life (lay and religious) and its various historical revisions begin to break down. This means a profound redefinition of the religious order and of the vows.

The vows would be redefined, as indeed has been happening for some time. Poverty thus shifts from avoiding worldly distractions to commitment to the poor. Celibacy shifts from rising above worldly impurities and the chains of family to commitment to a broader fertility, whose generation is mediated spiritually through the wider community. Obedience in turn shifts from reinforcement of the social structure through suppression of the self to personal response to the historical call of the Spirit and openness to the harsh demands coming from the way of the cross.

Yet there is still a role for the priestly or cosmic mediations of classic spirituality. This comes from a renewed emphasis on the contemplative vocation, as we see in the Buddhist-Christian encounter. Contemplation becomes the antidote to the loss of bearings and of depth in Western activism.

These thoughts are not new, nor original, but need to be seen in relation to the new root metaphor taking shape. The religious order becomes now the servant of creativity for the prophetic call of the whole Church. The whole Church in turn embarks on a path of prophetic creativity in the midst of profound social crisis. And finally the vows become not alternatives to the normal Christian pattern, but ways of showing all Christians the deeper meaning of their baptism.

There is a new model of *evangelization* emerging as well. In the classical model, the social elites (aristocracy) and the social center (Europe) were the source of evangelization, while the poor and the colonies were the object. In the more modern model of evangelization, as mentioned earlier, the pattern became on the Protestant side more individualistic (personal conversions) and on the Catholic side more institutional (e.g., training in Catholic schools), but in both cases increasingly focused on the middle class as the mediator.

In the post-modern model, it is the poor and oppressed who are the source of evangelization, as Monika Hellwig has begun to explore elsewhere in this volume.

This does not mean that the rich and powerful are rejected simply because evangelization comes from the poor and oppressed, any more than the classical evangelization model meant rejection of the poor and oppressed. But it does mean that the rich and powerful, in order to be converted, need to hear the Gospel from the poor and oppressed. As Jesus taught us, that is difficult but not impossible.

This has special significance too for the middle classes, for they can cast their lot upward or downward. They can see themselves as lesser versions of the rich and powerful, vicariously identify with them, strive to reach their heights, and even look down with fear and contempt toward the poor and oppressed. Or they can look downward and see themselves as closer to the poor and oppressed, and see the rich and powerful as more structurally alienated from the source of the Gospel. This is their choice precisely because they are in the middle, and the religious and social consequences are profound.

In sum, the face of God begins to appear to us in places we did not expect—in the face of the poor, the imprisoned, the tortured; in the face of woman who labors under sexism; in the face of people of color who bear the burden of racism; in the face of the third world and its massive poverty; in the face of the earth itself. These are the sources of evangelization.

Conclusion

Thus we have reviewed the historical life of three root metaphors—organic, mechanistic, and now artistic—in the social and religious history of the West. Each has its strength and each its weakness. It is not a question of absolutizing one, but rather of discerning historically the role of each in the present period. The judgment has been made that the mechanistic metaphor, which came to dominate the West, has exhausted its spiritual resources and is turning demonic. But grace-bearing energies are arising in a way that retrieves some aspects of the organic roots, recasting them in a communitarian and dynamic way. This has been called the artistic metaphor. It is implicitly the source of energy and vision for faith communities in the world today. Indeed, small communities are precisely the bearers of this new metaphor.

There is no question here of eliminating earlier dominant metaphors and making the new artistic metaphor all-powerful. All three are always simultaneously present, but the question remains: Which will be the ordering metaphor, the dominant one? What we have now is a contest for dominance between the reigning mechanistic metaphor and the ascendant artistic one. The artistic metaphor should not crush the mechanistic one, only reduce its power within the society and provide aesthetic guidance for it. This is the root issue in our social and religious crisis.

The rise of the artistic root metaphor carries at its foundation the rise of a new spirituality for the post-modern world. Out of this new spirituality, a renewed Church and a renewed society, indeed a renewed civilization, may one day arise, but not without the journey into the wilderness and the agony of the cross. The Spirit is unleashing new energies of creativity and their birth pangs are now upon us. The seeds are germinating in small communities.

NOTES

1. For this probing of the artistic root metaphor, I am indebted to the foundational work of Gibson Winter in the field of religious social ethics. This essay is a further development at a deeper level of my earlier work with Peter Henriot, S.J., on more technical dimensions of social analysis: *Social Analysis: Linking Faith and Justice* (Washington, D.C.: Center of Concern, 1980).

2. David Tracy, *The Analogical Imagination: Christian Theology and the Culture of Pluralism* (New York: Crossroad, 1981).

3. Avery Dulles, "The Meaning of Faith Considered in Relationship to Justice," in John Haughey (ed.), *The Faith That Does Justice* (New York: Paulist Press, 1977), pp. 10–46.

Part III

Interaction with the Theological Tradition

While they begin with experience, the new forms of theological reflection we have been examining do not describe or explain their experience without reference to the Scriptures and various elements of the Judaeo-Christian traditions. In Part III we turn our attention to ways in which contemporary stories and analyses of experience can be brought into dialogue with the more traditional sources of revelation for mutual enlightenment and guidance. The living God has interacted with our sisters and brothers in the human family for millennia. Their experience, understanding, and response can be enlightening for us.

In Chapter 9, Jouette Bassler describes precedents in two biblical communities for the type of theological reflection on experience carried on in the action/reflection groups that participated in the Woodstock study. She focuses upon the ways the major images of Christ that dominate Paul's Corinthian letters and John's Gospel were chosen and how those images in turn shaped the life of those communities and set them in distinctive ethical and spiritual directions. From those examples she suggests ways in which we can come to greater conscious awareness of our own operative Christologies and their influence upon our life choices.

The biblical evidence she unfolds reveals fascinating aspects of the theological reflection of two early Christian communities and encourages our own prayerful efforts. Bassler invites us to look seriously at the relative ineffectiveness of a spirituality that is imposed from outside the community, that is not evolved by the community itself through its own processes of theological reflection. She also points out the danger of a community spirituality that is not somehow kept in honest dialogue with the "outside," with the larger Church community. Her focus on Christological models brings us, with a renewed sense of their social-ethical importance, to confront the words of Jesus: "Who do *you* say that I am?"

In Chapter 10 Avery Dulles joins the ranks of those who see this era in the Church as a time of radical, even epochal, change. The recognition of cultural pluralism and the sorry realization of centuries of cultural imperialism in the name of religious evangelization are calling the Church to move beyond its European forms to become an authentically global reality. The immensity and difficulty of that task are driving the Church, in Dulles' words, "back upon the deepest wellsprings of its own life." He calls for a type of corporate theological reflection resembling that discussed in this volume. He sees it as "perhaps the only method that offers solid hope for mutual understanding and agreement among believers who differ profoundly in their explicit principles and who speak in diverse theological idioms."

For guidance in this task, Dulles reflects upon the Council of Jerusalem (Acts 15:1–35) where the early Christian community first faced the problem of cultural pluralism over the question of the circumcision of Gentile converts. The results of his meditations are both supportive and challenging for the theological reflection of action/reflection groups in the Church today.

John Godsey also sees this as a time of significant change in the Christian churches and sets himself the task of locating the action/reflection groups within the changing Church. In Chapter 11 he details several of the ways rapid socio-cultural change has affected the Church's sense of its identity and mission in the contemporary world. He then suggests to both the members of action/reflection groups and to the rest of the Church that we look upon these groups as concrete parables of what the whole Church is to become: witness to and servant of God in its witness to and service of the world.

If these small Christian communities committed to the search for justice are to be concrete parables for the Church at large, their theological reflection must be carried on with care. The last two chapters in this volume could be considered essays in the ethics of knowing or discerning. They are tentative explorations, in the light of the experience and analysis presented in the previous chapters, of the ways theological reflection should be done.

In Chapter 12 Larry Rasmussen sets out to identify the essential components of theological reflection in a community committed to being "Christians in earnest." He argues that it must take place within the context of a community deeply grounded in the story of Jesus—the normative story for Christians—and active in shaping the identity and sense of reality of its members in accord with that story. Good character formation and openness to Christian conversion are central to discerning theological reflection. He then calls for a type of communal reflection which takes full advantage of the special insight available to communities from their particular beliefs, experiences, symbols, loyalties, commitments, their immersion in their social and historical setting. An echo of Joe Holland's essay is heard when he describes this new type of ethical reflection by reference to an "artistic" metaphor. At the same time, he points out the need to balance the tendencies to subjectivism and group bias characteristic of this type of ethical reflection. He recommends complementing it with a type of critical analysis using principles of impartiality and universality developed in a more juridical or legal model of ethics and with consultation with other Church groups and members of the world community.

Jim Hug picks up the framework outlined by Rasmussen and fills it in with a number of more specific details. Chapter 13 offers a survey of practical components intended to help different groups who must design their own methods of careful theological reflection to fit the variety of different contexts within which they find themselves. It describes the type of prayerful openness necessary for good Christian discernment. It then outlines several types of self-reflection and consultation aimed at liberating the intuitive insights born of full involvement in the pursuit of a more Christian world (the "artistic" model of ethical reflection) while at the same time identifying and correcting the biases that can be introduced by the physical, psychological, sociological, political, economic, historical, and cultural influences in any situation. In the course of that discussion, Hug suggests a way of moving into a type of explicit theological analysis of experience which is available to all, no matter what their level of theological education.

This final chapter represents an attempt to bring together in a synthetic way many of the insights given to the Woodstock taskforce in the course of this project.

9
Theological Reflection: New Testament Antecedents and Models

Jouette Bassler

Christian action/reflection groups use Christological models in their reflective processes. These models are not identical and often they are not even consciously formulated or employed. The appropriation of a model may rest on accidental factors such as the history and experience of the community or its individual members. Alternatively, it may be the product of deliberate biblical study. Whatever its origin, the prevailing Christological model shapes the ongoing life of the community, for every model leads in distinctive ethical and spiritual directions. The consequences of this are profound, for the ethical and spiritual life of a community can be influenced or changed by the Christological models it embraces. The goal of this essay is to develop an awareness of this interaction of theological reflection, Christological model, and ethical impulse by studying some of the early Christian communities that generated the Christological models we find in the New Testament documents.

Such a study seems relevant for two main reasons. First, it will show us biblical communities engaged in theological reflection. The Christological models found in the various New Testament documents are themselves the result of early Christian reflection and are rooted in the experiences of the communities. Thus the study should provide us with some New Testament analogues to the contemporary activity of theological reflection. Second, however, it will reveal the potential influence of a model on a community. Once these models were generated out of the experience and prayerful reflection of the communities, they exercised a detectable influence on the ongoing structure and ethics of these communities.

It is beyond the scope of this essay to explore all the Christological models presented in the New Testament. Instead, we will focus on two: the model of the crucified Christ that Paul presents to the Corinthian church and the model of the transcendent Son of God that appears in the Gospel of John. A consideration of the particular goals of this essay dictated this choice.

1. Because theological reflection is theologizing out of experience, we need to know about the particular experiences brought by these communities to their reflective activities, and especially about any conflicts that might have shaped these experiences.

2. Because we have no access to the actual process of reflection in these communities, we must evaluate it on the basis of the theological results it produced. Thus we need information about the Christological models that evolved out of the experience/reflection processes in these two communities.

3. In order to test our claim that Christological models contain an ethical component, we need information about the structure and ethics of these early communities.

On all three counts these two biblical examples qualify for close examination. We have a wealth of information about the communities lying behind these documents; the Christological models presented in them are distinctive and exciting; the ethical ramifications for the communities are particularly clear and somewhat provocative.

The recovery of the communal experiences lying behind these biblical documents is facilitated by a recent surge of interest in the social setting of early Christianity. This interest goes far beyond earlier attempts that described this setting in highly generalized (and idealized) terms. Now the focus is on the social settings of specific early Christian communities such as Corinth, Antioch, or rural Palestine. To uncover these settings, New Testament scholars are turning to archaeology to supplement New Testament data and even more to the social sciences for help in interpreting these data.[1] This blending of the disciplines of biblical scholarship and sociology is akin to, but not identical with, the recent interest in social analysis as a primary component of the hermeneutical circle of action and reflection.[2] In the latter, social analysis of a contemporary situation is used to critique previous assumptions and to suggest opportunities for new action and reflection. In the former, sociology is used to heighten the sensitivity to the social data embedded in ancient texts and to suggest models for interpreting those data.

This new sociological expertise in biblical scholarship allows us to uncover with some certainty the very specific experiences of particular biblical communities. We can then attempt to correlate the experiences of a biblical community with the theological insights generated there. Thus we are able to see with remarkable clarity the interaction of experience and reflection in communities that existed some two thousand years ago. An awareness of this early Christian union of experience and reflection and the theological conclusions it generated should be of interest to those currently engaged in the same activity.

A distinction must be made between the Christological models of the Johannine and Pauline literature that we will examine. The Johannine model was a real one, a working understanding of Christ that affected the lives of the individuals in the Johannine community in a very profound way. In contrast, the Pauline model can only be described as a potential one. It is not at all clear that it had an immediate effect, indeed any effect at all, on the community for which it was initially developed. The significance of this can only be assessed at the end of this essay.

This approach to the biblical documents, which asks of them sociological and historical as well as theological questions, has one fundamental presupposition that needs to be clearly stated. The Christian acknowledges that the Bible contains the word of God. This word, however, is transmitted through human instruments, who reveal much about themselves and their own social history through the words they choose, the incidents they relate and omit, and the way they relate them.[3] Thus two separate sets of questions can be asked of any biblical text. On the one hand, one can ask what revelation is being given about God and God's will for the people. On the other hand, one can also ask what sort of community was the bearer of this revelation. Thus theological as well as sociological information is contained and intertwined in every document. This is most obvious in the case of the Pauline letters, where the specific circumstances of the writing are always clearly visible. It is, however, no less true for the Gospels, including the Gospel of John.

Finally, since we are concerned here with biblical paradigms and Christological models, I would like to insert a cautionary word about paradigms and models. A paradigm or model, even a biblical one, should not be conceived as necessarily a model to be imitated. A paradigm can also interpret what is going on—that is, it can also open up for us negative possibilities of a given situation and thus serve as a warning as well as a guide without relinquishing its status as the word of God.

PAUL AND THE CORINTHIAN CORRESPONDENCE

In 54 or 55 A.D., Paul wrote to the church in Corinth a letter packed with practical and theological advice. This advice clearly stemmed from Paul's theological reflection, and this reflection in turn was rooted in experience. In this example, however, the experiential aspect of the reflection process had two distinct components: the experience Paul brought to the Corinthian situation and the experience of the Corinthian community itself.[4] We need to consider these in turn.

What personal experience did Paul bring to this situation? Certainly his conversion comes immediately to mind, that thrice-described, dramatic reversal in which Christianity's severest persecutor became its most zealous proponent.[5] Indeed, so significant was this transformation of villain to saint that ever afterward Paul's conceptual categories seem to have been affected by it, for he constructs his arguments always in terms of polar opposites—law versus grace, flesh versus spirit, works versus faith. Surely this experience as well as his participation in the apostolic council[6] and other events too numerous to mention influenced Paul's message to his churches. Yet I would like to focus on another, more obscure episode in Paul's life that seems to have had a particular impact on his response to the situation in Corinth.

In his second letter to Corinth, Paul mentions a mysterious, minor, but annoying physical handicap—Paul calls it a thorn in his flesh—that seemed to interfere with his apostolic effectiveness (2 Cor

12:7–10). Paul reports that three times he asked for divine intervention to rid him of this affliction. Ultimately, he arrived at the understanding that through this affliction God was bringing him a
profound theological message, the way of strength through weakness.[7] This insight, itself gained through prayerful theological reflection, Paul brought to his Corinthian labors. Yet profound as this
insight was, it seems to have remained somewhat dormant until Paul
encountered the particular situation at Corinth. Something about
this church and its experience caused Paul to make his earlier theological insight, now clothed in Christological terms, the central metaphor for Christian existence. Thus we need to consider the situation
and experience of the Corinthian church as it interacted with Paul's
personal experience.

The experience of this community was as traumatic as Paul's,
but in a vastly different way. Consider the evidence in the letter.
Paul's First Letter to the Corinthians reveals quarreling factions promoting various spiritual heroes much as one might champion a political figure or an athletic hero in the secular world (1:10–12). It
reveals members of the young Christian community hauling their fellow Christians to court, following the secular laws of the city (6:1–8).
We see the message of Christian freedom being interpreted as a li-
cense for libertinism as the community of saints reveled in the sea-
port morals of the city of Corinth (5:1–13; 6:12–20). The letter shows
members of the Christian community using their knowledge that
idols are mere fabrications (8:4) in order to justify participation in
"empty" pagan religious ceremonies. Although such participation
was probably necessary for social advancement in Corinth,[8] it was
also causing the spiritual destruction of the Christian brothers and
sisters who had not yet reached the same level of theological maturity (chapters 8 and 10). We see the community celebrating the Holy
Eucharist using the secular banquet customs of the day in which the
affluent enjoyed a full and elegant meal while the indigent received
the host and the cup, but no more sustaining fare (11:17–34).[9] Finally, the letter reveals a community that exalted certain showy but in-
dividualized spiritual gifts, such as glossolalia, to the neglect of other
more prosaic charisms that would contribute more to the well-being
of the community (chapters 12–14).[10]

This was obviously a community nearly torn apart by factions, by social and religious stratifications that produced economic and spiritual elitism, by a preference for individual achievements rather than community wholeness.[11] Most of these divisions were caused by the arrogant and self-centered perspective of the more affluent members of the community. They alone could afford expensive and disruptive lawsuits and the elaborate meals accompanying the Eucharist, and they alone needed to participate in pagan religious ceremonies to secure their social position. Thus the new community of Christ was dominated too much by old social structures and influenced too little by the new spiritual reality of participation in the body of Christ. Invidious distinctions and customs from pagan life were infiltrating and nearly destroying church life, especially distinctions between the "haves" and the "have-nots" in both the economic and the spiritual spheres.

Paul was well aware of the social situation in Corinth, but he seems to have received most of his information from the social perspective of the "haves." Though these people were probably the numerical minority in the church,[12] they seem to have had a disproportionate influence in church affairs. For example, they were the initiators and authors of the letter to which Paul responds in First Corinthians.[13] As such, they obviously considered themselves to be speaking for the entire Church, for the snippets of this letter that Paul quotes reveal no tolerance of or consideration for an alternative opinion or perspective. "All of us possess knowledge," Paul quotes them as saying (8:1), yet clearly there were those in the Church who did not share this knowledge (8:7). Throughout the letter this unmoderated perspective "from above" appears as Paul's primary source of information about the situation in Corinth. In spite of this, and though Paul himself was one of the "haves," both with regard to his financial independence[14] and his theological and spiritual maturity, his response was consistently from the opposite perspective, the perspective of the silent "have-nots," the perspective "from below." Paul seems to have been influenced in this by his own earlier experience.

This social disruption of the community by a perspective that exalted religious and economic power and prestige desperately needed a correcting perspective, the perspective Paul had acquired in his earlier encounter with God. Thus Paul offered to this community the same message of strength through weakness that God had offered to him, but now expressed in Christological form: "For I decided to know nothing among you except Jesus Christ and him crucified" (2:2). God's power and wisdom are revealed through weakness, not strength. This message relativizes all division and all arrogant elitism. God works the divine purposes through the folly of the cross (1:18–25), not through the power of the empire. Thus, on the sociological level, it is not the elite few who legitimate and define the Christian community. It is instead those who reflect in their sociological or ecclesiological status the ignominy of the cross and its message of power through weakness, that is, the foolish, the weak, the low and despised in the world, even those who, from the dominant perspective, literally "are not" (1:26–29).

Paul's response to the situation and experience of Corinth, his response from the perspective of the "have-nots," was thus derived in part from his own earlier experience and his reading of the social reality in that community. Paul did not advocate the transformation or overthrow of external social institutions and hierarchy. He did, however, expect the young Christian Church to transcend divisive social factors *within its walls.* With an emphasis on power through weakness, expressed Christologically through the message and model of the crucified Christ, Paul strove to eliminate all self-centered boasting, all divisiveness, and all arrogance. He demanded that the situation be viewed not from a position of power but from the cross, which, because of its message, corresponds to a perspective from below.[15]

The crucifixion, however, was more than power revealed through weakness. Viewed from a slightly different perspective, it was also an act of self-renunciation on behalf of others (15:3). Thus the crucified Christ not only provided a negative comment on the self-centered and self-assured stance of the community, but it also provided a much needed positive model for behavior in Corinth. The litigant was therefore urged to suffer fraud rather than destroy the community with lawsuits (6:7). The one strong in his or her knowledge that idols have no existence was urged to forego acting out of this knowledge if another Christian were harmed by that act (8:10–13; 10:24–29). Christian freedom was interpreted as an invitation not to hedonism but to a higher mode of living that includes the freedom to renounce freedom itself if others are harmed by it (9:1–27). Spiritual gifts were to be appraised not by their showy qualities but by the service they rendered to others (14:4, 18–19). Finally, the mutuality of love was promoted as the highest gift, one which transcends all boasting and individualism (13:4–7). In all of this, the Corinthian community was called explicitly or implicitly to follow the model of the crucified Christ. "Be imitators of me," said Paul after describing his own self-renunciation, *"as I am of Christ"* (11:1).

The model thus called the community away from its own self-glorifying, schismatic tendencies and attempted to unite it in a mode of mutual, self-giving concern for all those for whom the primal act of self-giving had occurred. To heighten this sense of concern the members of the community were reminded of the brother and sister for whom Christ died (8:11), just as they themselves had been bought with a price (6:20; 7:23). This call to mutuality climaxes in the metaphor of the body that Paul developed to emphasize the bonds uniting all those who have participated in the death and resurrection of Christ (12:12–26).

This emphasis on the crucified Christ is not an occasional feature of First Corinthians. It is the central theme of the letter from the opening presentation of the paradox of the cross to the final discussion of the resurrection. More than in any other letter Paul hammered home this concept here as the focal point of Christian existence.[16] This particular emphasis arose, as we have seen, in part from Paul's experience, which included a dramatic divine reminder of the theological message of strength through weakness. It also arose in part from the experience of the Corinthian community, whose destructive theology of exaltation provided an appropriate, almost urgent, theological context for developing fully the Christological and ecclesiological ramifications of Paul's original insight.

It is important to note, however, that the model of the crucified Christ was not the product of community reflection. It was offered by Paul in response to the community's situation as a helpful focal point for their subsequent reflective activities. In this matter Paul conforms to the model of the classical prophets.[17] Like the Old Testament prophets, he received an insight from God, one with both theological and ethical ramifications. Again like the classical prophets, he proclaimed this word to an errant community. Finally, like the prophets, he seems to have had his word rejected by those for whom it was initially framed. It is not at all clear that Paul's attempt to impose his model on the community at Corinth was entirely successful, no matter how appropriate the model might have been.

Certainly later Christianity would have been theologically impoverished if Paul had not developed this model with such forcefulness, for it has had a lasting effect on subsequent theologians. Nevertheless, the short-term effects of Paul's effort were not so impressive. Paul's second letter to the community reveals, if anything, a hardening of the Corinthians' earlier position. They are no longer merely pursuing a theology of glory and power, but have now turned actively against the apostle who brought them the alternative message. Indeed, they despise him for the weakness he preached and displayed (2 Cor 10:10). The church has turned instead to new apostles ("false apostles" in Paul's view) whose message and actions corresponded more closely to their preferred perspective.[18]

If Paul ultimately won the church over to allegiance to his model and message,[19] the period of allegiance seems to have been relatively brief. By the time Clement, the third bishop of Rome, wrote his epistle to the Corinthian church in the year 95 A.D., some forty years after Paul's last letter, the community had already returned to its schismatic, contentious, self-seeking ways and required once again the apostolic message of compassion, humility, and self-control.[20] Paul's attempt to impose a model on this community from without must be judged a short-term failure. Much more effective in modifying the structure and response of a community is a model, such as the Johannine one, that arises out of the experience of the whole community.

THE JOHANNINE COMMUNITY AND GOSPEL

At first glance it is not easy to extract from the Gospel information about the communal experiences behind this presentation of the story of Jesus. This is primarily because the reader, reasonably enough, tends to focus on the message the Gospel intends to convey, that is, on the story itself. Yet when one considers the differences among the four Gospels, it should become clear that since the foundational story is the same, the differences in presentation must derive from the different experiences and situations of different communities. Each evangelist wrote, on one level at least, for a particular Christian community. Thus he presents the story in a particular way to make it relevant to the needs and experiences of that community. Mark strengthened a martyr Church by stressing that the path to Jesus' glory led through suffering, and that each Christian must bear his or her own cross. Luke stressed the universal content of Jesus' message in order to meet the needs of his primarily Gentile community, while Matthew highlighted Jesus' links with Jewish expectations for his Jewish-Christian community. In a similar way, one can see behind the particular Johannine emphases reflections of this community's past experiences and contemporary situation. Like the Pauline community, the primal experience of this community seems to have included conflict. In this case, however, the conflict was not initially intramural; it arose between the newly formed church and the synagogue that had once been its home.

The task of uncovering the experiences lying behind the Fourth Gospel is both complicated and enriched by the nature of this Gospel. Like the other three it is the product of a single individual (an individual, one might add, of extraordinary theological power and insight). Yet this individual has incorporated into the Gospel material deriving from various stages of the community's history. Indeed, one Johannine scholar has compared this Gospel to an archaeological tell because of its numerous literary strata, each of which can be mined for the communal interests and experiences that it reflects.[21] These different strata thus provide insights into the unfolding history of the Johannine community.

Like many early Christian groups, the Johannine church was initially formed and nurtured within the religious womb of the synagogue. It is therefore not surprising that the earliest detectable attitudes toward Judaism in this Gospel are positive. Jesus is presented as the fulfillment of the synagogue's messianic hopes, and as such he is shown attracting and holding many followers (1:19–51).[22] Yet alongside this evidence of continuity and harmony with Jewish expectations there are other passages that speak of Judaism with the strongest possible hostility and sense of alienation (2:23–25; 8:31–59). Here Jesus is portrayed as totally incomprehensible to the Jews (8:25). What has happened to the community to transform so completely the tone and tenor of various layers of this Gospel? Between these two Christological stages there probably occurred a trauma of separation that left its indelible mark on this community and on the pages of this Gospel. We need to explore this decisive episode of the Johannine community's experience.

As long as the Johannine "church" remained attached to the synagogue, its members considered themselves, and were considered, loyal Jews. They were at the same time firm in their conviction that Jesus was the long-awaited Messiah.[23] Yet the Christological convictions of these early believers did not remain long at this level. Theological and sociological factors combined to influence a move to a more profound understanding of Jesus' mission and nature. Their experience of the earthly Jesus and the resurrected Christ, their reflections on this experience, and their reflections on the Sacred Scriptures in the light of this experience led to a new insight. Jesus, they realized, is also Son and as such he enjoys a functional equality with God (3:24–25; 5:17–29).

Such a conviction, however, challenged the fundamental monotheistic convictions of the synagogue and thus inevitably led to conflict. What form this conflict took can be deduced from certain passages within the Gospel. Chapter 9, for example, retells a story about Jesus in a way that is particularly revealing of the trauma experienced by the community. In Chapter 8 of the Gospel, high Christological claims are made about Jesus. Not only is Jesus acclaimed as the light of the world (8:12), a title that corresponds to Old Testament messianic expectations (Is 9:1; 49:6; 60:1–3), but he is also described as the giver of life (8:12), a role traditionally reserved in Judaism for the Creator. Moreover, Jesus announces in this chapter his heavenly origins (8:42) and even uses the divine "I AM" to refer to himself (8:28, 58), a clear allusion to the Name announced to Moses on Mount Sinai.[24] Clearly the implied identity here between Jesus and God exceeded the limits of compatibility with Jewish monotheism. We learn in Chapter 9 that expulsion from the synagogue was the penalty for confessing Jesus to be this Christ (9:22, 34–35), an event that is likely to be as true for the Johannine church as for the earliest followers of Jesus.[25] Indeed, the Johannine community had surely experienced just this trauma of expulsion, and the hostility may have escalated to the level of actual persecution (16:2–3). Excluded from their former religious matrix, perceiving little but hostility from the surrounding (Jewish) society, this young church felt exceedingly alien and threatened in the world and brought this shared experience and this common feeling to their reflection.

This experience of alienation seems to have led this community to further insights into the nature of Jesus. Just as they felt alien to and alienated from the religious hierarchy and the world they knew, so too was Jesus alien to the world, but in a far more profound sense.[26] Their experience, they realized, was simply a reflection of Jesus' experience, though worked out on a vastly different level (17:14, 16). Through their own sharp experience of alienation and distance from their world, this community was able to perceive Jesus' distance from the world, expressed in theological terms as his transcendence and pre-existence (1:1–5). Thus this community arrived at a magnificent Christology by the union of experience and reflection into a mutually reinforcing cycle: experience led to insights into Jesus' exalted nature, these insights led to expulsion from the synagogue, and this new experience generated even higher Christological insights that increased the hostility of the synagogue. We are sometimes blind to the level of this accomplishment. The high Christological statements of this Gospel—the divine Word become flesh, the Son of God who is one with God in both will and being—became normative for the later Church creeds. Among the contemporary New Testament documents, however, there is none that reaches the Christological insights of this Gospel. Theological reflection on a traumatic experience here achieved some rather splendid results.

Yet this experience and this model of Jesus as transcendent Son of God and Word become flesh had other ramifications for the Johannine community, especially for its ethical response to the world. The soaring statement of John 3:16 ("For God so loved the world that he gave his only Son, that whoever believes in him may have eternal life") generally sets the tone for the reading of this Gospel. Yet if a strict numerical tally is kept, the number of pejorative statements about the world will be seen to outweigh by far those reflecting the sentiment of this verse. The world is generally perceived in negative terms. It cannot understand this transcendent, "alien" Christ and therefore rejects him, just as it rejects and persecutes his "alien" followers (15:18–21; 16:20). The tone is not completely dark, for the evangelist has set positive statement alongside negative and the world continues to be viewed as the necessary arena of missionary activity (10:16; 12:47; 17:20–21). Nevertheless, a certain distancing from the world has undeniably taken place. One gets from this Gospel a sense of somewhat perplexed isolation (14:22) that is enhanced by the model of Christ as transcendent, alien, and often-rejected Son.

Related to this is an ethical development evident in the admonitions of this Gospel. United as this group was by their common experience of the barriers separating them from the world and its religious matrix, there was a tightening of the bonds of concern for each other. This attitude seems to reflect the intense concern of the Johannine Jesus for his own (chapters 14–17). Thus the Fourth Gospel arrived at the purest statement of the command for mutual love (13:34–35; 15:12–17).[27] Indeed, the community was structured on the concepts of brotherhood and sisterhood, friendship, and mutual concern. The many commandments that characterize the other three Gospels are reduced in this Gospel to the one commandment, "Love one another."[28] The command to love each other even supplanted in this community and its Gospel the command to love one's enemies (Mt 5:44–48; Lk 6:27–36). All the moral energy of the community was directed, under the difficult conditions that prevailed, toward mutual concern and support. Thus in the face of external hostility, the community turned inward where it found joy and peace and support through strong bonds of internal love.

We see, then, in the Fourth Gospel a general sense of alienation from the Jewish world. Is there also evidence of a sense of alienation from the developing mainline Church?[29] Certainly this question needs to be balanced with the observation that all of early Christianity fits the classical description of a sect, especially insofar as it defined itself by contrast with the established religious institutions. The Johannine community shared this characteristic to a high degree, but the particular question raised by the Johannine literature is the relationship between its community and the emerging Catholic Church.[30]

This question is raised primarily by the enigmatic figure of the Beloved Disciple. This figure is never named, is never called apostle, and is never mentioned outside the Fourth Gospel. In John's Gospel, however, he appears in several passages that can only be described as displaying one-upsmanship with the apostle Peter. The most dramatic episode is perhaps the unique Johannine tradition of the race between Peter and the Beloved Disciple to the tomb of Jesus, where the Disciple was first to the tomb and first to believe.[31] One is sorely tempted to view this episode as having an allegorical level of meaning above and beyond the historical value it might have, especially since the other episodes involving the Beloved Disciple have the same tone. This disciple clearly seems to be the hero of the Johannine community, and Peter just as clearly represents the apostolic Church. Does the story indicate a sense of competition between two religious traditions? Certainly the evidence suggests that although the Johannine church and the Petrine or apostolic churches were aware of being a part of a larger unity, they remained somewhat separate under that general umbrella.[32]

As a result of this relative ecclesiastical isolation, the Johannine community seems to have experienced an intensification of its distinctive theological patterns. The later[33] Johannine epistles show clearly this particular aspect of the Johannine story. They represent an attempt to defend the community against the exaggerated theological position that resulted from this intensification process.

The author of 1 John, for example, argues against a view that denied or ignored Jesus' human existence: "Every spirit which confesses that Jesus Christ has come in the flesh is of God, and every spirit which does not confess Jesus (come in the flesh) is not of God" (4:2–3). This heretical claim probably evolved in a distorted but logical way from the high Christology of the Fourth Gospel, which focused on the transcendence and pre-existence of God's Son.[34] For this to happen, however, certain features of the Gospel's portrait of Jesus—his omniscience, his unity with God, his control over his destiny—must have been highlighted while other passages affirming Jesus' humanity were ignored. This Christological distortion could only occur if the influence of mainline Christianity, which rigorously affirmed both the humanity and divinity of Christ, were restricted. As we have seen, the Fourth Gospel shows evidence of just such a restricted interaction.

Some within the community resisted this development, most notably the author of the First Epistle. But by the time of this letter, the situation had already reached the point of irreversible schisms. The author refers to the deviant circles as liars (1:12; 2:4, 22), as dwellers in darkness (2:9, 11), as children of the devil (3:8, 10), as murderers (3:15), as ruled by the spirit of antichrist (4:3), and as consumed by hatred of their brothers and sisters (4:20). These harsh epithets are applied to those who were once part of the Johannine community (2:19). That community, though initially united by strong internal bonds of communion, was ultimately sundered by some continued theological reflection unmoderated by an exchange of ideas with other Christian communities.

The Johannine story thus closes on a desperate note. It began with a unique experience that led through reflection to a profound and magnificent Christological insight. But if uniqueness was this community's greatest fecundity, it also proved to be its greatest threat as portions of the community, apparently in relative theological isolation, carried these insights to heretical levels.

CONCLUSIONS

The two examples we have explored indicate that experience and conflict had profound effects on the theological reflections of these two early Christian communities. The biblical documents reveal a living process: the theological or Christological insights preserved in the New Testament were influenced by experience and these insights in turn influenced the ongoing life of the Church. Clearly we find here an encouragement, if not a mandate, for the contemporary process of rooting theological reflection in experience. It is not really the purpose of this essay, however, to initiate this type of activity. The practice of theologizing out of experience seems to be well established.[35] Rather it is to be hoped that this essay can help to clarify some aspects of this contemporary reflective process. Perhaps the discussion of the Pauline and Johannine Christological models and their ethical implications will encourage communities to develop a greater awareness of their own operative Christologies.

The two models discussed in this essay do not, of course, exhaust the variety of New Testament Christologies. The Gospel of Mark, for example, is close to Paul when it presents Jesus as the Suffering Servant of Deutero-Isaiah. The predominant features of the

Matthean Christ, however, stress his authority as *Kyrios* (Lord) of the Church, while the Lukan portrait gives more emphasis to his graciousness, tenderness, and compassion. The Letter to the Hebrews presents Christ in his role as intercessory High Priest, while the Book of Revelation depicts him as Christ Militant. The New Testament provides us with many images of Christ to use as contemporary models. Each model will have different implications for communal self-understanding, for moral response, and for relationships between community and surrounding culture. To determine which model influences a particular contemporary community, one could consider the clues provided by its liturgical life. Which biblical passages are most often turned to? Which divine epithets are most often employed? Which Christological images are most often evoked in prayer or worship? Questions such as these should uncover the prevailing Christological model.[36] Further reflection might reveal how this model is influencing the spiritual and ethical actions of this community or suggest the need to supplement one model with another. Exploration of the biblical roots of a particular Christology might uncover fruitful new challenges inherent in it.

This process, however, needs to be undertaken with some care. The various New Testament Christologies arose, as we have seen, in certain historical settings. They were to some extent shaped by these historical settings, though certainly not limited to them. Indeed, they could not function as the Word of God if they could not be appropriated by later generations. Nevertheless, the transfer of a Christological model from its original context to a contemporary one cannot be done without introducing some distortions. It seems reasonable to conclude, however, that these distortions will be minimized if a Christology from a particular historical setting is used in an analogous contemporary situation. This is not to say that a community should only seek Christological models that reinforce its prevailing tendencies. We must be open to challenges and criticisms from the biblical tradition. Yet a model that arose in communities with experiences similar to our own can challenge us in particularly relevant ways without suffering undue distortion in our appropriation of it.

So far we have spoken only of the biblical roots of Christological models and the contemporary appropriation of these models. However, the biblical process that we have uncovered and the multiplicity of biblical models should generate an openness to new Christological and theological concepts arising out of current theological reflection. Women, for example, played an important role in early Christianity, but for a variety of historical reasons their voices are muted in the biblical witness. This should not automatically invalidate the Christological and theological insights arising today out of their experience. On the other hand, even the results of this sort of contemporary theological reflection can be enriched by a return to the biblical witness. For example, although Paul was speaking of the Corinthian congregation as a whole, his insistence that the perspective from below is the one validated by the message of the cross should speak to those who today feel marginalized by Church or society. Yet his letters also indicate the limitations of prophetic criticism from the outside. Likewise, the Johannine experience of alienation and internal bonding could speak to many contemporary experiences, though it also suggests the benefits of keeping various lines of ecclesial communication open during the reflection process.

NOTES

1. A comparison of generalized studies of early Christianity, such as those of R. Bultmann (*Primitive Christianity in Its Contemporary Setting* [New York: World, 1956]) and H. Conzelmann (*Geschichte des Urchristentums* [Göttingen: Vandenhoeck and Ruprecht, 1969], with recent works by E. A. Judge (*The Social Pattern of the Christian Groups in the First Century* [London: Tyndale, 1960]), A. J. Malherbe (*Social Aspects of Early Christianity* [Baton Rouge: Louisiana State University, 1977]), W. A. Meeks and R. L. Wilken (*Jews and Christians in Antioch in the First Four Centuries of the Common Era* [Missoula: Scholars, 1978], and G. Theissen (*Sociology of Early Palestinian Christianity* [Philadelphia: Fortress, 1977]) reveals the more sophisticated methodology as well as the increased specificity of this new approach.

2. For a discussion of the role of social analysis in theological reflection, see the essays by Joe Holland and James Hug in this volume.

3. For a more lengthy statement of this crucial point, see the splendid essay by R. E. Brown, " 'And the Lord Said'? Biblical Reflections on Scripture as the Word of God," *Theological Studies* 42 (1981):3–19.

4. For a more general discussion of this experiential component, see the essay by Thomas Clarke in this volume.

5. Acts 9:1–10; 22:4–16; 26:9–18.

214 TRACING THE SPIRIT

6. Avery Dulles presents some reflections on this council in Chapter 10 of this volume.

7. K. Stendahl presents an excellent discussion of this event in his essay, "Paul at Prayer," *Interpretation* 34 (1980):240–249.

8. See the study of this behavior in Corinth by G. Theissen, "Die Starken und Schwachen in Korinth; Soziologische Analyse einer theologischen Streites," *Evangelische Theologie* 35 (1975):155–172.

9. Theissen has also studied the sociological implications of this behavior in "Soziale Integration und Sakramentales Handeln; Eine Analyse von 1 Kor. xi: 17–34," *Novum Testamentum* 16 (1974):179–206.

10. K. Stendahl presents a short but sensitive study of glossolalia, covering both the New Testament evidence and contemporary manifestations, in his excellent monograph, *Paul among Jews and Gentiles and Other Essays* (Philadelphia: Fortress, 1976), pp. 109–124.

11. See J. C. Haughey's excellent essay on individuality versus community in the Corinthian church, especially as it surfaces in the eucharistic behavior there: "Eucharist at Corinth: You Are the Christ," in *Above Every Name: The Lordship of Christ and Social Systems,* ed. T. E. Clarke (Ramsey: Paulist, 1980), pp. 107–133.

12. Paul's analysis of the Corinthian community does not preclude the presence of some affluent persons, though earlier commentators assumed that it did: "Not many of you were wise according to worldly standards, not many were powerful, not many were of noble birth" (1 Cor 1:26). Indeed, a careful examination of the letter betrays their influential presence; see G. Theissen, "Soziale Schichtung in der korinthischen Gemeinde: Ein Beitrag zur Soziologie des hellenistischen Christentums," *Zeitschrift für die neutestamentliche Wissenschaft* 65 (1974):232–273.

13. In chapters 7–14 Paul is responding to a series of questions from the Corinthian church which reached him in a letter (7:1) conveyed, perhaps, by Stephanas, Fortunatus, and Achaicus (16:17). (J. C. Hurd has done an impressive job of reconstructing the contents of this letter; see *The Origin of 1 Corinthians* [New York: Seabury, 1965].) For an analysis of the social standing of these three men as well as the perspective of their letter, see Theissen, "Soziale Schichtung," pp. 232–273 and "Starken und Schwachen," pp. 155–172. Paul also had a second source of information about the community, "Chloe's people" (1 Cor 1:11), who reported the presence of quarrels and factions within the community. It is not clear who these people were, what their relationship to the Corinthian church was, and what other information they may have supplied, though chapters 5–6 may deal with problems they mentioned (5:1).

14. Recently, careful research has established that Paul's social level

was at least a comfortable one, not that of the impecunious day laborer some of his statements seem to suggest. See R.F. Hock, "Paul's Tentmaking and the Problem of His Social Class," *Journal of Biblical Literature* 97 (1978):555–564.

15. An elaboration of this concept in terms of the hermeneutical privilege of the poor is found in Monika Hellwig's essay in this volume.

16. Paul certainly does not ignore the crucifixion in his other letters, but nowhere else does it have the insistent centrality and particular message that it does in the Corinthian correspondence. The crucifixion is not an important issue in 1 Thessalonians; in Galatians it receives more emphasis (Gal 2:20), but it is used there primarily to develop the idea that the cross means the end of the law (Galatians 3), not to illustrate the Corinthian paradox of strength through weakness. As in the Corinthian letters, the parenesis in Romans is focused on mutual concern and communal upbuilding (Rom 12:1–15:13). In Romans, however, Paul appeals to Old Testament quotations as the warrant for his advice (12:19; 13:9; 14:11; 15:3, 9–11), not to the figure on the cross. Only in Philippians do we find the same combination of a call to humility and concern for others with a reminder of Christ's act of humility and self-sacrifice (Phil 2:6–11), though there is a somewhat greater emphasis here on subsequent exaltation. This letter was probably written at about the same time as the Corinthian letters; see G. S. Duncan, "Philippians," in the *Interpreter's Dictionary of the Bible,* 4 vols., ed. G.A. Buttrick (Nashville: Abingdon, 1962), 3:787–791.

17. Paul consciously places himself within the prophetic tradition by describing his own call with the words Jeremiah used to record his (Gal 1:15–16; cf. Jer 1:5).

18. From Paul's second letter to Corinth we get a portrait of these newcomers as apostles who possessed showy charismatic gifts (12:1, 12), who wielded power and authority over the church (11:19–21), and who boasted excessively of their accomplishments, thereby forcing Paul into an emotional but ironic counter-boast (10:13–12:21).

19. Many scholars feel that Second Corinthians is a composite letter, made up of fragments of several letters deriving from this period of stormy relations with the church. Certainly the abruptly shifting tone of the letter would seem to support this thesis. In particular, the tone of relief and reconciliation pervading 2 Cor 1:1–9:15, so different from the angry and hurt tone of chapters 10–13, may indicate that the earlier chapters actually derive from the end of this period and reflect a happy resolution to the conflict.

20. See, e.g., *1 Clement* 5:17; 13:1–4; 44:1—47:7.

21. J.L. Martyn, *The Gospel of John in Christian History* (New York: Paulist, 1978), p. 90.

22. *Ibid.*, pp. 9–54, 93–102.

23. The messianic expectations of late Judaism were primarily national-istic: with God's help a Davidic (human) ruler would purge Jerusalem of its heathen overlords, lead the people of Israel to power, and then rule them with justice and compassion. See, e.g., the classic study by S. Mowinckel, *He That Cometh* (Oxford: B. Blackwell, 1956), though the Dead Sea Scrolls have changed the picture somewhat.

24. "Then Moses said to God, 'If I come to the people of Israel and say to them, "The God of your fathers has sent me to you," and they ask me, "What is his name?" what shall I say to them?' God said to Moses, 'I am who I am.' And he said, 'Say this to the people of Israel, "I AM has sent me to you" ' " (Ex 3:13–14). Here it is assumed that God's name, Yahweh, de-rives from the Hebrew word *'ehyeh*, which means "I am." E. Käsemann rather aptly describes the Johannine portrait of Jesus as "the God who goes about on earth" in *The Testament of Jesus according to John 17* (Philadel-phia: Fortress, 1968), p. 27.

25. Indeed the situation was considerably more acute for the Johannine church, for in 90 A.D. the synagogue authorities introduced a special curse on heretics (the *Birkat ha-Minim*) into their liturgy to enable them to identi-fy and expel those who believed Jesus to be the Christ. See J.L. Martyn, *His-tory and Theology in the Fourth Gospel* (New York: Harper & Row, 1968).

26. Many factors, not least of which is Old Testament Wisdom specula-tion, have influenced John's unique Christology. For the purposes of this es-say, I have highlighted the role of experience and focused on sociological factors. See Martyn, *Christian History,* p. 106; W.A. Meeks, "The Man from Heaven and Johannine Sectarianism," *Journal of Biblical Literature* 91 (1972):44–72, esp. p. 69.

27. Though this is expressed in generally masculine terms, it is clear from the emphasis on women in this Gospel that they were a strong part of the community that was urged to "Love one another." See on this R.E. Brown, "Roles of Women in the Fourth Gospel," *Theological Studies* 36 (1975):688–699; reprinted in *The Community of the Beloved Disciple* (New York: Paulist, 1979), pp. 183–198.

28. *Ibid.*, p. 131.

29. We are considering a period that is simply too early to apply the usual labels of orthodox, heterodox, catholic, etc., and my somewhat awk-ward terminology reflects this impasse. Clear lines were only really drawn during the great second century debates.

30. Compare, e.g., the conclusions of R.E. Brown, *Beloved Disciple,* pp. 13–17, 88–91 and W.A. Meeks, "Man from Heaven," *passim.*

31. 20:2–10; see also 13:23–26; 18:15–16; 19:26–27; 21:7, 20–23.

32. One could also mention the rather striking differences in both form and content that distinguish the Gospel of John from the other three Gospels. These differences raise the possibility that this community was unaware of some traditions shared by the other three evangelists, or that John's community did not value the same traditions. In either case some physical or intellectual or theological separation seems indicated.

33. The earlier debate over whether the epistles antedate or postdate the Gospel seems to be moving toward a consensus on the latter.

34. Brown, *Beloved Disciple,* pp. 109–123. In other areas as well, most notably ethics, eschatology, and pneumatology, there seems to have been movement from the Gospel message to untenable conclusions, but these developments are not as important to us here.

35. See, for example, the description of the various action/reflection groups in Chapters 2 and 3 of this volume.

36. The essay by James Hug in this volume provides further insights into this discernment process.

10
An Ecclesial Model
for Theological Reflection:
The Council of Jerusalem

Avery Dulles, S.J.

In the history of the Church there has been an ongoing tension between the quest for inner unity and the quest for inclusiveness. As Jouette Bassler points out in her study of New Testament Christologies, these two tendencies were both at work in the primitive Church.[1] Paul's Corinthian converts, according to his letters, were overinclined to accept ideas and customs which Paul judged pagan and irreconcilable with the Gospel. In the Johannine churches, on the other hand, preoccupation with inner unity and with fidelity to their special traditions was carried to a point that bordered on sectarianism, separating them not only from the world and from Judaism but also, in a measure, from other Christian communities. Theological discernment was to some extent applied to overcome these tensions, but neither the Pauline nor the Johannine communities possessed ideal conditions and structures for such discernment.

As Christianity moves toward the end of its twentieth century, the debates in the primitive Church might seem to hold only diminishing interest. But many Christians, seeking answers to contemporary questions, find unexpected riches in the New Testament. Like their New Testament forebears, believers of our own day are faced by new and unprecedented challenges. The world of their own religious past seems to be crumbling before their eyes. In nearly every country of the world, the inherited cultural patterns are being challenged by radical innovation. And Christianity itself, for the first time in history, is becoming not simply a European or Mediterranean export but an authentically global phenomenon. According to Karl Rahner, the current emergence of a truly worldwide Church constitutes a major qualitative break that has no comparable precedent except the passage from Jewish to Gentile Christianity in the first century.[2]

Facing up to the cultural pluralism of the Church in his day, Paul deemed it appropriate to do away with circumcision as a rite of initiation for Gentile converts. Christians who accepted this innovation soon regarded themselves free from the Mosaic law and the observance of the sabbath. Subsequently they found themselves accepting the transfer of the Church's center from Jerusalem to Rome and adopting new canonical Scriptures, which we today call the New Testament. The transition to a genuinely worldwide Church in the highly fluid culture of the late twentieth century may well call for comparable changes in teaching and organization. If Rahner is correct, the ancient culture of Western Europe, which has provided the institutional base for Catholic Christianity since patristic times, is scarcely more authoritative for the dawning age than was the ancient Jewish culture for the time when Gentile Christianity was beginning to take shape. Called to something resembling a new beginning, the Church must exercise a "Pauline boldness" (as Rahner puts it) in breaking with many continuities which up to this time have seemed self-evident.

To negotiate the present transition without inner schism or loss of identity will by no means be easy. Decisions cannot be reached by a simple appeal to approved doctrinal or canonical texts, for the adequacy of such texts is the precise point at issue. Driven back upon the deepest wellsprings of its own life, the Church must engage in a kind of corporate theological reflection resembling that discussed in the present volume. To establish dialogue among radically different theologies which admit of no reconciliation on the level of conceptual logic, all statements must be interpreted and assessed in relation to the basic experience that underlies the most fundamental Christian formulations—as Thomas Clarke suggested in Chapter 1. Theological reflection is perhaps the only method that offers solid hope for mutual understanding and agreement among believers who differ profoundly in their explicit principles and who speak in diverse theological idioms.

In primitive Christianity, as analyzed by many contemporary scholars, radically different outlooks co-existed without a rupture of communion or conflict on the level of faith. To maintain unity the early Christians made use of techniques similar to what is today called theological reflection. In the present chapter I shall illustrate this by an examination of the apostolic council described in Acts 15:1–35. The opposition between Jewish and Gentile Christianity which occasioned this council may be seen as paradigmatic for many of the tensions experienced in our own time.

Whether the meeting Luke here describes can properly be called a council may of course be disputed. It is not so designated in Scripture. While it does not satisfy the definition of a council that one might find in a text of canon law, it does exhibit the essentials of a council as theologically defined by certain authors. With Jerusalem, among other assemblies, in view, Heribert Mühlen defines a council as "the gathering of Church representatives, which through deliberation, common effort, and decision, serves the unity of the Church in the power of the one Holy Spirit made present in the Church as a whole."[3] The meeting at Jerusalem, though not generally listed as one of the ecumenical councils, is the closest biblical analogue to the general councils of subsequent centuries, from Nicea to Vatican II.

To anyone acquainted with modern biblical scholarship it goes without saying that the historicity of the details in Luke's narrative cannot be taken for granted. According to the more common opinion, Luke has here combined two related incidents: an apostolic conference at Jerusalem attended by Peter, Paul and other "pillars," and a decree subsequently issued, presumably by James and the authorities of the Jerusalem church, regulating the conduct of Gentile Christians in communities partly made up of Jewish Christians. In his own writings Paul gives no intimation that he was aware of the "apostolic decree" summarized in Acts 15:20, 29 and 21:25.[4]

Following a wide consensus in modern scholarship, I shall assume that Luke in Acts intends to exhibit "how the message of salvation, the Gospel of Jesus Christ, was revealed to 'all flesh,' how it reached the 'ends of the earth,' and how God's favors came to be bestowed upon 'foreigners'—in a word, how the apostolic preaching turned toward the pagan world."[5] Luke, therefore, is not content to be a chronicler. He intends to show that this new orientation was willed by God and guided by the Holy Spirit, and thus that it fulfilled the messianic prophecies.

The Council of Jerusalem, standing at the very midpoint of Acts, occupies a position in the narrative comparable in some ways to the "confession of Peter" in the Synoptic Gospels. It terminates the first half of the story, dominated by Peter and the Jerusalem church, and introduces the second half, recounting the great missionary journeys of Paul, and culminating in Paul's ministry at Rome.

Luke, quite consciously, presents an idealized account of the dealings between Antioch and Jerusalem. The conciliar process, as he portrays it, affords an exceptionally useful paradigm for arousing the attitudes and suggesting the processes needed to handle controversies that may later arise within the Christian community. By including Acts in its canonical Scriptures, the Church vouches for its abiding value.

I shall not here attempt a strictly exegetical commentary aimed at reconstructing the exact historical details or the precise meaning intended by Luke when he wrote this or that phrase. Rather, I shall focus on what the text might seem to suggest to modern Christians who read it in the light of their own experience, especially in view of what it might have to say about the processes by which current disputes in the Church could be resolved. In my opinion this text provides biblical precedent for many of the principles set forth in the standard literature on theological reflection and especially in the discussions of corporate discernment as utilized by St. Ignatius of Loyola and the tradition of spirituality that stems from him.[6]

"This created dissension and much controversy . . . " (15:2)[7]

The council originates from a dispute in the local church at Antioch, occasioned by interference on the part of visitors from Judea. The dispute impaired the harmonious relations within the local church and among local churches, and was therefore detrimental to the very being of the Church as a communion whose members, standing in the fellowship of the apostles (Acts 2:42), must have "one heart and one soul" (4:32). Luke's ecclesiology in this matter reinforces the strong insistence on unity in the Pauline and Johannine writings. Paul is adamant on the subject: "Let there be no factions" (1 Cor 1:10). For John the disciples of Jesus must maintain a mutual union patterned on that of Jesus and God (Jn 17:21).

The application is obvious. A polarized church is a scandal, contradicting the very essence of the Church. When quarreling breaks out among Christians, remedial measures must be taken so as to achieve a reconciliation that does justice to the legitimate concerns of all parties. Such reconciliation was a principal objective of the reflection process here to be examined.

"It was decided that Paul, Barnabas, and some others should go up to see the apostles and presbyters in Jerusalem about this matter" (15:2)

The dispute, provoked by visitors from Judea, could not be resolved at the local level without assistance from the church of Jerusalem, which, as the apostolic founding church, retained a certain responsibility for the communities that had arisen from itself. Antioch, moreover, apparently recognized the legitimacy of Jerusalem's concern in matters which were of more than local import.

This co-responsibility of universal and local leaders for the welfare of individual churches remains a permanent feature of Christianity. In the whole body of Christ, the members must have care for one another, and structures must exist for achieving universal solutions to problems which are universal. The principle of subsidiarity, which has been prominent in twentieth century Catholic social teaching, has ecclesiological implications.[8] According to this principle the local church must be allowed to reach decisions on purely local matters, where it can effectively do so. Conversely, according to the same principle, matters that cannot be handled locally, or those affecting the Church as a whole, must be resolved with the participation of persons who can speak for the universal Church.

A certain analogy might be drawn between the Council of Jerusalem and the Synod of Dutch Bishops held at Rome to review the affairs of the Dutch church on January 14–31, 1980. This synod in its closing statement expressly invoked the memory of "the apostles grouped around Peter in Jerusalem to decide crucial questions at a decisive moment of the life of the newborn Church (cf. Acts 15:6)."[9] The Dutch synod, however, differs from that of Jerusalem in that the local bishops were summoned to Rome rather than going there freely to resolve questions they did not feel capable of handling without the help of the parent Church. Such a summons by higher ecclesiastical authority, although entirely proper, runs the risk of failing to bring about consensus in the local church.[10]

"They made their way through Phoenicia and Samaria, telling everyone about the conversion of the Gentiles as they went. Their story caused great joy among the [believers]" (15:3)

In these words we can detect the high value placed on solidarity among local churches. Far from being content with mutual isolation, they were eager to tell their stories to one another and to seek out reactions. The representatives from Antioch were strengthened and buoyed up by the joy that their testimony evoked in other local churches.

Any particular group in the Church that ceases to communicate frankly and openly with others, or chooses to disregard the reactions of others, risks being led into serious delusions, as history abundantly confirms. Ronald Knox in his *Enthusiasm* provides a mournful chronical of deviations.[11] A new chapter in that history could be added, perhaps, by St. Benedict Center, a group which, in the late 1940s, placed itself under the exclusive direction of Fr. Leonard Feeney and refused to accept advice or direction from anyone outside the group.[12] The Center ended up in schism, with its director under excommunication, but in the 1970s, fortunately, wiser counsels prevailed. Father Feeney and the majority of the members were reconciled to the Catholic Church and gave up their exclusivist stance. Far from negating the value of the previous experiences of the group, this resumption of communion made it possible for, and incumbent upon, the rest of the Church to take those experiences seriously as pertaining to themselves.

The text we are now considering teaches not only the importance of seeking reactions from independent ecclesial communities but also that of being concerned with the well-being of groups other than one's own. Instead of becoming totally absorbed in its own particular agenda, an authentically ecclesial group will strive to share the concerns of other communities, and will praise God for the good things coming about as a result of other movements. In this way each group, while preserving its own distinctive agenda, can avoid onesidedness and fanaticism.

"Some of the converted Pharisees then got up and demanded that such Gentiles be circumcised and told to keep the Mosaic law" (15:5)

The conflicting responses in the Jerusalem church are the immediate occasion for the council which, in allowing "much discussion" (15:7), evidently gave each side the opportunity to argue its case. The apostles and presbyters, in seeking to arrive at the truth of the matter, did not dismiss either party without a full hearing.

Where efforts are being made to arrive at the truth in a disputed matter or to reconcile mutually opposed parties in the Church, it is advantageous for the reflection group to include believers of different perspectives. Elsewhere I have proposed four criteria for the selection of reflection teams dealing with theological questions:

> In the first place, all must be sincerely committed to the gospel, for the aim of the process is to decide what belief or course of action most accords with the revelation of Christ. Secondly, the team must constitute a community: they must have a common language, a capacity to understand one another's statements, and a good measure of mutual trust. Thirdly, they must be open to change their ideas and lifestyles if the results of the discernment call for this. Finally, to guard against onesidedness, the team should normally include persons of different temperaments, backgrounds, and specializations. For the dynamics of discernment, it has often been found beneficial to have different age groups and sexes. In short, everything should be varied except the one essential—concern for resolving the issue at stake in the light of the gospel.[13]

In an interesting essay entitled "Farewell to Descartes," Eugen Rosenstock-Huessy calls for the abandonment of Cartesian intellectualism, with its egocentricity, in favor of a more social and life-oriented epistemology. Authentic knowledge, he insists, arises out of situations in which people expose themselves to challenge from other points of view. For Descartes' *"Cogito ergo sum"* (I think, therefore I am) he proposes to substitute the formula, *"Respondeo etsi mutabor"* (I answer even though I shall be changed).[14]

All too often, in disputes between parties, each disputant is interested only in convincing the other. All wish to speak, but no one wishes to learn. Each party complains that the other is defensive, arrogant, self-serving, and unwilling to listen. Such complaints are not always unjustified. But when tempted to complain, each group would do well to ask itself whether it is prepared to accept correction—whether it is ready to acknowledge the beam in its own eye.

"At that time the whole assembly fell silent" (15:12)

At many points in his Gospel and in Acts, Luke calls attention to the need of silence and prayer before important decisions are made—for example, before Jesus chooses his twelve apostles (Lk 6:12) and before the early community selects a successor to Judas (Acts 1:24). In the present text it is unclear whether the silence is the result of the fact that no one can answer the arguments of Peter or is a space deliberately made for wordless converse with God. The two possible interpretations are not, of course, mutually exclusive. In any case, the observations of Alfred McBride are pertinent at this point: "This gathering was far more than parliamentary procedure or sophisticated debating. It was an hour of discernment which demanded that the noise of [people's] voices cease from time to time, so that minds might dwell on the Lord and hearts listen to the Spirit."[15]

The role of silence in the decision-making process has been honored in the tradition of many Christian groups, notably the Society of Friends. In the method of discernment recommended in the Ignatian tradition, each participant is expected to pray silently for a while after the arguments for each side have been presented, and to express a personal opinion only after having assessed the arguments in solitude. After the reasons pro and con a given course of action have been stated, each person "must discern the new movements of the Holy Spirit . . . resulting from the new evidence. . . . To discuss with others would bring about distractions and also the risk of lobbying and debating."[16]

"They listened to Barnabas and Paul as the two described all the signs and wonders God had worked among the Gentiles through them" (15:12)

Having listened to Peter's opinions based on his own experience (as previously recounted in chapters 10 and 11), the assembly was now eager to hear the testimony of those who had witnessed the wonderful events that the Holy Spirit was bringing about in Antioch.

The reports of Barnabas and Paul strikingly confirmed the lessons independently learned by Peter. So, too, in our own era it might be found that similar convictions were arising in different parts of the world as a result of similar experiences in unrelated basic communities. If so, this would be a phenomenon calling for theological discernment on the part of the whole Church.

In a number of key texts, Vatican Council II recalled the Church's duty to "scrutinize the signs of the times and to interpret them in the light of the Gospel."[17] In its Pastoral Constitution it declared that the Church, led by the Spirit of God who fills the whole earth, "labors to decipher authentic signs of God's presence and purpose in the happenings, needs, and desires" in which the members of the Church are involved.[18] A little later in the same document, the Council pointed out that it is the task of the entire Church—pastors, theologians, and laity—"to hear, distinguish, and interpret the many voices of our age, and to judge them in the light of the divine word."[19] Many of the recent developments in theology and in Church practice have been occasioned by dialogue between the Church, as a community of faith, and the world, considered as a secular community. In our day the Church cannot responsibly withdraw from this dialogue, which furnishes ample themes for theological reflection.

Those who seek on behalf of the Church to discern the significance of recent trends are often tempted to base their judgment on what conforms to their own previous ideas of what the Holy Spirit would be likely to do. Great openness is needed to be convinced by the testimony of those who have experienced something new and unprecedented. But if God can say, "See, I make all things new" (Rev 21:5), we should be prepared to admit that God, though always faithful to the covenant, is not bound in a rigid or exclusive way to follow previously established patterns. Otherwise there would be no need to discern the signs of the times.

"When they concluded their presentation, James spoke up" (15:13)

The discourse of James and the apostolic letter that follows are generally connected with the second of the two incidents apparently telescoped in Luke's account. It is hard to know whether James, in presenting his "mediating" position, speaks more as advocate or as judge. In the discernment process, unlike the judicial process, the roles of witnesses, advocates, and judges are not sharply distinguished. The group that exchanges experiences and reflections overlaps or coincides with the group that decides. Those who will be responsible for the decision previously involve themselves in the debate and forthrightly present the reasons inclining them to one position or another. The same flexibility of roles is admitted in modern Church councils, in which the assembled bishops are expected to act first as witnesses, reporting on their experience in their own dioceses, then as theologians, giving reasons for their positions, and finally as judges, in voting. In ecclesial reflection groups, the standard process resembles the conciliar rather than the judicial. The discernment can be upset if the arguments on which participants base their conclusions have not been frankly proposed and subjected to criticism in the discussion stage.

"The words of the prophets agree [with Peter's opinion]" (15:15)

Throughout the discussion appeals are frequently made to the Holy Scriptures, which serve as a common ground accepted by all participants. The converted Pharisees, as we have seen, argue that the Gentiles who become Christians should be circumcised and required to observe the Mosaic law in its entirety. In this demand they would seem to have reason on their side. The Christian Church claimed to believe in the God of Moses. If Christian converts were to be dispensed from the law of Moses, and from the circumcision on which Moses insisted (Ex 12:48), was not the Church in contradiction with itself?

We are not told how Paul and Barnabas answered this biblical argument, but we can surmise their line of reasoning from Paul's treatment of the law in Romans and Galatians. Paul contends that the law cannot be unconditionally binding since Abraham was justified by faith without circumcision and observance of the law (Gen 15:6; cf. Rom 4:4 and Gal 3:6–7). Further, Paul grounds his doctrine of justification by faith in a Christological interpretation of the prophecy of Habakkuk, "The just shall live by faith" (Hab 2:4; cf. Rom 1:17; Gal 3:11).

James, for his part, combines a liberating principle from the prophets with a restrictive principle from the law of Moses. He cites Amos 9:11–12 to prove that God is calling the Gentiles to become a new people of God (15:14–17). But at the same time he invokes the law of Moses as a basis for imposing on the Gentile converts those precepts of the law that were considered obligatory for Gentiles who resided with Israelites (15:19–21; cf. Lv 17:8—18:18).

In any discernment process careful attention must be paid to God's word in Scripture, for it contains the authoritative testimony in which the Church is permanently rooted. Scripture, however, can easily be misused. Conservatives, appealing to the law, can run the risk of falling into legalism. Progressives, appealing to the visions of the prophets, can fall into libertinism or antinomianism. Each party tends to select texts that confirm its own positions and to ignore the texts adduced by its adversaries. James sets a pattern by judiciously selecting themes from the legal and the prophetic traditions and by applying them creatively to the situation of his day.

All too often people suppose that Scripture has no authority for them unless they can cite authoritative texts that speak apodictically to their own questions today. If this were true, the authority of Scripture would constantly diminish as the social situation becomes more remote from that of biblical times. But the authority of Scripture can also be indirect.[20] Where the Bible does not textually answer our questions it often provides models and metaphors, parables and paradigms that work on our heart and imagination as well as on our discursive thought. By showing how men and women of faith, under very different circumstances, found God's will for themselves, Scripture can help us to do likewise within our own situation. If individuals and communities allow their identity to be shaped by prayerful reading of the Bible, they can often gain the strength and insight needed to discern God's call for themselves. As Thomas Clarke has put it,

Theological reflection needs to be creative as well as critical. Our recourse to distinctively Christian sources provides light and energy not only for a moral and religious appraisal of the present and of ourselves in the present but also for the discovery of alternative futures. Here the Scriptures are particularly powerful in their ability to spark the Christian imagination to new dreams for our humanity.[21]

"It was resolved by the apostles and the presbyters, in agreement with the whole Jerusalem church . . ." (15:22)

The final decree, as Luke presents it, is drawn up by the official leadership, but not without the concurrence of the general membership of the local church, who are in attendance. Yves Congar points out that the different roles of the apostles and presbyters on the one hand, and of the multitude on the other, set a pattern for the discipline that was to prevail in later centuries. He mentions especially the African provincial councils of the third century, the procedure of which is indicated by the rule that Cyprian, bishop of Carthage, set for himself "to decide nothing without your advice [that of the presbyters] and the people's agreement."[22] Congar concludes that although the laity do not form part of councils habitually or by right, "they can do so when they are able to supply useful information and when the matters to be discussed concern them."[23]

John Henry Newman popularized the idea that consultation with the laity can be highly useful to Church authorities not only in practical decisions but even in arriving at decisions about dogmas to be defined.[24] Vatican II, which recognized the unanimous consent of the faithful as a sure sign of the Holy Spirit,[25] pointed out how believers, through their own prayerful experience of the life of faith, as well as through the authorized preaching of their pastors, are able to achieve a continually deeper penetration of the abiding Christian message.[26]

A proper distinction between the roles of pastors and other members of the Church, with due respect for the distinctive contributions of all who are spiritually gifted, is essential for an orderly process of discernment. Rules worked out centuries ago for episcopal synods and ecumenical councils should not, however, be rigidly imposed on contemporary pastoral councils and informal reflection groups. In our own day there would seem to be a greater need than previously to involve the members of the Church in shared responsibility for decisions that affect them. Pope Paul VI called attention to this need in his letter, *A Call to Action* (1971), and the same thought runs through the Pastoral Instruction on Social Communications issued by the Pontifical Commission for the Means of Social Communication with the approval of Paul VI in 1971. According to the latter document, "Those who exercise authority in the Church will take care to ensure that there is a responsible exchange of freely held and expressed opinion among the people of God. More than this, they will set up norms and conditions for this to take place."[27] Reflection groups in which clergy, laity, and religious all take an active role can be a timely implementation of this directive.

"We have heard that some of our number without any instructions from us have upset you with their discussions and disturbed your peace of mind" (15:24)

The apostles and presbyters are careful to distinguish what is done by instruction from them and what others take upon themselves to do without authorization. In the following verses they praise Barnabas and Paul as loyal Christians who have "dedicated themselves to the cause of our Lord Jesus Christ" (15:26).

Throughout the centuries the intemperate zeal of self-appointed custodians of orthodoxy has never ceased to be a problem for the Church. In our own day a so-called "third magisterium" has stirred up trouble, defaming some who like Paul and Barnabas seek to serve the Church by responding in creative ways to new and difficult questions.[28] It remains a responsibility of Church authorities to repudiate heresy-hunters who meddle in matters beyond their competence, and to vindicate the good name of those who have been unjustly defamed.

"We have unanimously resolved . . ." (15:25)

The Greek term *homothymadon*, here translated "unanimously," could also mean "assembled in one place," but as Luke uses it, it seems generally to mean "with one mind or purpose." The common mind of the group is attributed in verse 28 to the Holy Spirit: "It is the decision of the Holy Spirit, and ours too . . ." Yves Congar remarks that it is the property of the Holy Spirit, by the very fact of being "spirit," to be able, while remaining one and the same, to become present and active in many persons. He quotes St. Ambrose as saying of the apostles: "They were different persons, but one in all their accomplishments, because the Holy Spirit is one."[29]

Church historians and theologians have repeatedly pointed out that conciliar discernment is not a parliamentary procedure in which representatives of particular interest groups bargain with one another in order to achieve a majority, even a slim one, and thus to vanquish their opponents. Rather, such a body seeks to grasp the intentions of the Holy Spirit for the whole group. Since the Spirit is one, the message must be one. Yves Congar has expressed this in a powerful paragraph:

> It is not the law of the majority but unanimity which is valid at a council. Naturally voting takes place at councils, too, because no other means of expression have yet been discovered, just as the only way we can test a pupil's knowledge is to let him take an examination. But this voting at a council is only a means for achieving unanimity; by means of a majority the true mind and directive of the Church as such is determined so that perhaps those few who had not yet perceived it could now—after it had been interpreted and determined—recognize it as a law binding upon all. Hence a council is not the sum total of the individual votes, but the totality of the consciousness of the Church. As in the first days, its ideal is *in unum convenire* (St. Cyprian, Epist. 55.6.1), namely, unanimity. When the bishops affixed their signatures to the decisions with *consensi et subscripsi,* they did not so much mean to say "I am in agreement" as "I share the consensus, that is, I espouse the unanimity."[30]

Congar is here speaking of ecclesiastical councils in which the decisions are made by bishops having a special grace of office. But the same principles are applicable, *mutatis mutandis,* to all ecclesial reflection groups. Speaking of community discernment in a Jesuit context, John Futrell writes:

> The atmosphere in this deliberation is one of communal seeking, not of debate. The purpose is not that one "party"

prevail, but that all discover the actual word of God to the whole community. One is not a representative of a faction, but a member of the community seeking with his brothers to find God together in a specific corporate decision. There are no "winners" or "losers" and, so, no disaffected minority at the end of a successful deliberation of true communal discernment. There is, rather, the unanimously shared peace of finding God together here and now in a specific corporate decision.[31]

Although unanimity is the ideal, it does not always come about as easily as one might think from Luke's idealized account. Consensus is sometimes achieved by the action of trusted leaders who, after hearing all the opinions, sum up the sense of the meeting in such a way as to evoke general satisfaction. A formal vote is not always necessary or desirable. When taken, it has the advantage of manifesting the consensus more clearly. But a vote can also have the disadvantage of hardening the differences of opinion, in such a way that a minority feels itself to be excluded.[32] By producing a "disaffected minority" some councils have sown the seeds of later conflict and schism. To mention only contemporary examples, one may think of the followers of Archbishop Marcel Lefebvre who reject some of the decisions of Vatican II, or the negative reactions of many Catholics to the Dutch Pastoral Council of 1968–1970, or even the milder opposition provoked by the Detroit Call to Action Conference in 1976. These cases seem to indicate that in modern society the liberal parliamentary model, with its mechanistic paradigm of parts exerting pressure on one another, may excessively politicize the process of decision-making.[33] The older organic models, in which trusted elders spoke for the whole community, often led more successfully to the desired unanimity. Even if it cannot be repristinated in its ancient form, this organic model, as portrayed in the story of the Jerusalem council, may suggest fruitful alternatives for the Church in our day.

"... *not to lay on you any burden beyond that which is strictly necessary* ..." (15:28)
In spite of the authoritarian tendencies that have manifested

themselves in the Church, freedom remains a fundamental Christian value, greatly esteemed by the New Testament authors. In well-known passages John and Paul extol the freedom given by Jesus and the Holy Spirit. Paul, in Romans and Galatians, develops his theology of freedom in opposition to the legalism of Jewish Christianity. In the Council of Jerusalem, as described by Luke, Peter argues against imposing the Mosaic law on the Gentile converts because such restrictions would be inconsistent with the belief "that we are saved by the favor of the Lord Jesus and so are they" (15:11). James contends that it would be wrong to set up obstacles to the conversion of the Gentiles through whom God is rebuilding the fallen house of David (15:16–19). It is not surprising, then, that the decree invokes the principle that no unnecessary burdens are to be laid on the Gentile converts.

The same bias toward freedom has resurfaced at many crucial turning points in Christian history. It was a central theme of Vatican II. According to the Declaration on Religious Freedom (no. 7), the usages of society "require that human freedom be respected as far as possible, and curtailed only when and insofar as necessary." The Decree on Ecumenism, quoting Acts 15:28, taught that for the preservation or restoration of Christian unity one must "impose no burden beyond what is indispensable" (no. 18).

Unfortunately this respect for freedom, which has always been a feature of authentic Christianity, has often been countered by a legalism resembling that of the converted Pharisees, as portrayed by Luke. Particular groups of believers, convinced that they know the way of righteousness, have a tendency to force their convictions on others by force or threats, and thus to minimize the zone of freedom. We are all familiar with the authoritarianism of the right that lays on the shoulders of new generations burdens "which neither we nor our fathers were able to bear" (15:10). We should be equally alert to detect the totalitarianism of the progressives, who sometimes impugn the motives and intelligence of Christians who do not agree with them.[34] The Church still has much to learn from the Council of Jerusalem which allowed Jewish and Gentile Christians to live and think differently and yet made provision, as we shall presently see, for their peaceful co-existence in one and the same communion.

"... *to abstain from meat sacrificed to idols, from blood, from the meat of strangled animals, and from illicit sexual union*" (15:29)

In spite of its option for freedom, the decree does impose some regulations—the four which, as we have seen from the discourse of James, were mandatory for Gentiles living in Israelite territory. The council accepted James' argument that these precepts must have been familiar to pious Gentiles living with Jews in places such as Antioch. The final decree thus respects what Joseph Fitzmyer calls James' pleas for "a sympathetic understanding of Jewish-Christian sensitivities."[35] In this sense, the settlement may be called a compromise between the positions of the Pauline and the Judaizing parties, neither of which probably achieved exactly what it had originally intended.

If freedom had been the only concern of the council, it could have simply allowed each party to go its own way, with the Jewish converts observing the Mosaic law and the Gentile converts ignoring it. This kind of permissiveness, however, would have undermined the common life and worship of the two groups of Christians and would have resulted in the kind of inconsistent conduct of which Paul accuses Peter in Antioch (Gal 2:12). Where the decree of Jerusalem was known and observed, there would be nothing to prevent a Jewish Christian like Peter from entering into table fellowship, and hence also into eucharistic communion, with the uncircumcised. Although there is no evidence in Paul's writing that he knew of the Jerusalem decree, it does not seem to violate the principles of his theology. He repeatedly insists that Gentile converts should respect the conscientious convictions of Jewish Christians. "If food causes my brother to sin," he writes, "I will never eat meat again, so that I may not be an occasion of sin to him" (1 Cor 8:13).

Nearly all councils end in compromises of one kind or another. This does not, or should not, mean that they straddle between truth and error, between right and wrong. Some compromises are constructive and enriching; they go beyond the insights that each party could have achieved on its own, and yet violate the principles of neither. Other compromises are simply dilatory or temporizing; they represent a measure of agreement and are open to future development. Still other compromises are ambiguous and misleading; they simply put contradictory and unreconciled principles side by side. A good theology of compromise will distinguish among all these, and other, types of compromise.[36] It will see the value of honest compromise for avoiding unnecessary rifts in the community and for preparing the way to future advances to be achieved through continuing dialogue.

In our age the Church is seeking to implant itself in a great variety of cultures. Problems similar to those at Antioch are arising in many parts of the globe. Freedom and pluralism must be allowed, but mere tolerance does not suffice to establish communion among those who differ. The kind of compromise enshrined in the Jerusalem decree retains its value as an example of successful mediation. Jerusalem teaches us that "progressive" groups must sometimes be willing to accept restraints out of respect for the conscientious convictions of those who adhere to more traditional ways. Such an acceptance can be viewed as a dilatory compromise, but at a deeper level it is an exercise of communal charity. To renounce the self-interest of one's own group or party for the sake of the spiritual good of others is compromise of the highest and most honorable kind.

This admonition, politely expressed, has been taken by some exegetes as a mere recommendation and as addressed only to Christians "of Gentile origin in Antioch, Syria, and Cilicia" (15:23). Acts 21:25, however, indicates that James and the Jerusalem authorities regarded the decision as imposing a true obligation on all Gentile Christians living in mixed communities, including Jerusalem itself. In a sense the decree was tied to a particular transitory situation. It would no longer be relevant when Jewish converts became a small minority in the Church. Yet the decree was not without dogmatic force. It implicitly taught that, contrary to the opinion of the Judaizing Christians, circumcision was not necessary for salvation (cf. 15:1).

In a time of rapid flux, when decisions cannot in every case be supported by cogent speculative arguments, Church authorities may increasingly be expected to teach by means of provisional and practical decrees which Rahner speaks of as "pastoral instructions."[37] As Rahner cautions, we should not hastily assume that because we do not have an infallible doctrinal pronouncement we have a mere expression of opinion which may easily be dismissed as lacking the force of law. Rather, we should ask ourselves whether the Holy Spirit may not be summoning the Church to common action and belief by means of provisional decisions which reject certain positions as contrary to the Gospel and leave open the course of future development. Unless there are serious reasons for conscientious protest or disobedience—a possibility that cannot be antecedently excluded[38]—such legitimate decisions by competent authority deserve to be respected and obeyed, even though, at some later time, they may be modified or forgotten.

"Thus were the representatives sent on their way to Antioch" (15:30)

A very important factor in the settlement of disputes is the manner in which the decision is communicated. In this case the Jerusalem authorities were not content to issue a bare decree. As we have already seen, they wrote a polite and encouraging letter in which they apologized for the earlier misconduct of some members of their own community. More than this, they sent two highly esteemed prophetic leaders, Judas and Silas, to impart the decision in a tactful and persuasive manner.

It is easy to think of recent cases in which substantively sound decisions by ecclesiastical authorities have been received with anger and resentment, either because the decision itself was phrased in an abrupt and legalistic style or because it was ineptly communicated. Communications are sometimes impeded by a certain type of popular journalism that stands to gain from suspicion and contestation. Reporters often depict Church authorities as autocratic and unbending, while glorifying dissenters as heroes and martyrs. Local reflection groups should be on guard against being misled by these or other stereotypes. Higher authorities, on the other hand, must take pains to smooth the way for potentially unpopular decisions by personal contact and quiet diplomacy.

"When it [the letter] was read there was great delight at the encouragement it gave" (15:31)

The incident ends on a typically Lukan note with mention of the strength and joy brought by the decision to the local church. More than most other biblical authors, Luke emphasizes the sentiments of consolation and peace which follow upon authentic spiritual experiences, such as the appearances of the risen Christ in the last chapters of the Gospel and the fervent practice of community life in the early chapters of Acts.

The process of theological reflection and discussion that had begun at Antioch with the unwelcome meddling of the visitors from Jerusalem now terminates at Antioch with the communication of the decree by duly authorized and competent emissaries. The reception of the decree is an integral part of the decision-making process; for if the decree had been rejected by the local church, the controversy would have remained unresolved.

In the Ignatian process of decision-making, the choice, once made, is to be submitted to a process of confirmation. As a result of choosing correctly, St. Ignatius believes, one "will often experience more abundantly within the soul lights, consolations, and divine inspirations."[39] By consolation he means "every increase of faith, hope, and love, and all interior joy that invites and attracts to what is heavenly and to the salvation of one's soul by filling it with peace and quiet in Christ. . . ."[40]

Extending the Ignatian discernment process to corporate decisions, contemporary spiritual writers hold that when the community has reached a sound Christian decision it will experience greater joy and strength in its communal life and undertakings.[41] Careful scrutiny is to be given to the consequences of living by the decisions. Does this build up the community and its members by bringing greater light, peace, vitality, and freedom into their lives, or does it on the contrary lead to darkness, discouragement, confusion, and tension? In any such evaluation, Paul's lists of the fruits of the good and evil spirits in Galatians 5:16–26 may profitably be consulted.

CONCLUSION

We have surveyed a biblical paradigm of corporate theological reflection dealing with a painful conflict in the early Church. The process led through frank discussion to a unanimous conclusion, peacefully accepted. The Council of Jerusalem, as described in Acts, has served as a model for many councils which have invoked the Holy Spirit and have claimed to act under the Spirit's guidance. Insofar as the Church itself is a "divinely convoked council," as some express it, the conciliar process should characterize the life of the Church as a whole. Every deliberation, to the extent that it is ecclesial, recapitulates the essential features we have traced in the conciliar reflection at Jerusalem.

If this be true, theological reflection should not be regarded as the exclusive prerogative of any particular organ in the Church—whether this be a small, voluntary, local reflection group or a conciliar assembly of high ecclesiastics issuing decrees in the name of the universal Church. The process of reflection and decision in its totality must transcend the distinction between pastors and laity, between local communities and hierarchical authorities.

As a paradigm, the Council of Jerusalem will be more appropriate for some situations than for others. Where there is question of a free and binding decision of the Church regarding its own inner life and discipline, the model will be especially apposite. Where the controversy concerns the Christian response to academic and social questions of a more technical character in which non-Christians as well as Christians are involved, the paradigm may be of more limited value; but its lessons, I suspect, will not be negligible.

It may of course be objected that the Acts of the Apostles deals with the formative period before the Church had fully developed its papal-episcopal structures, its body of established doctrine, and its New Testament Scriptures. The Council of Jerusalem does indeed have certain special features that cannot be exactly reproduced under modern conditions. But one may argue that for this precise reason the Jerusalem experience has special value in our own day. For, as mentioned in the opening pages of this chapter, we live in a time of radical questioning and of new beginnings.

In response to current needs, the methods of corporate theological reflection, already familiar to Luke, are being perfected and reactivated in our time, especially in countries that feel culturally distant from the "old world" in which Catholicism has been most at home for many centuries. The small reflection groups that have sprung into being in various regions may be compared to mountain streams that arise where the glaciers begin to melt. As they gradually descend toward the inhabited plains below, these streams change course, combine, and grow in volume, until at length they turn into mighty rivers that carry all before them. In the providence of God the reflection groups studied in this volume may play a significant role in preparing the paths of some future council—call it Vatican III or Jerusalem II—in which their testimony, like that of Peter or Paul at the first Jerusalem meeting, may help to shape the consciousness of the universal Church. But, if the Council of Jerusalem is any indication, the proposals of local reflection groups will presumably be modified and matured by dialogue with Christians more committed to traditional ways.

NOTES

1. See the preceding chapter of the present volume.

2. K. Rahner, "Towards a Fundamental Theological Interpretation of Vatican II," *Theological Studies* 40 (1979) 716–27.

3. H. Mühlen, *Morgen wird Einheit sein* (Paderborn: Schöningh, 1974), p. 45. In this work, which builds on the recommendations of the Faith and Order Commission meeting at Louvain in 1971, Mühlen makes extensive use of Acts 15 as a model of conciliarity.

4. Readers who wish to pursue the problems of historicity in greater detail may consult standard commentaries such as E. Haenchen, *The Acts of the Apostles* (Philadelphia: Westminster, 1971).

5. J. Dupont, *The Salvation of the Gentiles: Essays on the Acts of the Apostles* (New York: Paulist, 1979), pp. 32–33.

6. For an introduction see John C. Futrell, *Making an Apostolic Community of Love: The Role of the Superior According to Ignatius of Loyola* (St. Louis: Institute of Jesuit Sources, 1970). The "Deliberation of the First Fathers" printed in Appendix I vividly illustrates how Ignatius and his companions arrived at certain basic decisions regarding their form of life.

7. Throughout this chapter Scripture will be quoted according to *The New American Bible* (Confraternity of Christian Doctrine, 1970).

8. The classical formulation of this principle may be found in Pius XII's encyclical *Quadragesimo Anno* (*AAS* 23 [1931] 203), quoted in English translation in W.A. Abbott (ed.), *The Documents of Vatican II* (New York: America Press, 1966), p. 300 (editor's footnote).

9. *Origins* 9:35 (Feb. 14, 1980) 557, 559.

10. The unfavorable reception of the Synod was noted by Cardinal Willebrands in his "Reflections on the Dutch Synod," *Origins* 11:10 (Aug. 13, 1981) 154–56.

11. R.A. Knox, *Enthusiasm* (Oxford: Clarendon, 1950).

12. See T.F. O'Dea, "Catholic Sectarianism: A Sociological Study of

the So-Called Boston Heresy Case," reprinted in his *Sociology and the Study of Religion* (New York: Basic Books, 1970), pp. 23–38.

13. A. Dulles, "The Apostolate of Theological Reflection," *The Way,* Supplement No. 20 (Autumn 1973) 118. In connection with the first criterion it is observed in a footnote: "This is not to exclude the participation of resource persons who, without being explicitly committed to the Christian faith, may be in a position to provide valuable information or criticism of the process of discussion" (note 12).

14. E. Rosenstock-Huessy, "Farewell to Descartes," *Out of Revolution* (New York: W. Morrow, 1969), pp. 740–53.

15. A. McBride, *The Gospel of the Holy Spirit* (New York: Hawthorn, 1975), p. 88.

16. J.C. Futrell, "Communal Discernment: Reflections on Experience," *Studies in the Spirituality of Jesuits* 4:5 (Nov. 1972) 175.

17. Vatican II, *Gaudium et spes* (Pastoral Constitution on the Church in the Modern World), no. 4.

18. *Gaudium et spes,* no. 11.

19. *Gaudium et spes,* no. 44.

20. On the indirect authority of Scripture see David H. Kelsey, *The Uses of Scripture in Recent Theology* (Philadelphia: Fortress, 1975), esp. pp. 122–23, 140–51.

21. T.E. Clarke, "Methodology," in *The Context of Our Ministries: Working Papers* (Washington, D.C.: Jesuit Conference, 1981), p. 8.

22. St. Cyprian, *Epist.* 14:4 (ed. G. Hartel), *CSEL* 3:2, p. 512.

23. Y. Congar, *Lay People in the Church* (Westminster: Newman, 1957), pp. 237–38.

24. J.H. Newman, *On Consulting the Faithful in Matters of Doctrine,* ed. by J. Coulson (New York: Sheed & Ward, 1962).

25. Vatican II, *Lumen Gentium* (Dogmatic Constitution on the Church), no. 12.

26. Vatican II, *Dei Verbum* (Dogmatic Constitution on Divine Revelation), no. 8.

27. *Pastoral Instruction on the Means of Social Communication* (Washington, D.C.: USCC, 1971), no. 116, p. 35.

28. R.E. Brown describes the "third magisterium" as "the massive presence of those who . . . would vie for authority in teaching with both bishops and theologians." See his "The Dilemma of the Magisterium vs. the Theologians—Debunking Some Fictions," *Chicago Studies* 17 (1978) 297; reprinted in Brown's *The Critical Meaning of the Bible* (New York: Paulist, 1981), p. 53.

29. St. Ambrose, *De Spiritu Sancto* 1.7.81 (*PL* 16:724). Cf. Y. Congar,

"The Council as an Assembly and the Church as Essentially Conciliar," in H. Vorgrimler (ed.), *One, Holy, Catholic, and Apostolic* (London: Sheed & Ward, 1968), pp. 67–68. The idea of the Holy Spirit as "one person in many persons" is a favorite theme of H. Mühlen, as may be seen from the work cited in note 3, above.

30. Y. Congar, "Die Konzilien im Leben der Kirche," *Una Sancta* 14 (1959) 161–62; quoted by Hans Küng, *Structures of the Church* (New York: Nelson, 1964), p. 34.

31. J.C. Futrell, "Communal Discernment," pp. 176–77.

32. See the wise cautions of G. Dumeige, "Jesuit 'Deliberation' and Discernment," *The Way,* Supplement No. 20 (Autumn 1973) 67.

33. See the contribution of Joe Holland to the present volume.

34. In the United States today, the attacks of "progressives" on the "Moral Majority" sometimes exhibit a regrettable intolerance.

35. R.J. Dillon and J.A. Fitzmyer, "Acts of the Apostles," *Jerome Biblical Commentary* (Englewood Cliffs: Prentice-Hall, 1968), sec. 45, no. 75 (vol. 2, p. 196).

36. For a morphology of the various types of compromise see M. Seckler, "Über den Kompromiss in Sachen der Lehre" in M. Seckler and others (eds.), *Begegnung* (Graz: Styria, 1972), pp. 45–57; reprinted in Seckler, *Im Spannungsfeld von Wissenschaft und Kirche* (Freiburg: Herder, 1980), pp. 99–109.

37. K. Rahner, "On the Theological Problems Entailed in a 'Pastoral Constitution'," *Theological Investigations,* Vol. 10 (New York: Herder and Herder, 1973), pp. 293–317.

38. There seems to be no reason we cannot apply to the Church the general principles enunciated by Karol Wojtyla before he became Pope: "The structure of a human community is correct only if it admits not just the presence of a justified opposition but also that practical effectiveness of opposition required by the common good and the right of participation. . . . Undoubtedly opposition may make the cooperation of [people] less smooth and more difficult, but it should never damage or prevent it" (*The Acting Person* [Dordrecht, Holland: D. Reidel, 1979], p. 287).

39. Ignatius of Loyola, *The Spiritual Exercises,* no. 213.

40. *Spiritual Exercises,* no. 316.

41. See, for example, Futrell, "Communal Discernment," p. 164; also J.J. Toner, "A Method for Communal Discernment of God's Will," *Studies in the Spirituality of Jesuits* 3:4 (Sept. 1971) 144–45.

11
Theological Reflection and the Mission of the Church

John D. Godsey

Today the churches of North America are caught in a raging sea of change. The transformation of society itself continues at a bewildering pace, the result of complex technological, social, economic, and political factors. Monetary inflation, nuclear threat, ecological fragility, computerization of life, the power of international cartels, unemployment, the arms race, racial and class tensions, competition with the Soviet Union, the rising expectations of third world countries—these are some of the elements that keep our world churning. Never immune from the problems of society, the churches themselves are feeling the effects of these unsettled times.

Besides being influenced from without by changes affecting the general populace, the churches have increasingly had to face problems peculiar to themselves. The process of secularization, begun as early as the Middle Ages but flowering since the eighteenth century Enlightenment, has brought an end to the so-called Constantinian era, when churches tended to profit from alliances with powerful governing authorities. To be sure, the churches of the United States are considered to be officially "disestablished" by the doctrine of the separation of Church and state, but what this has meant, practically speaking, has been an alliance, especially of the mainline Protestant churches, with the middle classes—an alliance which has by no means been totally salutary. Often it has meant that the churches have become too comfortable within a bourgeois milieu and have tended to lose their concern for the poor.

The far-reaching impact of the Second Vatican Council on the Roman Catholic Church has been overwhelmingly positive, but, as could be expected from such a major "updating," it has also had some negative results on the U.S. scene. These run the gamut from conservative resistance on the one side to liberal disappointment that the changes did not go far enough on the other. Most distressing, perhaps, has been a sense of confusion and disorientation on the part of many that has led to considerable disaffection and loss in the ranks of clergy, religious, and laity alike.

Other significant developments on the religious scene in recent times have been the rise of third world churches and the decreasing dominance of the "Christian West," the emergence of liberation theology in its third world, black, and feminist forms, the revival of world religions, the changed relations between Christians and Jews after the holocaust, and the resurgence of fundamentalist groups like the "Moral Majority."

Rocked by change from within and without, the churches of the United States are being forced to inquire afresh about the wellsprings of their existence and to act creatively to meet the challenges that confront them in the world. They have had to ask again the fundamental questions: What is the Church? What is its purpose? What is its mission? What must it do? True, these are not new questions. They have been addressed by Vatican II and by the ecumenical movement, and the Church has always faced and always will be facing them. But now they must be asked by Christians in the United States with a special urgency, for the situation of the churches is rapidly changing and in many respects the future of the world appears to be more grim.

This project of the Woodstock Theological Center on theological reflection as it is understood and practiced by various groups of Christians who are actively committed to social justice is timely indeed. It recognizes that theological reflection is proceeding apace among such groups, and it offers an opportunity for critique and mutual enrichment between those on the battle line, so to speak, and those whose profession has been to think theologically. This essay aims to focus the question of action/reflection on the mission of the Church in and to the world.

THE ACTION/REFLECTION GROUPS

The types of church groups included in the Woodstock Theological Center's Project on Theological Reflection vary significantly, but they have in common their social concern. They therefore represent the cutting edge of the prophetic ministry of the Church as it attempts to influence governmental policy toward the building of a just, participatory, and sustainable society both at home and abroad. As such, they serve as catalysts for change among the larger churches, promoting a broader and deeper understanding of the mission to which God is calling the Church in our day. The groups function as "signs" within the masses of acculturated Christians. This is the case whether the group is Catholic, Protestant, or interdenominational, and whether it belongs to a specific church (e.g., the Catholic Church's Campaign for Human Development and the Friends Committee on National Legislation), is an independent organization, although perhaps closely tied to a church (e.g., NETWORK, the Center of Concern, the Churches' Center for Theology and Public Policy, and the Foundation for Community Creativity), or functions as an independent church (e.g., the Church of the Saviour and Sojourners).

The commonality of concern among these groups appears in their statements about their goal or purpose. NETWORK is essentially a Catholic social justice lobby that communicates and organizes to effect systemic change by influencing national legislation on issues that touch the powerless. The Friends Committee likewise attempts to affect national legislation so that the social, economic, and political aspects of life will be conducted in love and justice. The Campaign for Human Development is an education-action program to combat domestic poverty by changing structures, policies, conditions, and institutions. The Center of Concern is an interdisciplinary team engaged in social analysis, religious reflection, and public education in issues of social justice. The Churches' Center for Theology and Public Policy is an ecumenical study center devoted to the analysis of serious issues that face the churches in the public domain. Community Creativity Incorporated is a consultative organization that aims to encourage the development of Christian groups and communities by fostering life-giving relationships between persons and structures. Eastern Mennonite College sponsors a Washington, D.C. seminar "to prepare students to serve, and be served by, the present society through direct participation in and observation of the institutional life and structures of the metropolis."

Two groups involved in the Woodstock Project share the other groups' concern for mission in and to the world but are special cases, in that they are Christian communities that carry on all the normal churchly functions and understand themselves to be churches of a special sort in the Washington setting. The Church of the Saviour was founded in 1947 by Southern Baptist Gordon Cosby as an ecumenical and interracial community that requires stringent commitment to disciplined spiritual exercises (the "inward journey") and to ongoing involvement in a corporate mission in the world, especially in the city (the "outward journey"). Commitment to the city, particularly to the poor among whom they live, also characterizes Sojourners, a community of families and singles who worship together and minister together in the city of Washington. Founded by Jim Wallis and other evangelical Christians whose social consciences were radicalized during the civil rights and anti-war struggles of the 1960s, the community also carries on a far-reaching literary mission through the publication of *Sojourners* magazine.[1]

What ties all of these action/reflection groups together—and they of course are representative of numerous other groups throughout the country—is their openness to the world as God's world in spite of its fallenness, and their belief that Christians must act to help change the world, precisely because of its fallenness.

THE MISSION OF THE CHURCH

The first thing to be said about the mission of the Church is that its mission is defined exclusively by its divine origin. That is, the Church does not generate its own mission but participates in God's mission to the world, namely, the reconciliation of the world with God as this has taken place in Jesus Christ. In this sense it can be said that the Church does not "have" a mission but "is" mission. Its very *raison d'être* is to be an instrument of God's missionary activity as this is carried out by the Holy Spirit today. If it were not engaged in mission, it would not be the Church.

While mission is utterly essential to a proper understanding of the nature and purpose of the Church, mission does not, in my judgment, exhaust the life of the Church. Besides being a herald of God's love to the world and a sign of that love within its midst, the Church carries on a life of worship and loving service internal to itself. It is commanded to love both God and neighbor, and although intimately related, neither of these loves is simply reducible to the other. In its prayer and worship the Church demonstrates a love of God that is directed to God alone, an honoring of God as God, the value of which is not instrumental but intrinsic. On the other hand, because this God is revealed in Jesus Christ to be a God who loves all humankind, forgiving sinners and enabling a new life of sacrificial love and justice among the peoples of the earth, love of God is never without a corresponding love of neighbor.[2]

God's mission for the Church is, above all, to be a witness to the new age of grace that was inaugurated by Jesus Christ. The Church is sent into the world to bear witness to the Gospel, the good news of Jesus Christ, and to call the world to obedience to the divine will for a new community of faith, love, and hope. The Church is called to bear this witness by both words and actions. If the Gospel proclaims God's wondrous self-giving, reconciling love for a fallen world and the formation of a new community following this "way" of love, then the Church's mere verbalization of the Gospel becomes incredible to the world if it is not accompanied by the deeds of love that characterize the Way.

The understanding of mission has changed notably during the twentieth century.[3] First of all, the missionary frontier used to be thought of almost exclusively in geographical terms. Missionaries from the churches of the Western world were sent to far-off countries in Africa and Asia to convert the heathen and to plant churches. This was undoubtedly a valid form of missionary activity in that day, although it suffered from its association with Western colonial expansion and the seemingly inevitable acculturation of the Gospel that accompanied the aura of dominance inherent in "Christendom." Gradually during this century the churches came to realize that the frontier with the unbelieving world is everywhere, that the missionary boundaries, while sometimes geographical, are also psychological and sociological, and, of course, always theological. The attitudes associated with colonialism and Christendom, while not entirely abolished, no longer prevail; the younger churches of Africa and Asia and South America now send missionaries to Europe and North America, and some contend that the "coming third church" will soon be the most influential Christian force on planet earth.[4]

A second change has entailed the move away from a strictly Church-centered mission to a more God-centered mission, that is, from a theology and strategy that viewed the purpose of mission to be primarily the expansion of the Church as the locus of God's kingdom on earth to a view that interprets the Church's mission as vital participation in God's hidden but powerful work of bringing *shalom* (peace, harmony) to all peoples throughout the world. In this view God is understood to be constantly at work in the world for its salvation, and the role of the Church is to discern the "signs of the times" and to join the divine work of salvation that is being wrought wherever love and justice and peace are happening anywhere in the world.[5]

This new view of *missio Dei* (God's mission), or what some prefer to call *missiones Dei* (God's missions), involves a changed interpretation of both Church and world. There is a new openness to the world, with the implied assumption that the world is not necessarily hostile to God and that "secular" affairs are at least equally the locus of God's saving work as are churchly ones. Furthermore, the Church is now understood not as a sanctuary which provides divine refuge from a hostile environment but rather as a sign that points beyond itself to divine happenings in the world that otherwise would remain hidden or obscure. As one author has put it, a sign is not an enclosure but a disclosure; it performs its function not by containing but by communicating, not by annexation but by representation.[6]

A third change, intimately related to both of the above, has to do with the relation of evangelization to mission, indeed with the nature or meaning of evangelism per se. For most "evangelicals," evangelism is synonymous with preaching, and preaching is the pre-eminent if not sole mode of missionary activity. Its goal is to convert or to change people and to bring them into the Church. To be sure, sometimes a distinction is made between evangelism and mission, in that the former applies to those at home who are no longer Christians, whereas the latter concerns those who are far off and who are not yet Christians. But this appears to be a distinction without any essential difference. On the other hand, "ecumenicals" of the mainline churches have tended to broaden the meaning of evangelism and to either supplement or supplant verbal proclamation with social and/or political action. The mission of the Church in this view has been expressed in such terms as humanization, advocacy, liberation, and participation in the development of humanity. The accent has been on changing oppressive structures and systems more than on conversion of individuals.[7]

The debate over the meaning and goal of the mission of the Church is far from over, and the split over the issues is to be found in Catholicism and Eastern Orthodoxy as well as in "mainline" and "evangelical" Protestanism. The three changes sketched above are in reality all interrelated and point to a basic shift over the past few decades in many churches' self-understanding and perception of the world. This shift has in large measure been forced upon the churches "from below," that is, from the perspective of the world's impoverished, disadvantaged, and oppressed. The predominant churches have for a long time tended to ally themselves with the wealthy and powerful, whether it be with the middle classes in the more democratic countries or with the oligarchies in the more authoritarian ones. Against this alliance an opposition has gradually grown which is made up of those who believe the Church should be in solidarity with the poor and the oppressed. A theology of liberation has been developed to expose what is considered to be an ideological captivity of the Western churches that will not square with the Gospel.[8]

This confrontation has been most intense between the Latin American churches on the one hand and those of North America and Europe on the other. Talk has gradually shifted from "development" to "liberation." A watershed occurrence for the Roman Catholic Church, by far the largest in Latin America, was the Second General Conference of the Latin American Episcopate (CELAM) at Medellín, Colombia in 1968. The documents that emerged recognized the institutional violence involved in the exploitation of resources and peoples by outside economic interests, called for "liberating education," integrated "conscientization" (consciousness-raising) into pastoral work, and urged solidarity with the poor in their struggles for self-determination and economic justice. These goals, which placed the Catholic Church on the side of the oppressed, were essentially upheld by the next conference of the bishops at Puebla, Mexico in 1979.

Many Protestants in Latin America have actively joined the movement toward liberation and have concurrently contributed to its theology and action. Meanwhile, the World Council of Churches, especially since its World Conference on Church and Society in 1966 and its Studies on the Missionary Structure of the Congregation (1962–66), has moved its interpretation of mission more and more to the side of those who seek justice for the poor and oppressed through systemic change. It has even made monetary grants to certain guerrilla groups fighting for liberation in Africa, albeit for food and not weapons. In the United States, during the 1960s and 1970s, movements and theologies dedicated to civil rights and liberation from injustice and oppression have developed among blacks, native Americans, and Hispanics, as well as among women.

God appears to be working through the churches and through worldly forces outside the churches to bring about this worldwide and revolutionary demand for redress and equity. As a result momentous changes are taking place within the churches. Nowhere is this more evident than in missionary theology and practice. Slogans such as "the Church for others" mark the changes that run the gamut from priests in revolutionary movements to the formation of "base communities" for the consciousness-raising of Latin American peasants,[9] from black power in New York City to anti-apartheid demonstrations in South Africa.

The watchword of liberation-inspired missions today is "praxis." This is not an easy word to define with precision. In the words of one commentator:

It most definitely does *not* mean technique or know-how or "putting faith into practice" or "making Christianity practical." Rather praxis is a complexity of awareness, consciousness, intentionality, vision, imagination and purposefulness in all of one's action *and* reflection. Praxis is revolutionary in the sense that it is a consciousness that sets one apart and alienates one from the prevailing cultural expectations or ideology such that one perceives the "false consciousness" of the present age and acts in ways calculated to change the social conditions which contribute to and give an air of credibility to that false consciousness.[10]

Mission, then, must be grounded in praxis, which entails commitment to and solidarity with the poor and oppressed. According to liberation theologians, "orthopraxis" is more important for the Church today than "orthodoxy"—that is, proper practice of Christian faith is more important than correct formulation of doctrine. Although this emphasis upon "praxis" is understandable, it is a mistake, in my judgment, to pit orthopraxis against orthodoxy. Right thinking and right acting are equally essential for the effective witness of the Church.

To sum up, the centrifugal mission of the Church is to be interpreted theocentrically, as based in the triune God's missionary activity in the world. That is, mission is grounded in the Christian doctrine of God and not in ecclesiology. Furthermore, although mission is essential to the Church, the life of the Christian community, which includes worship, cannot be reduced solely to its mission. Again, missionary activity requires both verbal proclamation and responsible social action. Deeds without words are ambiguous, words without deeds ring hollow. Next, mission to persons and mission to social structures are equally required. Finally, it is my conviction that one's understanding of mission will inevitably be greatly influenced by one's view of the world, a subject to which we now turn.

CHURCH-WORLD RELATIONS

Groups of Christians engaged in God's mission in the world will be affected for good or ill by their basic attitude toward that world. If the world, defined now as that space or human experience that is "not Church," is considered to be a place of darkness dominated by the powers of evil, then the tendency is to fear or to hate it, and thus either to avoid it as much as possible or to enter the hostile territory to do battle with evil, realizing all the time the risk of "crucifixion." If, on the contrary, the world is looked upon essentially as God's good creation but one that has been adversely affected by human sin, then it will be approached with a feeling of solidarity and at least a modicum of optimism.

The term "world," of course, has more than one meaning. In its simplest sense it refers to the whole of created reality, but in the New Testament it often designates humanity in rebellion against God or even a personal power that possesses humankind. The same Johannine writings, for instance, can at one point declare God's love for the world (Jn 3:16) and at another admonish Christians not to love the world (1 Jn 2:15).[11] In the same vein, Christians are often said to be "in the world but not of it," by which is meant that they, like all other human beings, are part of God's creation and yet they are not to be dominated by and give their ultimate loyalty to that which is created but rather to the Creator and Redeemer, God.

In his book *Christ and Culture,* H. Richard Niebuhr presents a helpful typology of five different ways Christ is understood to be related to culture, or, for our purpose, how Church and world are related.[12] At one end of the spectrum we have "Christ against culture," *radical Christians* who perceive the world as a realm under the power of evil, a region of darkness to be avoided. At the opposite end we find "the Christ of culture," *cultural Christians* who feel at home in the community of culture and find in the world a mixture of movements and institutions, some good and some evil. Between these extremes Niebuhr places the majority of Christians in a middle position which has three branches: the *synthetists* of "Christ above culture" who affirm both Christ and culture, although Christ is far above culture; the *dualists* of "Christ and culture in paradox" who view culture as godless and unavoidable but whose real interest is in the dualism between the righteous God and sinful human beings; and the *transformationists* of "Christ the transformer of culture" who look upon the world as corrupted good rather than simply bad, and who, because of God's ongoing creative activity in the world, believe that the world can be transformed for the better.

One of the most revealing aspects of Niebuhr's analysis is the conception of sin involved in each type. For radicals, the world, dominated by animal passions, is the chief locus of sin, whereas the Church, as the holy communion, can be free of sin. At the other end of the spectrum, however, cultural Christians tend to locate sin mainly in social institutions, evil being confined to selected bad institutions. They believe it possible that sin does not reach into the depths of human personality. Individuals who obey the laws of God are able to be free of sin in "a citadel of righteousness in the high place of the personal spirit."[13] Both these otherwise dissimilar groups have in common the rejection of the idea of "total depravity," in the sense that sin, with its effects, extends to all humans and involves all of human nature. Instead, they believe that there can be a realm free of sin.

All three types in the middle of the spectrum have a more serious view of sin and thus of the human predicament. Sin is considered to be universal and radical, a rebellion against God that ends in egocentricity and alienation. Salvation is believed to be possible only through God's redemptive action centered in Christ's death and resurrection. For synthetists, God operates in both Church and world, and the Church rejoices to cooperate with civic virtues and just institutions, but salvation comes only through the sacramental grace it imparts. Dualists see sin mirrored in the cross, and from that perspective they declare all humans and their works infected with godlessness and therefore corrupt. In this situation, Christians can be spoken of only in paradoxes, as simultaneously sinners and yet justified through faith in Christ; they must live by the Gospel alone in a society that is unconquerably immoral. Transformationists join synthetists in a more hopeful attitude toward culture than the dualists exhibit. For them, sin involves a radical departure from God and a clinging to a created good; humans and their culture are corrupted in the sense of being warped, twisted, and misdirected; and through God's present activity in history, persons and their societies can be converted and changed for the better.

In his book, Niebuhr's discussions of these types of relations between Church and world are extensive and rich with illustrations. But even in the sketches above it becomes apparent that the typology is a useful one for judging the attitudes of churches and groups of Christians toward and their involvement in socially-oriented activity to change unjust conditions in the world. From the outset, however, we must recognize that U.S. churches, even those traditionally classified as sectarian, demonstrate an astonishing amount of cultural conformity—a phenomenon known as "civil religion." The various traditional Church-world stances of the churches tend to differ considerably from their present-day positions. Furthermore, counter-cultural prophetic protests, exemplified recently by the civil rights and anti-war movements, have generally cut across denominational boundaries. The effect of these protests, supported by a growing theology of liberation, has been salutary. The pricked consciences of many members of the churches have caused them to re-examine their churches' social policies in the light of oppressive realities, the increasing political conservatism in the country, and the frightening shift from "social welfare industrial capitalism" to what has been called "national security industrial capitalism."[14]

Considered in terms of Niebuhr's typology, most of the action/reflection groups encountered in the Woodstock Theological Center's Project are to be located, in my judgment, within the categories of "Christ above culture" or "Christ transforming culture," although probably no group represents a pure type. The Sojourners, for instance, would probably locate themselves in the "Christ against culture" type, and yet they exhibit none of the withdrawal and perfectionist traits normally associated with radical Christians and are in reality close to the "Christ and culture in paradox" position. The one type, it seems, that is unrepresented among these groups is that of "the Christ of culture," and in this they clash with the prevailing tendencies of much of U.S. Christianity.

THEOLOGICAL REFLECTION ON WORSHIP AND MISSIONARY ACTION

Theology is that function of the Church whereby critical rational attention is focused on the work of the people of God. That work in the broad sense is liturgy (*leitourgia* in common Greek parlance means a public work or service), which includes both devoted worship of God and faithful service for God in the world. Theological reflection is a necessary moment in the undulating life of the Church between worship and missionary action. Its task is to aid the Church to respond in the best possible way to Christ's twofold commandment that we should love God wholeheartedly and should love our neighbors as ourselves. The task is a critical one, because the Church must always make its decisions in the light of the Gospel, that is, on the basis of God's word revealed in Jesus Christ and interpreted in the tradition of the Church. The task is an ongoing one, for the world situation to which the Church must speak and in which it must act and be acted upon is forever changing.

Theological thinking is taking place in the churches all the time, and it is by no means confined to professional theologians and clergy. Every Christian is, or at least should be, a theologian in some degree, namely, to the extent that he or she thinks about God in relation to the world and about the world in relation to God. Groups of Christians who share intensively in communal life and missionary activity of a social and political kind also should share the labors of theological reflection, for each member can contribute from his or her experience both of the world and of the Gospel. This has proven to be the case with those groups that have been involved in the Woodstock Project.

Experience can never be separated from theological reflection, because those who reflect are existing historical beings whose very language and process of thinking have been shaped by cultural experience. In theology, reflection on human existence and reflection on the contents of divine revelation are interrelated, and the crucial questions have to do with who is doing the reflecting, whose experience is being reflected upon, how the revelation of God is conceived, and what is to be considered normative or authoritative. Contemporary theologians interested in liberating humans from oppressive social conditions and in changing the world to a condition of *shalom* are insisting that theological reflection be widened to include more and more lay Christians, especially those who are experiencing oppression. They are demanding that scientific social analysis be a regular part of the reflective process, and they are arguing that the central thrust of divine revelation is found in the biblical stories of the exodus of the Hebrew slaves from Egypt and of Jesus' announcement of the intent of his ministry when he read from the Book of Isaiah in the synagogue at Nazareth: "The Spirit of the Lord is upon me, because he has anointed me to preach good news to the poor. He has sent me to proclaim release to the captives and recovering of sight to the blind, to set at liberty those who are oppressed, to proclaim the acceptable year of the Lord" (Lk 4:16–19).

In the churches today there is a dangerous division between personal pietists and social activists, between those who believe Christian faith has to do primarily with saving the souls of individuals and those who believe it requires active work for justice and peace in society. The danger of the former group is that they will emphasize personal nurture and spiritual disciplines and perhaps even humanitarian relief but will accept the status quo in society, with all its systemic and structural injustices. The danger of the latter group is that they will become so engrossed in the problems of the world that they will neglect the wellsprings of prayer and worship which strengthen and guide their actions.

Such a dichotomy is, of course, harmful and unwarranted. The Bible, in my judgment, witnesses to a triune God who in love seeks *both* the conversion and growth toward maturity of individuals *and* the establishment of the divine kingdom as a community of love, justice, and peace. Furthermore, the Bible views the human being as a creature who is fully human only when in a right relation to others, that is, in a free relation of love to God and to neighbors. There are, in reality, only individuals-in-community and communities-consisting-of-individuals. Sin, which is essentially rebellion against God, also always involves the breaking of the loving relation to the neighbor and the neighborhood. Thus it ends in egocentricity and individualism.

As Jesus Christ's own earthly-historical form of existence (Karl Barth), the Church, to be an effective witness, must follow the Lord's own life-pattern of withdrawal for worship and prayer and of moving out to witness by word and deed in the midst of society. If the Church is to be an efficacious sign of God's coming kingdom, then its theological reflection must be done in a pattern regularly related to individual and communal worship on the one hand and work for a more just and humane society on the other.[15]

THE CHURCH AS SERVANT

The greatest danger in defining the Church lies in reducing it to something less than it is. The Church is—a mystery! Or, to say the same thing differently, the Church is *of God,* which means there is a divine dimension to this human community that distinguishes it from every other human community. To be sure, that this is so is a matter of faith: the trustful conviction that the Church is called by God, grounded in Jesus Christ, and empowered by the Holy Spirit. The Church, then, is fundamentally a movement of the Spirit; it lives by divine grace and knows that it is upheld solely by the presence and promise of the triune God.

However, the Church is not only of God; it is also made up of quite ordinary human beings whose earthiness and creatureliness and fallibility are only too evident. The Church consists *of people*—people with a variety of gifts and limitations who, because of Jesus Christ, have embarked on a new way of life that has as its goal eternal life in the kingdom of God. They know that, in spite of their unworthiness, God is on their side, has forgiven their sins, has mysteriously turned their lives in a new direction, and has given them a special responsibility toward the world. That responsibility may perhaps best be summed up by two words: witness and service, although no words can adequately connote the richness and variety of the Christian vocation. But this much is certain: the Church is commanded to witness to the love of God for the world as this has been revealed in the life, death, and resurrection of Jesus, and to serve the world by ministering to its needs, especially the needs of those who are weak and downtrodden. As God has loved the world in Christ, so too the Christian community is to love the world on God's behalf.

The Church, like the sons of Zebedee in the Gospel story, is always tempted not to serve but to lord it over others. Such self-aggrandizement was specifically prohibited by Jesus who admonished his disciples in these words: "It shall not be so among you; but whoever would be great among you must be your servant, and whoever would be first among you must be your slave, even as the Son of Man came not to be served but to serve, and to give his life as a ransom for many" (Mt 20:26–28). Of the various models of the Church today, that of servant is probably the most appropriate for our time—as well as the most difficult to fulfill.[16]

The Church is called to serve God in the world by proclaiming the Gospel and by taking the side of "the least of these"—Christ's brothers and sisters who are hungry and thirsty, who are strangers in the world, who are naked and sick and in prison (Mt 25:31–46). That is, Christ has promised to be present and active in two specific locations in the world: wherever his liberating word is preached and enacted and wherever there are those in need of food, drink, and clothing, of friendship, healing, and liberation. The Church is to function as Christ's servants in both these situations, realizing that Christ is *already there* through the power of the Spirit and thus that through this service the Church is brought into communion with its Lord, who himself rules by serving.

The strategic importance of action/reflection groups such as those encountered in this Project is that they provide concrete examples of the servant model of the Church. They are keenly aware that God calls the Church to proclaim the good news of reconciliation in Christ and to work for justice and peace in society, but they also know that to perform this mission they need the constant guidance and empowerment of the Spirit. And so they pray together, worship together, reflect together, and struggle together to accomplish the will of God in the world. In this way they help overcome the stultifying dichotomies within the churches between activists and pietists, clergy and laity, blacks and whites, women and men, rich and poor. They work for egalitarian race, sex, and class relations, economic sharing and cooperation, non-violence, and non-cooperation with institutions in society that endanger the human family. They deliberately widen the basis of the ministry to include all the faithful, and in a communal life committed to new social, economic, and political possibilities they challenge the world to new directions and help shape the Church of the future.

When functioning effectively as communities of love that go forth to serve God and their neighbors in a broken world, action/reflection groups become like a light set upon a hill that illumines the darkness of the world and like leaven that transforms its structures. Thus they truly embody the Church and become "parables of missionary action."[17] In their life together and life for others they become a sign or sacrament of Christ's presence in and for the world. They represent "hope in action,"[18] which, after all, is a good definition of mission.

NOTES

1. For more detailed information on the various groups, see William Newell's chapter in this volume.

2. See John Haughey's discussion of the function of prayer and functionless prayer in Chapter 5 of this volume.

3. For a history of the developments in missionary theology, see David J. Bosch, *Witness to the World: The Christian Mission in Theological Perspective* (Atlanta: John Knox Press, 1980), Chapters 16 and 17. Also pertinent is J. Verkuyl, *Contemporary Missiology: An Introduction* (Grand Rapids: Wm. B. Eerdmans Publishing Co., 1978), Chapter III.

4. This is the thesis of Walbert Buhlmann in his *The Coming of the Third Church* (Maryknoll, N.Y.: Orbis Books, 1977).

5. These views are prominent in J.C. Hoekendijk, *The Church Inside Out* (London: SCM Press, 1966), in Thomas Wieser, ed., *Planning for Mission: Working Papers on the New Quest for Missionary Communities* (New York: The U.S. Conference for the World Council of Churches, 1966), and in *The Church for Others: Two Reports on the Missionary Structure of the Congregation* (Geneva: World Council of Churches, 1967). See also Johannes Aagaard's "Mission after Uppsala 1968" in Gerald H. Anderson and Thomas F. Stransky, C.S.P., eds., *Mission Trends No. 1* (New York: Paulist Press and Grand Rapids, Mich.: Wm. B. Eerdmans Publishing Co., 1974), pp. 13–21.

6. William B. Frazier, M.M., "Guidelines for a New Theology of Mission," in Anderson and Stransky, *op. cit.*, p. 27. Thomas Clarke's discussion of experience as a source of divine revelation throws further light on this issue. See Chapter 1 of this volume.

7. The terms "evangelicals" and "ecumenicals" is used by David J. Bosch in contrasting two missionary models: *op. cit.*, Chapter 4.

8. Monika Hellwig's essay in this volume is a helpful survey and evaluation of the various claims about the importance of the poor for the Church.

9. Alfred Hennelly describes and discusses these "base communities" in Chapter 3 of this volume.

10. Lee E. Snook, "The Uses of Experience in Recent Theology," *Word and World: Theology for Christian Ministry*, 1/3 (Summer 1981), p. 297.

11. For further elaboration of this point, see Jouette Bassler's chapter in this volume.

12. H. Richard Niebuhr, *Christ and Culture* (New York: Harper and Brothers, 1951).

13. *Ibid.*, pp. 112f.

14. Three stages of industrial capitalism, from "Laissez-Faire" to "Social Welfare" to "National Security," are convincingly outlined in Joe Holland and Peter Henriot, S.J., *Social Analysis: Linking Faith and Justice* (Washington, D.C.: Center of Concern, 1980).

15. John Haughey and Joe Holland also discuss the tension between personal pietists and social activists in their chapters.

16. For a helpful discussion of various models, see Avery Dulles, S.J., *Models of the Church* (Garden City, N.Y.: Doubleday & Co., 1974).

17. Thomas Wieser, "Introduction," in Thomas Wieser, ed. *Planning for Mission,* p. 11.

18. This is Hans Jochen Margull's definition, as given in Thomas Wieser, ed., *Planning for Mission,* p. 34.

12
Community Reflection

Larry L. Rasmussen

Early in his career as a Reformer, Martin Luther attended to liturgy. He proposed three kinds of Mass as part of a reforming church. By the time of the writing cited below, he had already published a revision of the Latin Mass, the *Formula Missae.* He does not contemplate further changes for the time being and only notes that it would be wrong to discontinue Mass in the Latin tongue. His attention next turns to the creation of a *Deutsche Messe, A German Mass and Order of Service,* "arranged for the sake of the unlearned lay folk ... with which we are now concerned."[1]

Luther's hope was that worship in the vernacular might move some "to believe and become Christians."[2] His picture of these "unlearned" and only half-believing lay folk is somewhat amusing but it is clear what purpose reformed liturgy was to play.

> These two orders of service [the Latin and German Masses] must be used publicly, in the churches, for all the people, among whom are many who do not believe and are not yet Christians. Most of them stand around and gape, hoping to see something new, just as if we were holding a service among the Turks or the heathen in a public square or out in a field. That is not yet a well-ordered congregation, in which Christians could be ruled according to the gospel; on the contrary, the gospel must be publicly preached to move [such people] to believe and become Christians.[3]

Yet the intriguing proposal is the third. This service should be

... a truly evangelical order and should not be held in a public place for all sorts of people. But those who want to be Christians in earnest and who profess the gospel with hand and mouth should sign their names and meet alone in a house somewhere to pray, to read, to baptize, to receive the sacrament, and to do other Christian works. According to this order, those who do not lead Christian lives could be known, reproved, corrected, cast out, or excommunicated, according to the rule of Christ, Matthew 18 [15–17]. Here one could also solicit benevolent gifts to be willingly given and distributed to the poor, according to Paul's example, 2 Corinthians 9. Here one would need a good short [catechization] on the Creed, the Ten Commandments, and the Our Father.

In short, if one had the kind of people and persons who wanted to be Christians in earnest, the rules and regulations would soon be ready. But as yet I neither can nor desire to begin such a congregation or assembly or to make rules for it. For I have not yet the people or persons for it, nor do I see many who want it. But if I should be requested to do it and could not refuse with a good conscience, I should gladly do my part and help as best I can. In the meanwhile the two above-mentioned orders of service must suffice. And to train the young and to call and attract others to faith, I shall—besides preaching—help to further such public services for the people, until Christians who earnestly love the Word find each other and join together. For if I should try to make it up out of my own need, it might turn into a sect. For we Germans are a rough, rude, and reckless people, with whom it is hard do anything, except in cases of dire need.[4]

The subject of this chapter is not Martin Luther's liturgical reforms. Rather, it is the life of "those who want to be Christians in earnest" and who, "earnestly lov[ing] the Word, [have found] each other and [joined] together." The form of this life together may be the kind of house church Luther here yearns for, or some other ar-

rangement of close Christian contact. It is, in any event, such communities of self-conscious efforts to live by "the rule of Christ" that
we have in mind.

Their worship life is not irrelevant, of course. On the contrary!
But it is not directed to attracting people to faith in the first instance
so much as it is celebrating the faith already claimed and proclaimed.
Some "rough, rude, and reckless" people, Germans or otherwise,
may even be allowed! They would only need be among "the kind of
people and persons who wanted to be Christians in earnest. . . ."

What would the components of such Christian community be?
What, at least, would be the essential components of *reflection* in
such Christian communities? That question sets the subject of this
essay.

GROUNDING IN THE JESUS STORY

We begin with the notion of story. Many in the community need
to know the normative story. We will call it simply "the Jesus story."
If no one knows the Jesus story, the community as a Christian community ceases to exist. Indeed, if the Jesus story is not remembered,
even for one generation, the entire Church would, as Church, expire,
at least until the story were rediscovered. No Jesus story, no Christian community.

But why story? Because of the nature of story and because
Christianity in its essence is a story. Like all stories, Christianity is,
in Frederick Buechner's words, "a time, a place, a set of characters,
and the implied promise . . . that something is coming, something interesting or significant or exciting is about to happen."[5]

In a very telling passage Buechner continues:

> If we whittle away long enough, it is a story that we come
> to at last. And if we take even the fanciest and most meta-
> physical kind of theologian or preacher and keep on ques-
> tioning him far enough—Why is this so? All right, but why
> is *that* so? Yes, but how do we know that it's so?—even he
> is forced finally to take off his spectacles and push his
> books off to one side and say, "Once upon a time there was
> . ." and then everybody leans forward a little and starts to
> ·listen. . . .[6]

What good stories—all good stories—do is draw us into their world. But more than that, what powerful stories do—like the Jesus story—is mold people's identities and their sense of world and reality. Powerful stories—like the Jesus story—create a basic orientation for those who are drawn into them. They shape our perception of life and hone our sensitivities. They help form commitments and nurture loyalties. They yield transforming insight. And they solicit our own involvement in pursuing the story further.

What the *Gospel* does, in and through story, is *"form and reform personal identities in a decisive (or transforming) way."*[7] Indeed, what defines the Church as Church is the shaping and reshaping of members' identities in accord with the Jesus story. The means are many—worship, prayer, study, play, conversation, celebration, grief—but the reality is that of joining the life particulars of gathered Christians to the life particulars of the Jesus story and to those who through the centuries have endeavored to align their own stories with his.

For this to happen, members of the community have to know the normative story. They have to tell and retell it in ways that "connect" with the story of the particular Christian community and the stories of its members. That means liturgy, whether "high" or "low," "formal" or "informal." Luther was not off the mark in pursuing liturgical reform early on. For liturgy is the ritual re-enactment of decisive parts of the formative story. It grafts the life of the present Christian community into the life of the tale of the centuries. One of the components of intentional Christian community, then, is the presence of people, lay or clergy, who know the story and can give meaningful shape to community life in the form of its liturgical enactment.

Despite its tenacity here, liturgy is not the only component of Christian community and its reflection; thus we turn to that remembering and telling of the story which takes the form of teaching.

"The teaching" was a prominent part of the earliest Christian communities. In the Pauline lists of gifts (*charismata*), only that of proclamation (or "prophecy") is mentioned more often than teaching. The proclamatory and the didactic gifts were central, though all gifts were considered vital. Indeed, what later came to be called "apostolic succession" was, in its origins, reference to a succession in teaching that stretched back to the community around Jesus. ("I learned from Polycarp, who learned from John ..." etc.) And, of course, a prime and perhaps first title for the one about whom the normative story is told is that of "Teacher." The Gospels are laced with phrases like: "On one of his teaching journeys round the villages ..." (Mk 6:7) and "When a crowd gathered round him once again, he followed his usual practice and taught them" (Mk 10:1). From the point of origins onward, teaching is crucial to the community. It is the community's telling and probing of the normative story, thinking it through and thinking about it, to the end that the community might be built up as a faithful community.

"Thinking" is no doubt too narrow a term, since the community teaches in many ways other than strictly verbal and cognitive ones. Drama and dance, music, story-telling and liturgical enactment and social action are, or can be, part and parcel of the community's rendering of the Jesus story to mine its many meanings. Open debate and table conversation are also media. Teaching is not communicated solely by way of the formal discourse of instruction and study, though that is a common form and a proper one.

Teaching is a community enterprise, even when abilities vary widely. Some will be better with the children, some will excel in non-verbal teaching, some will write, some will raise the needed and unaddressed questions, some will listen especially well.

If there are professionally trained theologians in the community, they are also there for its teaching life. It cannot be underscored strongly enough that the lives of such persons should be *organically linked to local Christian communities* and their work *should root in that tie.* The "full-time theologian" must know his or her community well, from the inside, since the task at hand is the community's collective appropriation of the faith. And that task cannot be done well apart from intimate touch with the realities of the community itself. A community is, after all, a community in its own particularity and not a replication in miniature of some Platonic understanding of "the Church."

The overwhelming tendency has been to let the doing of theology fall to the pastor as local theologian and to the professor as theologian in university and seminary centers of learning. But there is no necessary fixing of the office there. In any event, the task is to root theology in the teaching life of the disciplined community in order to enhance the whole community's abilities to understand and articulate the faith it professes. The measure of success would be the proliferation of lay theologians within the community. The measure of failure would be the isolation of theologians in universities and seminaries and the existence of pan-clergy study groups.

COMMUNITY REFLECTION

We now move to the essay's subject proper—community reflection.

The Jesus story "is a many-sided tale."[8] Indeed, there is not one story but four in the New Testament canon itself, and others beyond. Moreover, the Jesus story is always an interpreted story. It was that in the very earliest Christian communities[9] and it remains that for communities today. The portrait of Jesus "changes" in the sense that it is rendered differently in different times and places—often by the same Christian community in the course of its own life. In fact, if the community is a living one, the expectation should be that of changing understandings, whether of the teaching of Jesus, the meaning of baptism, the understanding of the Eucharist, the sense of the community's mission, or whatever aspect of the story is under consideration.

Yet this living, developing, changing Jesus story is also *the* normative one for the community. And here enters an important community task: to ask *why and on what grounds* the community has chosen the rendering of the normative story that it has, and *why and on what grounds* it has shifted in its understandings.

This is the *critical* element in community reflection, its most probing undertaking. There is no safe place beyond the reach of the "why" question and one should not be sought. If a particular community has shifted emphasis from political engagement as its impassioned articulation of the faith for its time and place to focused pastoral nurturing of the "internal" life of the community, then we should want to know why and on what grounds. A reply that the community has been so led by the Spirit is not an answer that stops with the statement itself; it is an invitation to further probing. Or, if the community has *not* made such shifts, then the question is *why* the chosen stance continues as the proper rendering of the Jesus story, given other possibilities either extant or imaginable. Indeed, good reflection is relentless. It even asks why the particular understanding of the Jesus story was chosen in the first place. This forces the community to "re-view" the old, old story and its appropriation of it.

At this juncture, community reflection sometimes joins dimensions of "conversion" or "transformation." It is not "prophetic" in the proper sense, since the prophet's word is one *to* the community, a thunderous "thus saith the Lord" that addresses the community face forward and with full force. Rather, we are talking of the community's exploration of its formative understandings. This is part of its ongoing teaching ministry. Differently said, it is not the heights of *kerygma* (proclamation) that are confronted here, but the very deepest reaches of *didache* (teaching). Yet the *outcome* is often akin to the prophetic challenge in that it entails significant change, even conversion.

When Paul, in Romans 12, exhorts the community not to be patterned after the current age, but "transformed" by the "renewing of your minds," he links the "remaking" of minds with the transformation of "your whole nature." Two things should not escape us here. Transformation occurs in community—in this case, the Church. (Paul's pronouns are all plural.) Secondly, transformation is by way of a change or correction of mind. In fact, this is the etymological meaning of the word for repentance that is attributed to Jesus himself.

Still, if significant change occurs, it is not because of the sheer fact of community reflection. It is because that community endeavor is organically tied to its socio-historical life. Negatively, it is because the community's theology has not gone the way of so much theology and become abstracted from the social location in which it arose.

Effective reflection, then, occurs only when it arises from the depths of the community's own life and returns there. It can come from outside only when "outside" is also vital "inside" (e.g., Paul to the church in Rome).

Here the basic Christian communities in Latin America teach us. A certain cycle is present in their life together. It has three "moments," though not necessarily in the following order.[10]

1. *Analysis.* One moment is community analysis. Questions are

raised in the community as it faces some specific situation in its life together. The questions may arise in response to some crisis—lack of adequate or affordable housing, the spectre of war, a tragedy in the lives of some community members, the threat of worsened unemployment. Or the occasion might be certain turning points in life— the celebration of a birth, a rite of passage into a next stage of life with its attendant responsibilities, the joy of a marriage, the change of careers, support for those struggling with divorce, grieving over the dying. Whether crisis events, the marking of human passages, or something else, one moment in reflection is analysis of the matter as raised in and by the community.

Often the initial step is simply recounting the story surrounding the matter-at-hand. This is crucial but it is not yet analysis. Analysis, as analysis, is a taking apart, a sorting, a probing and puzzling. It requires specific skills if it is to be done well—the use of tools for social analysis, psychological analysis, historical and cultural analysis. But these are no more locked into the arcane ways of "professionals" than theology is captured by professional theologians. With a little help, which can usually be found in or acquired by the community, illuminating analysis can be done.

2. *Scripture and Tradition.* Another moment is biblical and reflective. The texts appropriate to the Church year, or other texts, are studied by the community as a whole with an eye to what they meant for the communities out of which they came and to which they were initially addressed. Secondly, they are considered with a view to the meaning they cast upon the studying community and its situation-at-hand.

The first entails exegesis. The community seeks to understand the text at the point of its origins and its movement and place in the canon. Matters of historical context, the literary nature and organization of the text, its theological dimensions—these are all pertinent dimensions. To uncover them may require special resources and training. But they can be attained and in fact are usually present in most communities in surprising degree. What we want to underscore again is the engagement of many in the community, perhaps all, and not assigning exegesis to one person or a small coterie of the like-minded. We also want to underscore another earlier point—meanings are frequently discerned and communicated non-verbally as well as verbally. A group which "acts out" via impromptu drama what it "hears" and "sees" in the texts often finds itself leading others into deeper levels of the story. (Here children can join in the teaching itself.)

Exegesis moves on, in community discussion, to the meaning of the Scriptures for the situation under discussion. The community moves between perceptions of the original meanings of the texts and perceptions of meanings for current concerns. What is the meaning, for us today? Arriving at that should entail consultation with the tradition. How have other struggling communities of faith understood this biblical word?

In any event, this second move is much like that which Luther named "living Word"—a genuine encounter with God-in-Christ, mediated by an encounter with Scripture, while one is grappling with the realities of some present concern.

The two moments described thus far—community analysis and wrestling with Scripture and tradition—are not as cleanly divided as our discussion has rendered them. Indeed, part of community reflection itself is awareness of the interplay. Any interpretation of Scripture and tradition mirrors the community's own profile and location. What is heard and seen in the texts, indeed what is *capable* of being seen and heard, is inextricably linked to the particulars of time and place, class, culture, sex, race, language, etc. And to be keenly aware of this is to introduce critical self-consciousness into the process of exegesis and interpretation itself.

At the same time, transforming insight ("revelation") often comes when an apparently alien perspective from another time, place and quarter invades—when, for example, a biblical text illumines the horizons of the present in a way the community didn't expect but which is readily recognized. Then the community's own self-awareness is enhanced by insights from elsewhere.

Community analysis becomes, then, part of the discussion that moves between the texts in their origins and the texts now in this community, and exegesis and interpretation help illumine the community's own world. The community's concrete experiences find their way into a living tradition and a living tradition finds its way into those experiences.

All of this is, in larger perspective, the grafting of the Jesus story into the community's story and vice versa. Darrell Jodock nicely captures a portion of what we have pointed to:

> To read the Bible as story is to sense the kind of response people made to God, the response of Israel at different periods, of the church in different places, the response of patriarchs, prophets, and apostles. This diverse set of responses becomes the stuff from which clear guidance for life style is fashioned. Yet even before such clarity is achieved there is a sense of the appropriate and inappropriate which comes along with the stories. This basic "sense" discovers in those stories neither readily transferable universal norms nor the irrelevant attitudes of an archaic document; it discovers there instead the profile of a life style along with the freedom to apply it creatively in the present.[11]

3. *Directives for Action.* Determining directives for action and creative application is the third moment in the cycle. It follows from the other two. Given analysis and given confrontation with the texts in the community and through the tradition, what is faithful response? That response may be directed both to the "internal" life of the community—its life together with one another—and its "external" life—its life as a community in the wider world. Both pastoral and missional dimensions are real in this moment. Both represent the quest for fitting action.

In sum, analysis, wrestling with Scripture and tradition, and directives for action are all *part of* community reflection and all entail teaching in and by the community *as a whole,* whatever the agreed-upon division of labor required to do the tasks well.

COMMUNITY INVOLVEMENT: IMPASSIONED ETHICAL REFLECTION

We must probe further. What has been written thus far could have been done quite apart from consultation with the Christian communities we contacted in this project. What has been said may be helpful *to* them but it is not new material drawn *from* them.

Their contribution is considerable and much of it directly intersects the subject of community reflection. The remainder of this essay gathers together the experience of many Christian communities around their *moral and ethical deliberation* in particular. Within the broad enterprise of community reflection, how do such groups come to clarity on the behavioral consequences of holding to the Jesus story? This is "ethical" inquiry. What, in different words, are the dynamics whereby the three "moments" described above provide guidance for shaping community character and conduct? (Character and conduct are the focal concerns of ethics.)

To begin our discussion is to distinguish the reflection we have in mind from the standard brands present in much literature and some practice. Community ethical reflection, arising from engagement, is an under-developed project. Where it is in fact done, it goes on without much critical attention to procedure. So these final pages will necessarily be exploratory and hopefully suggestive, rather than the passing along of a matured tradition.

We start with a gloss on "knowing." For the communities we have spoken with, knowledge is closely tied to engagement and the particulars of community experience. It is the kind of knowing that comes by immersion rather than detachment, by participation rather than distanced observation. It is existential and intimate. Its materials are those of the members' own identities, interests and traditions, experienced with a sense of immediacy around specific events and occasions. Other materials are drawn upon only if it is expected that they will be illuminative for community engagement and nurture. This is knowledge out of a story-in-process in which those who use the knowledge are part of the tale itself.

Much theological/ethical knowledge and reflection has *not* proceeded from such immersion in local community experience and has not taken seriously the particular kind of knowing there involved. The "grassroots" theologizing of which we speak appears quite different from that which takes place in seminaries and in the groves of academe.[12]

How has deliberation proceeded in "professional" circles (i.e., in university and seminary quarters)? A certain cast is seen there, probably explained by the following concerns.

For a long while in Western traditions there has existed a deep suspicion of individual and group interests as distorting and corrupting factors in moral judgment. From Augustine to Reinhold Niebuhr writers have underscored the profound skewing and self-serving impact of our particular loyalties upon our perception and judgment. That I am white, male, bourgeois, American, capitalist, and Protestant is regarded as strong grounds for suspicion rather than as the locus of moral resources for valid and vital moral knowledge and deliberation. So the tradition has it that "good ethics" proceeds in such a way as to minimize the impact of particular interests.

A tradition that stretches back even further is that of ethics as the quest for the *universal* right and good. That which can be regarded as right and good for all, that which can be willed for all, has real moral integrity. If we add to this the strong influence of modern science upon our way of knowing, then it becomes clear why impersonal rationality or "objectivity" has become a hallmark of much ethical reflection. Modern science prizes knowledge that is as free as possible from the observers' biases.

Under these influences, morality with the most integrity is morality which is as free as possible from subjective beliefs and from group bias, which can be formulated from a point of view capable of being held by anyone of rational mind, and which can be applied to all.

Differently said, moral judgments should not depend for their validity only upon the particular truth claims of particular communities and traditions. Indeed, what is ruled out is reliance upon experience exclusively bound to the unique time and place of the moral agent. The peculiarities of the person's own story—community, class, race, sex, nationality, creed, etc.—are to be "transcended" when seeking valid moral judgments. It is important to point out that this understanding of proper ethical formulation does not deny experience as a source of morality, but it abstracts from it to a very high level and judges it by what is assumed to be a commonly held faculty of relatively untainted reason.

Given these concerns for the universally valid, and given the suspicion about individual and group bias, the most congenial style of moral deliberation has been one we shall call "juridical." In this tradition, ethical reflection proceeds best when it resembles the operation of good law. And good "ethicists" resemble good lawyers, judges and juries.

Analogies should not be pressed too firmly or too far, but we can venture at least the following as descriptive of such ethics, Christian and otherwise. All persons and cases of a like character ought to be judged alike. The materials of judging are moral principles which are at their best when they are generalizable and can be agreed to by all on the basis of "disinterested" reason. Those doing the judging are at their best when they set aside the passions of their own history and seek instead to view the case at hand from the point of view of the impartial observer. Objectivity and detachment, though alternating with empathy, are key virtues for those who are to render a moral verdict.

Great attention is given to "the facts." It is imperative that evidence be sound and thorough, including what can be known about motives, conditions at the time, extenuating circumstances, and so on. The use of impartial and universal norms is matched by a search for all the possibly pertinent data in the case at hand.

The procedure, then, is to move from a high level of abstraction and objectivity, where moral norms exist apart from individual and group identity, to application in specific cases, with all their particularity. It proceeds by way of careful logic that appeals to the impartial rationality of a jury which tries to keep the interests of its own members from intruding in ways that would distort an "objective" outcome.

A strong case for ethical reflection in this mode has often been made, and we will return to its strengths. For the moment, it is perhaps apparent that it does not wholly "fit" the style of the close Christian communities of which we speak, even when they employ it. In such communities it is, after all, precisely the *particular* beliefs, experiences, symbols, loyalties and commitments which are the source of moral vitality and the strongest influences in moral deliberation. Furthermore, the community feels they *should* be. Highly specific interests and intimately held symbols are what animate decision-making. And at base it is the normative Jesus story—a particular story that cannot be exchanged for a different story—that sets the framework for the community's ethics. To somehow "transcend" or bracket the particulars of the normative story and the community's specific expression of it is to leave behind precisely that which is regarded as morally significant.

There are analogies which suggest themselves as illuminative for thinking about moral deliberation in such communities. One is the manner in which decisions are made within relationships of intimacy—a family, for example, or among close friends. Within intimate relationships moral sensitivities develop over time as part of the relationship itself. The non-transferable factors of the relationship itself are morally vital—the parent's relationship to the child, one friend's to the other, the grandchildren's to the grandparents, one lover's to the other, etc. Whole sets of obligations are learned and understood. Moral norms are involved, of course, but they are internalized as part of an identity and "story" fashioned in the course of the growing relationship itself. These norms are invoked, even if not articulated, when the ethical question emerges, "What should we do now in this case?" The reply is often as much "sensed" as argued, and what is sometimes called "intuition" becomes a highly significant way of knowing. Rational deliberation might very well take place but it never cuts its ties to what is intuitively sensed as "fitting in" with the salient relationships.

To the degree that life in a close Christian community approaches the dynamics of an extended family or the life together of close friends, this ethics of intuition in *koinonia* will likely be as prevalent as the juridical style.

Another pertinent analogy is the esthetic one. An artist "knows" in a different way from the scientist or lawyer. There is very careful attention to craft and technique, of course, but the entry into what is significant is by self-attachment and profound immersion, rather than purposefully distanced observation. Imagination and empathy are especially critical to knowing. Discernment of what the artist regards as "real" is the outcome.

There is logic, to be sure, but it is not so much the kind captured in syllogism and deduction, or even induction, as it is the logic of seeing things in their patterned relationships or imagining them constituted in a different way which yet holds together. "Story" and "vision" and "the whole" are more precise names for what is morally significant than are "law," "principles," "the case" and "the facts."

We might add that everything just said about the esthetic as a way of understanding can be said with equal force for mystical and contemplative traditions. Discernment is the key. And it comes by way of immersion, empathy and imagination, themselves assisted by a disciplined craft, by the "arts" of meditation.

At this juncture no proposal is offered that sets forth a combination of the familial and the artistic or mystical as a way of conceiving community ethics. But a plea is made that close Christian communities become more self-conscious about how they actually do, or might, proceed in such fashion. It would be a service to all if we were more sophisticated about the dynamics of moral guidance that proceeds from community intuition and common discernment, from joint immersion in common action, from shared feeling and vision, and from the shared sensibilities that are nurtured in the *koinonia.*[13]

Short of a detailed explication, we can sketch a general theory that combines the juridical and the artistic/familial. In this theory, these are not distinctive choices so much as tiers for community moral knowledge and ethical reflection.

First or basic moral knowledge is that acquired in intimacy and intense engagement. It is the knowledge that arises from deeply self-involving relationships. It is knowledge rooted in the experience of caring and being cared for, of acting and being acted upon in close community. It is filled with touch and voice and gesture and symbol and eating and drinking and playing and worshiping, the very texture of life. All the senses are engaged, character is shaped and re-shaped, attitudes and dispositions are formed and reformed, outlooks are fashioned and refashioned. It happens in one's most basic communities and is more affective and perhaps even mystical than it is cognitive, although the cognitive is also engaged and vital.

This is where Christian ethics is itself rooted. It is the ethics of an impassioned story, that of God-in-Christ. What matters is the passion and the details—God in the flesh of a particular Jew in Galilee during certain years of a human epoch under the Romans, announcing a specific message, joining certain people for table fellowship, asking of followers a particular way of life, meeting a certain kind of death on a given Friday, rising from the tomb of another Jew, breaking bread together again with his community, and on and on. The formative and normative story is inextricable from the details and from life-in-community. So are the ethics. The power is lost if the story is "summarized" in universal doctrine and principles that take on some life of their own.

Our conclusion is that the Christian community should plumb the depths of its particular story, keep returning to it, rather than set the details aside or abstract the universal from them.

If the affective and the particular is the ground level of community knowledge, is there also a strong place for the cognitive and the juridical? Yes—even an indispensable one. What roots in passion and moves to compassion can still be terribly wrong as an actual moral judgment. More is involved, and more is necessary, in making sound decisions. Powers of critical analysis and adjudication, and the ability to step back and see with a different eye, are hedges against intuition gone awry. Too, the juridical style's procedures for testing fairness (similar cases treated similarly), and its checks upon the constant tendency of individual and group bias to distort and corrupt, secure for community moral deliberation what the ethics of passion usually do not. A persistent Socratic and juridical strain thus complements a *koinonia* ethic. (From its side, the *koinonia* ethic knows far better the grounds of moral vitality and the power to move persons to action.)

CONCLUSION

Perhaps the best way to conclude this essay is to set forth succinctly the ways in which a close Christian community functions in the moral life of its members. This will draw together elements from the essay as a whole but arrange them in a manner which highlights moral dimensions.

1. The community is a shaper of the moral identity of its members. The Jesus story, as expressed in the life of the community, becomes the moral nexus for deciding fitting character and conduct. The life of the community as a whole—worship, play, common action, conversation—helps form the moral profile of the members. It was not an error to begin this essay with the central activity of the gathered community—liturgy. It is a vital component in the forging of community identity, including moral identity.

2. The community is a bearer of moral tradition. This is closely

connected to the forging of identity, of course. Moral growth and maturity includes "membership" in a moral tradition and being aware of that tradition as a part of us. This does not mean an uncritical stance. But it does mean being rooted. The moral tradition allows members to locate themselves among possibilities, and it supplies much of the content for their ethic.

3. The community is a community of moral deliberation. As the community faces decisions and probes directives for action, as it does analysis and weighs responses, it invariably engages in moral deliberation—"What ought we to do, on what grounds, for what reasons, and toward what ends?" "What are our responsibilities?" "Which course of action best reflects who we are as people of God?"

Here specifically ethical reflection probes the Christian moral life in much the same way that the earlier mentioned reflection pressed toward the baseline understandings of the normative story. That is, as the community uses certain moral norms and makes moral appeals, ethical reflection will want to know *why and on what grounds* these norms are invoked and these appeals are made. If some particular notion of justice or love is invoked for moral guidance, community ethical reflection will want their articulation and assessment, and their connections to the Jesus story. Ethical reflection will press for justification of the community's moral choices, in the sense of not only giving good reasons for the choices, but giving good reasons for the moral baselines *beneath* the community's moral choices. Eventually that will push the community to the very ground of its ethics in the Jesus story itself. Here ethical reflection passes over into basic community convictions and commitments.

Ethical reflection, then, is inherently self-critical. It keeps asking the probing "why" question. It insists upon scrutiny of the grounds of moral authority. It is best done in examination that is open to public debate, to pros and cons and vigorous argumentation. And when the community as a whole does it, it forecloses on the possibility that moral authority will reside, uncriticized, in only certain offices or persons.

Nonetheless, the danger remains that the community will be subject to that distorted perception which is based in shared interests and commonality of mind and argument. For this, two correctives are available and necessary. One rests in membership in the universal

Church itself. This translates as an openness to, and exchange with, other understandings of the Jesus story and other styles of the Christian life. These can check the persistent tendencies of a close Christian community to be sectarian, to identify its particular community as "the Church." The other check is "the world" as a constant partner in conversation and, indeed, as a locus of God's revelation. The word from "without," often a corrective and a teaching word, is crucial to the community.

4. The community is, finally, an agency of action, both as a collective entity and through the engagement of its members severally. The "moments" of which we spoke earlier were not their own end— analysis, confrontation, directives. Nor are the above moral functions of the community ones that exist for themselves. All exist for the purpose of faithful response, for Christians "in earnest" who profess the Gospel with hands as well as mouth (to call to mind the opening quotation from Luther).

Community reflection is, then, in the service of the community as tools for its mission. But the community's service is not to itself, in the end. Nor is its mission its own. Reflection is a part of loving God and neighbor "with all one's mind." If it is not this, it is in vain.[14]

NOTES

1. *Luther's Works: Liturgies and Hymns,* ed. by Ulrich S. Leopold, general editor Helmut T. Lehmann (Philadelphia: Fortress Press, Vol. 53, 1965), p. 63.

2. *Ibid.*

3. *Ibid.,* insertions in parentheses mine, made for the sake of clarity.

4. *Ibid.,* pp. 63–64.

5. Cited by Darrell Jodock in "Story and Scripture," *Word and World,* Vol. 1, No. 2 (Spring 1982), p. 132, from Buechner's sermon, "The Annunciation," in his *The Magnificent Defeat* (New York: Seabury, 1966), pp. 58–59. The discussion of story in this essay is indebted to Jodock's helpful article.

6. *Ibid.,* p. 133, citing Buechner, p. 59.

7. See the discussion, "The Church as Community Context," in Birch and Rasmussen, *Bible and Ethics in the Christian Life* (Minneapolis: Augsburg, 1976), pp. 125ff. The quotation is from p. 129.

8. Stanley Hauerwas, *A Community of Character* (Notre Dame: University of Notre Dame Press, 1981), p. 52.

9. See the essay in this volume by Jouette Bassler.

10. For a helpful, more elaborated discussion, see the chapter in this volume by Alfred Hennelly, S.J. Social analysis is discussed in the chapter by Joe Holland.

11. Jodock, *op. cit.,* p. 138.

12. See the chapter in this volume by Thomas Clarke, S.J., especially the conclusion and note 1.

13. Rather extensive work along this line is already present in the chapter in this volume, "Christian Moral Discernment," by James E. Hug, S.J.

14. While I have not borrowed directly from the following for this essay, I want to acknowledge helpful conversations with Professors John Howard Yoder (Notre Dame University) and Walter Bouman (Trinity Theological Seminary) in July 1981 at Holden Village. The writing of Daniel Maguire, especially *The Moral Choice* (Minneapolis: Winston Press, 1978), has also been instructive. See also John Godsey's reflections on Church and mission in Chapter 11 of this volume.

13
Christian Moral Discernment

James E. Hug, S.J.

How can we use theological reflection to make discerning judgments? The search for liberating methods is a preoccupation of our age. It is a living concern among religious groups working for social justice as well. But can the question be answered?

It is clear, first of all, that no simple answer can be given. The interviews shaping this volume of studies have revealed a rich diversity of groups. They range from new ecumenical churches to agencies of mainline Catholic and Protestant churches, from educational institutions primarily concerned with the personal formation of students to political lobbies organized to bring the voices of the churches to bear on the formation of national policy and legislation, from groups committed to developing full Christian community life together to people who coalesce from a variety of community bases to cooperate in specific tasks. They are large and small, complex and simple. They have diverse goals and contexts. They operate in different time frames and under different pressures.

From this diversity, a variety of methods of theological reflection and decision has emerged. The methods have been developed in the light of the challenges of specific contexts and tailored to serve the people and goals involved. Although they all bear a certain family resemblance, it would be a mistake to blur over their specific differences as though these were unimportant. I will not attempt to develop a single, comprehensive method for so many different groups and settings.

Nonetheless, there is value in bringing together in summary form reflections on a few of the elements that seem important whenever religious people try to bring their faith and values to bear on the options facing them. In this chapter, then, I will try to sketch as concretely as possible the central "family traits" observable in the better methods of theological reflection. Each group must develop these elements into a method which fits its context, meets its needs, compensates for its particular weaknesses, draws upon its unique resources, and responds to its aspirations.

    The traits of discerning moral judgment developed in this chapter are tailored for Christians deeply involved in issues of justice—whether they are primarily concerned with personal formation and conversion or with social development and transformation. The processes discussed aim at drawing out the special insights and sensitivities to value which passionate concern makes possible while eliminating as much as possible the limitations and biases traditionally identified with such subjective involvement.[1]

    These elements of Christian moral discernment are important either before or after an action is decided upon. Before the decision they can help a group test its "leanings" for their appropriateness to the situation. After the fact they provide touchstones for evaluating the decision, thereby contributing to informed planning for the future.

    The raw material for this discernment, then, can be found in either the spontaneous intuitions, emotions, and inclinations to specific actions felt within a group as it is drawn toward decision (*before* the fact) or in the institutions, policies, and actions in which a group has embodied its moral judgments (after the fact). Students develop verbatim reports of ministerial situations and gather with others to gain deeper insight into their feelings and actions and to plan more effective pastoral responses. The federal government proposes a sudden social revolution through skillful manipulation of the budget process and lobbying groups gather to examine their instinctive reactions, clarify their hopes, choose their battles, hammer out their strategies. A local church community takes time to evaluate its program for unwed mothers of the region developed the previous year. Feelings, desires, passions, instinctive inclinations, actions, programs, institutions—these provide a sort of "revelation in the rough." They are rich in spontaneous faith, embodied theology. They are intelligent, loving, intuitive responses to life emerging from the pre-conscious regions of the human spirit, shaped by individual personality, group loyalties and traits, local contexts. They carry the limits, biases, commitments—the sin and grace—of human life. The elements of Christian moral discernment gathered in this chapter are designed to help in the continuing effort to recognize the creative/redemptive activity of God in human history as it invites and enables us to respond.

PRAYERFUL OPENNESS

It is important from the very beginning to establish a context of prayer, one which will help to relieve as much as possible the pain, needs, and everyday cares of the people present.[2] Spontaneous moral judgments, inclinations, and responses arise from and are shaped by those personal needs, cares, desires. Discerning evaluation of them requires re-entry into a prayerful consciousness of God which brings with it loving dispositions rooted in religious experience and oriented as fully as possible to God and all that God loves. This is the dispositive function of prayer described by John Haughey in Chapter 4.

These dispositions can be characterized in various ways. There is a restored sense of inner peace and strength. Calm trust replaces anxieties—and the body relaxes noticeably. A renewed sense of identity and mission—personal, corporate, Christian—gives a feeling of "coming home." There is a relaxed and broader consciousness of the situation which is more appreciative of all the values it contemplates and less in need of controlling, possessing, or organizing them. There is greater openness to surprise. There is less spirit of competition with other people and more joy and gratitude for their gifts and successes. These dispositions are generally rooted in a deeply felt experience of being known, forgiven, loved, chosen by God.

This fuller integration into consciousness of the religious reality of the situation has several important consequences. First, it tends to free the creative intuition and response of the individuals. Dominant emotions focus and direct our conscious attention while unconsciously selecting associated images, interpretations, and action responses from the memory and imagination. So, for example, judgments or responses made while in the grip of anxiety over one's safety will be geared principally to self-protection. Those made in anger and intense personal pain tend to be tailored ruthlessly to ease the pain or exact retribution. Those made under the feeling of oppression frequently focus only upon the power relationships in the situation. In some situations such responses are appropriate; in others they are not. In those situations where they are appropriate, restoration of a loving, contemplative state of spirit rooted in one's experience of God will confirm them. In those situations where the responses are inappropriate, a loving contemplative look will tend to call forth intuitions and associated interpretations or responses more sensitive to the broad range of values actually present in the context.

Secondly, this prayerful disposition can free the individuals to listen to each other more receptively and sensitively. In such an atmosphere, personal fears are quieted and individuals are freed to speak their intuitions and feelings. This prepares the way for a discerning corporate response which is far wiser, more nuanced, and more constructive, enriched by the unique contributions of the individual members.

Finally, this atmosphere, in relaxing the need to argue one's viewpoints or control the direction of discussion, allows trends and movements to emerge from the group and tends to sensitize its members to them.

In general, then, the entry into prayerful openness is an indispensable context for good Christian discernment. It draws the participants into better touch with the full reality of the situation. It tends to free their perceptions, spontaneous judgments and responses from the preoccupying grip of immediate anxieties by bringing them under the guiding control of their best personal and loving dispositions toward God, each other, and all creation.

Obviously, dispositions which touch so deeply into the emotional life of a group and its individual members are not called forth magically at times of crisis or decision or evaluation. They cannot be recalled if they do not exist. In one way or another, then, most groups attend to the general Christian formation and development of their members. They encourage personal prayer with the Scriptures, spiritual direction, retreats, common prayer, journaling, study of theology, or some combination of these. They urge attention to the religious dimension of personal experience and the sharing of these contemporary stories of good news. Those groups committed to developing deeper community life together frequently celebrate the story of God's activity as it has shaped their corporate existence and situated them in the sweep of the larger Christian story. The deliberate nurturing of religious consciousness in a group makes the recollection of a contemplative, loving disposition possible.

Even with a foundation of this type and a fairly developed sense of personal and corporate religious identity, this disposition is not easily "switched on" with any depth. *Remembering* experiences of God and of prayerful openness is not the same as *entering* deeply into them and being renewed in them. That deeper renewal is only rarely triggered by a simple opening prayer or the reading of a passage from Scripture. Time must be taken for all to recall and re-enter the history of God's activity with them individually, as a community or working group, and as part of the larger Christian community in history.

Many different methods have been developed to facilitate deeper recovery of Christian dispositions in discernment processes. Choice of a place to meet which is in a restful setting away from telephones and the intrusion of daily problems can contribute in subtle, important ways. Some groups have places that have become sacred for them in the course of their history together. Return to those places can facilitate inner renewal. Some groups use extended periods of personal prayer; others recount personal stories or the story of the group; others use the rituals developed by the group or common to their tradition. The means chosen usually reflect the denominational and cultural characteristics of the groups. The Friends' Committee relies on receptive silence; charismatic groups find nurture in more expressive and ecstatic forms of communal prayer. The clues to the best methods for any particular group are there to be discovered in the experience and testimony of its members. They must discover together those processes which help them recover the loving contemplative openness which marks union in the Spirit. Experimenting with different forms of prayer may help to open groups to new dimensions of the experience of God.

Finally, while concern for these dispositions should mark the very beginning of Christian discernment processes, it must not be confined to the beginning. They should constitute the atmosphere or "psychic space" within which all the other moments of the process move. They usually require nourishment by some rhythm of personal and communal prayer running throughout the deliberations. It is important that all members of a group have the freedom to invite a time of prayer whenever the atmosphere of loving, contemplative dispositions is eroding.

SELF-REFLECTIVE MOMENT

The inner dynamic of the self-reflective moment is in itself relatively simple. It involves two movements: raising to consciousness the factors which influenced the intuitions, inclinations, or actions which are the subject matter of this reflection, and, in the atmosphere of prayerful openness, accepting, complementing, modifying, or rejecting those influences.

This dynamic is, however, seriously complicated by the web of interwoven influences which shape every human response. I can only offer a sketchy glimpse of the main personal, interpersonal, and societal factors that are potentially a matter of concern here. Even that sketch may seem frustratingly vast and time-consuming to people with a passion for justice urging them on to action. Nevertheless, I want to underline the fact that this is only an explicit statement of the forces already implicitly shaping our responses. A few moments of reflection on them can free us to accept or modify those influences. If we fail to take that time, we run the risk of accidentally putting our passion for justice at the service of values we would not consciously choose.

Physical Factors

Physical factors influence human responses in important, but often overlooked, ways. They can shape dispositions, expose or hide certain types of data, stimulate the imagination or inhibit it, foster investigative processes or short-circuit them.

A moment of reflection should assess the specific ways in which physical factors actually influenced the intuitive inclinations and responses. In any given situation, the number of significantly formative physical influences may be small or large. It could include the health and general condition of each of the participants, their weariness or freshness, the pressures of time, the relative comfort of the room, the arrangement of the furniture, the quiet or noise, the air quality, the impact of the suburban or inner city setting. The list is potentially enormous; the *actual* formative influences are the important ones.

When a community in a prayerful contemplative disposition becomes aware of the ways in which physical factors have shaped their spontaneous inclinations and actions, they can also become aware of a sense of resonance or dissonance, a feeling of being satisfied with those influences or of wanting to compensate for them by changing the response in some way. There is no single ideal physical setting for discerning Christian judgment and response. Some find their responses more authentically Christian when shaped by the physical context of the poor; others require more peaceful or comfortable settings—even in order to identify in a loving way with the poor. It is important to keep in mind that there is enormous room for self-deception here. Insulation from the actual experience of the poor can seriously distort even the most well-intentioned efforts on their behalf. The smells, sights, and sounds—the daily struggles—of poverty not only fuel a greater sense of urgency in the work for social justice. They also stimulate the imagination to shape programs in ways that hotel meeting rooms or bureaucratic offices cannot duplicate. Perhaps recognition of the subtle dangers involved here would counsel beginning with a bias toward poverty and simplicity—one that could be modified later as experience might require.[3] In the last analysis, the felt testimony of the prayerful, loving disposition attending to the effects of the physical influences is the best judge of what is conducive to discerning Christian judgment and response.

Psychological Factors

Spontaneous inclinations and judgments bear the clear imprint of the psychological dynamics of the individuals and groups involved. The more we understand these dynamics, the more we will be able to recognize their influence on our judgments and evaluate it.

A variety of psychological schools provide helpful insights and types of analysis. A number of groups we interviewed make some use of the Myers-Briggs Personality Indicator.[4] It is based upon Jung's analysis of personality types according to preferred fundamental attitudes (introversion or extraversion), types of perception (sensation or intuition), and approaches to judgment (thinking or feeling).[5] It can

indicate personal strengths and suggest certain characteristic problems of perception and evaluation which plague each personality
type. These weaknesses require conscious, deliberate attention if bias
and partiality are not to reign unnoticed. Introverts, for example,
tend to be more attuned to the interior life and its influences but to
overlook or underestimate institutional and social influences. Intui-
tives are more sensitive to the possibilities in a situation and to the
principles or truth behind the facts, but weak in attention to detailed
factual data. And so on. The Myers-Briggs Indicator can also be
used to profile strengths and weaknesses in the makeup and processes of groups.

Developmental psychologists such as Erik Erikson, Lawrence
Kohlberg, Carol Gilligan, and James Fowler have identified stages of
human development which shape perception and judgment.[6] These
stages reflect a progression of meaning structures and ultimate concerns. The underlying meaning structure and concern at any single
stage focus attention, organize past experience, and give rise to spontaneous interpretations and reactions. In other words, they influence
what we notice, what we consider important in it, and how we respond. Such basic concepts as justice, sin, grace, salvation, and
church tend to shift in meaning from stage to stage. Different forms
of logic become possible and characteristic at different stages. Systemic social analysis, for example, is beyond the developmental abilities of many people, even many adults. Different types of community
become possible and necessary at different stages. Different experiences of God have some correlation to different stages of development.

Clearly, then, some sensitivity to developmental factors operating in a situation can be very illuminating. Students at a religious college struggling with their religious identity can be expected to
perceive, interpret, and evaluate a political crisis in ways predictably
different from an older, more established group comprising a lobby
such as NETWORK.

Awareness of these psychological factors and a variety of others
such as sexual traits and roles, brought in a prayerful spirit to the
spontaneous inclinations and judgments, can help reveal how appropriate they are to the total context.

Sociological Factors

Concern for the analysis of a great variety of social influences on personal judgments has grown dramatically in recent years among religious people involved in ministry for justice.[7] Attention to which sociological groupings are influencing judgments and which are not can often provide clues to the special insights or the blind spots in our perceptions. These groupings can include social divisions based on such factors as class, race, ethnicity, sex, sexual preference, age, religion and form of "church" life, and geography. Various combinations of these influences can instill such emotions as anger or apathy, a burning sense of injustice or severe anxiety about being deviant or controversial—emotions which guide judgments in very different directions.

It can also be instructive to ask which groups benefit from specific inclinations or actions, which suffer them or pay their costs, and how these factors reflect or counteract the prevailing patterns of relationship between groups in this society. The analysis of Reaganomics as welfare for the rich and the military at the cost of the poor, women, blacks and other minorities is an obvious example of this type of reflection.

A loving, contemplative disposition will call for wider, more inclusive consultation and will move to counter obvious prejudices and inequities in whatever ways are necessary.

Political Factors

Political analysis observes power relationships and the exercise of power. These have great importance within the discerning group as well as within and among the other groups and institutions active in the situation. Good political analysis will take care to include the national and international political actors who directly or indirectly influence the local situation.

In reviewing a particular inclination or action, this type of analysis should attempt to uncover the power system and its workings: how power is distributed (within each group and within the context as a whole), what patterns of organization and leadership are operating (both formal leadership and informal), who participates effectively in decision-making and who is without effective voice, who profits from the decisions made in these ways and who suffers.

All these factors, implicit in every situation, affect spontaneous intuitions, inclinations, and actions. Self-critical reflection should seek awareness of how these influenced the first response of the community and how a loving, prayerful disposition might move to bring about fuller participation and more universal care for all involved in the episode.

Economic Factors

There is little need today to highlight the importance of economic factors in human society. Sources and flows of capital (or the lack thereof), resources and the means of production, distribution networks and consumption patterns are part of the daily bread of life. Adequate critical reflection must include an effort to grasp and evaluate the system underlying the various economic dimensions of a situation and influencing all its participants.

The more obvious concerns are rather easily raised: Are this group's inclinations or actions inappropriately governed by its own economic needs or desires? What are the effects of this line of action on the poor? Who profits and who suffers in this situation?

The subtler concerns are much more easily overlooked. The sources, security, and levels of economic support usually dictate the education, types of experience, and social circles that a group identifies with. Those factors help to shape the questions they ask (and do not think or dare to ask), the interpretations of social reality they espouse, the types of goods and services they expect, need, seek, and become unwilling or unable to live without. It is neither accidental nor surprising that the rich interpret economic problems according to supply-side economics or development theory while the very poor are sensitive to the structural dependencies built into the present system and are calling for much more radical change.[8]

Most of the groups interviewed for this study showed some attraction to a poorer life-style and greater identification with the poor as a way to live Gospel values and free themselves for more responsive and discerning Christian love. It is in part a testimony to the subtle power of economic factors that by their own admission so few have been able to follow that attraction.

Cultural Factors

Only recently have people in social justice ministries directed serious energies toward cultural analysis. This type of self-critical reflection attends especially to the symbolic elements which shape the self-image of a group, a people, a nation. Art, music, everyday language, sciences, movies, literature, the media, educational programs and institutions—the embodiments and carriers of culture abound and give a certain distinguishable character to the way of life of the individuals and groups who share it.

Mainstream U.S. culture, for example, tends to be characterized by a pioneer mentality which values the "new and improved," the scientific or technological breakthrough. It is a technical, secular, consumer culture which prizes efficiency, pragmatism, planning, competition, and success—which it measures largely by the accumulation of power and wealth. It defines freedom in terms of individual rights or liberties. It cherishes the image of being "Number One" in the world in all it holds important—from military power to the commitment to peace, from standard of living to the protection of "liberty and justice for all." It verges on severe individualism while trying to maintain commanding leadership of the Western world. It is struggling to reassert its innocence and value in a difficult political and economic period. Currently it seems to be trying to avoid recognition or acceptance of the ways that the role and position of the United States in world affairs are changing.

Groups within a society reflect the dominant culture in varying degrees and manners while at the same time generating particular cultural characteristics of their own which express their uniqueness and modify the dominant cultural expressions in their setting. Part of the purpose of the Eastern Mennonite College year of study in Washington, D.C., for instance, is to induce a shock of cultures leading to a more socially conscious integration of the Mennonite heritage. This is intended to enable the students to address their Christian message to the U.S. culture more effectively.[9]

Good moral discernment requires prayerful attention to the images, concepts, myths, philosophies, and modes of thinking and valuing which are implicit in spontaneous inclinations and actions. Such contemplation can reveal what cultural factors are actually operative in the group's response and how well that response fits with the more deeply religious dispositions of prayer. The explicitly theological dimensions of this cultural analysis will be discussed more extensively in the last part of this section.

Historical Factors

Perhaps here more than anywhere else, the intertwining of these factors or types of analysis is apparent. There is an important historical dimension to each of the elements already reflected upon, and the category "historical factors" includes them all as dimensions of its complex totality.[10] Events in one's personal history, trends in the life of a community, sociocultural and political movements, national tragedies and triumphs all linger in memory and imagination to shape interpretations and responses in the present and form expectations and hopes for the future. People who struggled through the Depression of the 1930s still relate to money, goods, and economic security in ways that show the effects of that experience. More recently, the Vietnam War and Watergate have changed families, organizations, and both domestic and foreign policy—and their impact is only beginning to be felt and understood.

It is important, therefore, to attend carefully to the historical events and trends—personal, local, national, international—exerting influence in the situation under discerning review. In the light of prayerful contemplative spirit, does their influence appear to have rendered the inclination or response actually appropriate to the context or in some ways anachronistic?

Theological Factors

Explicit reflection upon the religious dimensions of life situations and human responses constitutes the central and distinguishing element of theological reflection. It is addressed here not as one element of self-reflective moment among others but as the one which attempts to unfold before us the deepest level of meaning that integrates them all. The physical, psychological, social, political, economic, cultural, and historical analyses uncovered facets and implications of the lived theology embodied in human response and interaction. They provide other languages for describing and drawing our attention to various elements of what is, in the final analysis, a graced experience of God immanent and/or a taste of sin.

Groups attempting an explicit theological analysis of their experience approach the task in a variety of ways. Some rely upon the personal prayer of their members to discover enlightening biblical analogies: "We look for our story within the Scriptures and Scripture within our story." Many read contemporary theology, searching for perspectives and analyses applicable to their situation. Some groups send representatives for formal theological education. Others bring professional theologians to the data of their reality for consultation.

All of these strategies represent attempts to deal with a problem of amateur vs. professional analysis. The quality of analysis depends not only upon the affective dispositions of the group but also to some extent upon the intelligence and sophistication of its training. There is not one single solution to this problem. All of the approaches mentioned have advantages and disadvantages. Without sifting through and evaluating the various approaches, I will simply suggest a way of moving into explicit theological analysis of experience which is available to anyone at any level of theological sophistication who undertakes the task.

This process begins with the recognition that all human life is a lived theology, a response—whether conscious or not—to God. Once the complexity and richness of that response have been exposed in narrative and more systematic analytic terms, an important clue to its theological meaning can be found in the dispositions and underlying concerns embodied there.

Explicit theological reflection can begin, then, by entering into the dispositions and underlying concerns to discover what images of God they evoke. Jouette Bassler has shown, for example, how Paul's experience of weakness and yearning for power evoked for him the image of the crucified Christ and of God as paradoxically strongest in weakness.[11] When Paul entered the Corinthian context, his earlier experience sensitized him to the power struggles there and called forth a response rooted in the same theological model. He saw God's wisdom and power working in the poor and weak, inviting the conversion of the powerful. The hostile context of the Johannine community stimulated its yearning for belonging and acceptance. In the prevailing atmosphere of those dispositions, they recalled the words and actions of Jesus which showed him (and them) in special relationship with God and fostered a supportive home community among them. God is seen as active in building a community whose internal bonds of love are God's fullest revelation to the world.

In other words, then, the intuitive responses to specific social contexts embody affective dispositions which are linked with experiences and images of God deep in the pre-conscious of the human spirit. By consciously entering into the affective disposition, we can draw upon a type of spontaneous "logic of the affections" to call into consciousness the sense of God from which and to which we are responding.

As Bassler indicated, the two models she described are far from the only two to be found. The Scriptures and the Christian tradition exhibit an array of images of God as varied as the range of human emotional responses to life and the specific historical and cultural contexts which have given them concrete form. This is simply another way of saying that God evokes and responds to the full range of human emotion in and through all the contexts of life's experiences. In response to the longing for security and strength, God has been experienced and named Rock, Fortress, King, Omnipotent. The yearning for justice has discovered God as Wrath, Prophetic Voice, Judge, Justice itself, Eternal Law. The restless, searching heart has found an Abba, a loving Father/Mother, an intimate friend.

Attempts to identify the most important names of God and integrate them issue in systematic theologies. A full systematic theology cannot be presented here. However, it is possible to sketch briefly several basic human experiences and indicate the images of God and the action inclinations characteristically associated with them by the type of "logic of the affections" I have mentioned.[12] This sketch does not claim to be complete; other experiences such as the sense of belonging, of community, or of tradition could be developed in a similar way. This presentation is intended as an illustration of this approach to theological reflection and as a potentially helpful tool for future work. I hope it will stimulate further reflection on the fundamental experiences of human life.

The foundational human experiences I suggest for contemplation can be expressed as a sense of dependence, a sense of grateful love, a sense of repentance, a sense of obligation, a sense of possibility, and a sense of direction. These are experienced in widely differing ways in human life and with a broad range of intensities. There are occasional "breakthrough moments" when the transcendence of one or more of the senses is deeply felt and something of God is vividly disclosed. There are the numerous small experiences of support, kindness, or forgiveness mediated by the people and events of our lives. There are the testimonies of members of our communities and the teaching of our traditions witnessing to profound experiences some have never felt personally at any depth. It is above all the breakthrough moments which reveal the transcendent God that invite us to see God immanent, mediated in the less intense daily experiences and in the witness of the community.[13]

A SENSE OF DEPENDENCE

A friend once related his most profound religious experience to me as waking up one morning and being deeply aware that he did not need to exist. His very existence was a fragile mystery. That experience opened his eyes to the radical dependence that marks everyday human life in ways so ordinary we usually overlook them. He realized his dependence on the air he breathes, the food and drink he consumes, the environment that supports their production, the friends he shares them with and who help him find meaning and love, the seeming coincidences which so frequently surround the vitally important events and relationships of his life. He was deeply alert to God as Creator, Source of life, fruitful, awesome, all-pervasive.

In the grace of such an experience, certain New Testament images of Jesus become much more meaningful and attractive. For example, Jesus was "in the beginning with God; all things were made

through him. . . ." He has initiated the new creation.[14] In his own
trust and reliance on God through success and failure, even through
suffering and death, Jesus revealed his own divine life.

Certain inclinations or dispositions flow from the depths of the
experience. There can be awe tending toward praise and worship.
There can be an awareness of personal limits and relativity—calling
for humility in claims to knowledge or moral certitude. There can be
a sense of trust in the Creator, giving a freedom and desire to act in
service of creation and Creator even when risk is involved. "Sin" is
recognized in the lack of awe, humility, trust; it is discovered in the
refusal to care for the earth and its peoples in the same spirit our
Creator shows.

A SENSE OF GRATEFUL LOVE

Even in the midst of suffering, Paul urged, "Dedicate yourselves
to thankfulness."[15] At the heart of the Christian experience is the realization, deeply felt, that God is love. Human life and all that it depends upon comes as loving gift from the Creator. Each human
being is known through and through and loved.

As the sense of being loved deepens, daily life becomes more
transparent to the gifts and actions of the Lover. The beauty of flow-
ers such as lilies in the field, the existence of adequate food, the availability of organizations and systems which make desired activities
possible and enjoyable, the acceptance and care of good friends and
lovers—almost anything can be a gift bearing God's love, an embodiment of God loving. Even such apparently ambiguous signs as the
falling of the gentle rain profiting the unjust at least as much as the
just becomes a clear evidence of God's patient, forgiving, unconditional love.

The power of that love is most clearly visible in Jesus who
preached it, embodied it in forgiving and healing touch, flared out in
anger at those who closed themselves against it, gathered a community characterized especially by the love of its members for each other. He died faithful to that love and overcame even death. God's love
does not remove the mystery of suffering and injustice in human life,
but it does show the strength and fidelity to overcome it and trans-

form it finally. That is celebrated as the heart of the new covenant by Christian communities in the Eucharist.

People with a deep sense of being graciously loved reflect that openly in their responses to life. They show a gentleness and grateful care for all that is given. They persevere in the struggle for justice with a certain inner peace even in the midst of apparent failure. There is a freedom and desire to give freely as they have freely received. Sin is seen in ingratitude, in lack of care for the elements of the created world, especially its people, in greed and unjust appropriation of the gifts given to humanity, in the refusal of love and the refusal to love.

A SENSE OF REPENTANCE

In the light of the generous love embracing us, we frequently become aware of dispositions, acts, subtle patterns by which we cripple the life and gifts within or ignore and abuse the people and creation around us. In those moments, a sense of sadness, of regret arises. Sometimes it is relatively brief and invites a simple word of apology to a friend. At others its intensity can disclose the deepest significance of all sin, its rejection of God. In the sense of repentance, God is experienced as Judge. This is not simply the projection of a harsh superego. It is a sense of being in touch with the source of all true moral authority. It is the dimension of the experience of the divine felt when God's loving generosity stands as a contrasting prophetic challenge to our normal inclinations and patterns of life.

Entering into the sense of repentance, we easily recall the first public words of Jesus calling for repentance and openness to God's rule over life. Images of Jesus extending gentle forgiveness to the woman caught in adultery and abandoned by everyone, even her partner in adultery, to the paralytic, to all who will accept it, take on special value. We hear again—in a new, more personal way—the prayer of Jesus for those whose refusal of God's love brought about his death on the cross: "Abba, forgive them, for they know not what they do."[16]

The sense of repentance brings with it a sense of personal weakness and a wiser, more critical self-awareness. The denial of one's sin is seen now to be itself a major element of sin. From the encounter with God's loving forgiveness, there is born a grateful desire to reform our lives. There is the Christian freedom to begin again in joy and persistent trust.

A SENSE OF OBLIGATION

Human life is full of obligation—to the environment, to family members and friends, to social institutions, to religious communities, to God. The things, events, and people of the world make constant demands on us. Failure to respond to those demands has its costs. Lack of care for ecological systems through strip mining, for example, results in flooding. Refusal to relax brings ulcers and other physical and psychic disabilities. Inability or unwillingness to relate vulnerably and lovingly with others brings increasing personal isolation or a succession of relationships marked by varying forms of domination and submission. Heavy dependence on foreign oil guarantees loss of power and freedom in international relations. Generations of exploitation of a population by the wealthy foments revolution.

Cooperation with the demands, on the other hand, promises rewards. Good care of oneself releases greater energy and enjoyment of life. Science and technology can enhance human life through their abilities to understand the ordering of nature and take advantage of it through cooperation with its patterns in various ways. The sense of obligation, then, is rooted deeply in the ordering present in reality.

The experience of felt obligation to the ordering discernible in creation has long been a dimension of the experience of God. The images of God ordering creation and giving laws for life come from the deepest layers of the Judaeo-Christian experience. God's law has long been seen as a gift revealing and facilitating free, full, successful, and happy human life. Matthew's Gospel presents Jesus as the new Moses revealing God's law with new clarity and brilliance. Paul holds up the cross as the embodiment of the true wisdom of God in the face of the foolishness of predominant contemporary perspectives and values. The doctrines of natural law (Catholic) and orders of creation (Protestant) attempted to articulate the obligations implied by the ordering apparent in life and to present them as revelations of God's law—indeed, of God's very being and activity.

The felt sense of obligation to God in the contexts of daily life promotes dispositions of openness and yearning for insight into the ways God is ordering life in those contexts. We want to know what God is doing and cooperate with it. Disorder, refusing to act in the pattern of Jesus or according to the will of God—these constitute the sinful dimension of human activity from the perspective of this experience of God.

A SENSE OF POSSIBILITIES

The order experienced in human life is not a static order. It is an ordering which continually evolves new possibilities and stimulates human creativity. A new job or a new friend opens a wealth of new contacts and opportunities. A moment of intense religious conversion carries the promise of a new way of life. Scientific breakthroughs generate sweeping changes in the way of life of a people. Change and newness have become the atmosphere we breathe, and future shock from the dizzying pace of change is a real cultural danger. At the edge of life as we know it, the possibility of newness of life in unimaginable form invites us.

It is possible to see disclosed in these and similar experiences the quiet work of the same God who opened an unexpected future for the slaves of Egypt and the Jewish exiles in Babylon. The image of God as Redeemer and Source of hope is central to the Judaeo-Christian tradition. Jesus understood his mission as bringing good news to the poor, proclaiming liberty to captives, offering recovery of sight to the blind and release to prisoners, and initiating a year of jubilee: establishing the promised new covenant. His death/resurrection stands as the ultimate sign of hope for all who have discovered God-Redeeming in Jesus—and in their own lives.

A sense of possibilities counters despair, setting up expectations for a better future. It heightens sensitivity to personal growth bringing new capacities to act. It fosters attention to new opportunities for creative action opening in the situations of life. Resistance to change and growth is seen as a manifestation of sin against the God who would make all things new.

A SENSE OF DIRECTION

In order to develop a sense of direction and some criteria for evaluating legislative programs, NETWORK took great care to define its shared vision for a preferred world. Clear articulation of that vision helps to evaluate congressional actions and guides NETWORK's responses.

That experience is replicated in a variety of forms throughout human experience. The objects of human love give direction to human action. If we are not discovering goals and responding accordingly, we are busy setting them for ourselves.

In that pervasive experience, it is possible to glimpse a disclosure of God as the final goal of creation and God's purposes as of central importance to human life. As Jesus expressed it, what profit is there in accomplishing goal after goal—even up to achieving mastery over the whole world—while missing the ultimate purpose of human life? Jesus is presented throughout the New Testament as uniquely able to teach the way to God, since he came from God and has returned to God. He is the first fruits of the new creation and all will follow him until all are one with God in Christ. Jesus has shown in his teaching and his life the way to discover and cooperate with God's purposes.

The experience of God as our destiny evokes a yearning to participate in and cooperate with God's purposes in life. It calls forth a care for all creation. It sensitizes us to the goals and goal-seeking present in the situations demanding moral discernment and provides a felt sense of direction by which to evaluate them. Sin is recognized in the refusal to order human life toward intermediate goals and by means which direct us toward God as our final fulfilment.

All six of these "senses" have been recognized through history as authentic dimensions of the Christian experience of God. The one God present and acting in human life creates and supports, loves, judges and forgives, orders, liberates, guides.

With this as a backdrop, the task of the self-reflective moment in theological reflection can be described simply. The inclinations or actions that are the subject matter of this discernment process emerge from certain dispositions and yearnings. Recognizing that these are related to dimensions of the experience of God, it is possible to ask what senses of God are actually operative here and now, grounding this particular response in this context. A prophetic response attempting to help the poor organize against redlining or unjust housing policies may seem rooted in a spontaneous, unconscious sense that God is judging the evil in the situation and opening new possibilities for action. In the contemplative moment of self-critical reflection, we attend to whether that interpretation "fits" with a more consciously prayerful openness to God. And we consciously recall the other dimensions of God to see if they illumine other traces of divine activity in the situation. Are we sensitive to any possible creative, supportive, loving, ordering, guiding facets of God's activity in interaction with all the people and organizations involved?

This expansion of religious consciousness makes possible a more perceptive and appropriate response to what God is doing. It will not, however, resolve all differences of Christian interpretation and response. In its history the Church has insisted that the most fundamental reality is God's love. Even divine judgment is understood as a challenge to human sinfulness flowing from God's love. But beyond that there has been no lasting consensus on which dimensions of the experience of God are more central to Christianity and carry stronger claims on Christian response. Even with a heightened awareness of the ways God seems to be creating and providing, loving, judging and forgiving, ordering, liberating, and guiding, different individuals and communities may respond differently in the Spirit of Christ. Influenced by significant life experiences, some may feel deeply moved to participate in the ordering activity by working for legislative reform. At the same time, others may feel moved to focus their energies on modeling the type of community toward which the God of hope seems to be moving and ordering the political forces in the context. Nonetheless, explicit reflection on underlying religious influences may modify initial responses by revealing more adequately what God is doing. And it should provide grounds for dialogue with other Christians about the range and limits of appropriate Christian responses in a situation.

These reflections move us toward other important moments in the process of Christian moral discernment. While they are as important and complex as the self-reflective moment, it will be possible to

Experience "a sense of"	Theological Reference	Christological Title	Moral Dispositions	Sin
Dependence	Creator	Word, New Creation	Awareness of finiteness, self-criticism; knowledge of limits, recognition of relativity; limits the claims to moral certitude. Awe, trust: confidence within the condition of finiteness; sense of responsibility, reliability.	pride, refusal to steward creation
Gratitude	Beneficent God, Good in Creation, Provident, Love	Redeemer	Reason for being moral; motivates and enables us to do good to others. Grateful gentleness, care, passion for good.	ingratitude, refusal to care, love; refusal of love.
Repentance	God as Judge Moral Authority	Justifier	Self-criticism and turning toward God's moral purposes; freedom to risk.	denial of own sin
Obligation	God as Orderer Sustainer of Life	Pattern, Model	Awareness of duties, obligations, personal and social accountability before the Orderer.	disorder, disobedience
Possibility	God as one who continues to act creatively and redemptively God of Hope	Sanctifier	Counters despair, fatedness; nourishes awareness of opportunities to avoid harm and benefit others, to direct events toward more just and benevolent ends.	resistance to change, growth
Direction	God as Telos, End of our creation, Final End, Destiny	Teacher, Way	Opens paths through the complexities of human experience toward an end which is both spiritual and moral; gives direction, longing to act and order life according to God's purposes, ends; love for God, creation; seeking to glorify God.	self-centeredness disorder

sketch them quite briefly since they build upon the issues already elaborated.

CONSTRUCTIVE MOMENT

The processes of the self-reflective moment raise to critical awareness the variety of forces shaping our spontaneous responses. They thereby help free us to respond consciously with the greatest integrity possible. In doing so, these processes also reveal the physical, psychological, social, political, economic, cultural, historical, and religious forces operating in the total context. In the constructive part of the discernment process, the community again turns its gaze toward the situation confronting it and attends to the felt response and interpretation which emerge from this heightened and prayerful consciousness. The initial spontaneous response which began our discussion is displaced by a felt response rooted in a more consciously enlightened and lovingly disposed consciousness.

Since limits, biases, and sin haunt even the most careful human responses, it is important to explain this second intuitive response and offer what honest justifications for it seem possible. In other words, it is still necessary to give reasons and arguments attempting to show the appropriateness of this response to the Christian identity of the group and to the activity and grace of God in the situation.

These arguments will spell out the physical, psychological, sociological, political, economic, cultural, and historical analyses implicit in the response. These analyses make the response reasonable in the light of the information and principles used in them. The arguments should also try to show how the response fits with the moral principles accepted by the community and with the stories and the theological synthesis which make up their religious vision.

The central concern here is whether the judgment/response can be grounded in the knowledge and beliefs of the community, whether it is logically coherent with them. This is not a deductive process beginning with the beliefs and trying to conclude to the appropriate action response. It is a reflective process beginning with the spontaneous inclination to action and attempting to clarify the theological and philosophical positions implicit in it. Relating those to the faith and principles of the community makes possible the confirmation of the response and/or the clarification and expansion of the community's faith through the intuitively grasped revelation of the contemporary context.[17]

The arguments offered will take different forms depending on what the community considers ultimately persuasive and authoritative. Catholics have traditionally based their arguments for matters of social justice on natural law considerations or on official teachings of the Church hierarchy which claims divine legitimation and guidance for its teaching. Both of these are gradually losing authority in the Catholic community under the weight of the insights and suspicions engendered by psychology, sociology, existentialist and personalist philosophies, critical economics, and analyses of historical and cultural relativities.

In the wake of this onslaught, many Catholics have joined their brothers and sisters in the Protestant communities who turn to the Bible for authoritative moral discernment. The problems here, however, are many and complex. At a time in history when elements of the U.S. community apparently find their inspiration in the texts justifying the brutal conquest of Canaan rather than in the liberation motif of the exodus, the difficulties surrounding appropriate and responsible use of biblical texts are in clear public view. There are many different biblical theologies written in and for a variety of communities, each struggling with its own problems in its own culture, through its various stages of development, and in its particular historical era.

There is, of course, always the danger of bad faith—of misuse of the Scriptures as a propaganda tool—even among believing Christians. But such dishonesty is only one of many possible explanations for differences among people who justify their moral responses by appeal to biblical texts. There could be and usually are many others rooted in the plurality of biblical witnesses and faith perspectives, the variety of levels of communication and types of literature involved, the range of historical, social, and cultural contexts then and now, and the plurality of backgrounds, needs, and orientations of those interpreting the texts.

There is not enough space here to enter into an adequate discussion of criteria for using Scripture well in moral discernment and argument.[18] For the purposes of this chapter, I suggest looking upon the Bible (and the other classic works of the Judaeo-Christian tradition) as an important collection of precedents available for personal formation, enlightenment and challenge. They represent attempts by Christians in other times and places to do what Christians today must do: discover, interpret, and respond to God active in the contemporary context. The faith interpretations of Scripture and tradition can provide helpful light and guidance if the context in which they arose is truly analogous to the present situation in substantial ways. Arguments attempting to justify moral responses biblically need to demonstrate the analogy involved. In the last analysis, however, analogies are always partial. The final authority which will accept or reject the applicability of specific biblical or traditional teachings to contemporary contexts will be the felt sense of their rightness or wrongness. The texts will have a "bite" to them and will assume power in the context only when they touch a deeply responsive chord in the individuals and the community. The final authority is indisputably grounded in experience.

In brief, then, clarification and justification of moral responses involve explaining (through the various types of analysis described earlier) what is happening in the context and what—in and through it all—God is doing and enabling. This clarification and justification should try to show that the actions or intuitive inclinations are coherent with the community's calling and with God's activity as these are being revealed in the present context and have been manifested in the past experience of this community and of Christians throughout the ages.

A SOCIAL TEST

I have urged the importance of overcoming narrow limitations and biased perspectives throughout this discussion of moral discernment. The value of consultation beyond one's own community—with other communities and groups within the Church universal as well as with other individuals and groups vitally involved in similar issues—should be apparent. The greater the variety of backgrounds, expertise, cultural formation, national allegiance, political, social, and economic status and persuasion, the greater the possibility of overcoming blind spots and distorting biases. The dangers of inbreeding are real—perhaps especially for groups committed to passionate partisan activity.

Such consultation with other interested, experienced, and involved groups can serve to confirm the inclinations, perceptions, analyses, and arguments of a discerning community. It can also complement, enhance, stimulate, challenge, and purify them through further discussion and prayer.[19]

This invitation to broader social testing of a community's moral instincts and reflection is not meant to be a ticket to paralysis. The urgencies of some social needs do not permit leisurely discerning consultation. But a community that is never willing to test its presuppositions and perspectives seriously by the experiences, values, and perspectives of a broad spectrum of people can hardly claim an honest openness in the Spirit of Christ to the activity and invitation of the God whose Mystery and Love encompass us all.

Personal and Communal Confirmation

The final judgment on an action or a proposed response remains inalienably with the discerning community. The contemplative attitude, self-critical reflection, imaginative reinterpretation, and consultation can only serve to prepare and guide a group. In the final analysis—again in a prayerful, loving mood—the group must sense for itself whether their felt judgment/response is integral to their personal and corporate religious calling and appropriate to the actual context. Does it "fit" with what God is doing and enabling them to do then and there to the best of their ability to discern it?

A number of the groups that participated in this study have evolved processes of consensus decision-making.[20] These processes reflect respect for the unique gifts of each community member and aim at safeguarding the potential prophetic witness of even the smallest lone voice.

All of these processes point to an important truth. Theological reflection discovers personal and group "vocations" in various situations. There is an important subjective element that is intrinsic to the reality. As a result, different groups—discerning wisely and well—could find themselves on opposite sides of a conflict. The perplexing differences among Christian groups are sometimes rooted as much in the Mystery of God's ways of working as in the sin or error of the groups involved. Mutual respect and openness to each other's roots in a common faith can provide the arena needed for creative reconciliation in the future and the development of new, redemptive directions.

CONCLUSION

This chapter began by asking how theological reflection might be used to guide work for social justice. The answer emerged as a survey of components important for the variety of different specific methods tailored to the needs of different groups and contexts.

Even when sketched out briefly, the complexity of these components is obvious—and perhaps a bit overwhelming. We are invited to develop extensive self-knowledge and openness, to master a great variety of careful analytic and interpretive skills, to foster as rich and developed an imagination as possible, to nurture a dedicated habit of loving response to the personal invitations of the God of Life.

It would be a clear mistake, however, to let a glimpse of the task inspire discouragement. Its rich complexity is a sign of its truth and value. In addition, we should remember that the development of the skills and knowledge is cumulative and shared by our communities. Personal and societal patterns discovered through long, painful effort in one situation frequently come easily and clearly into view on first glance in later situations. Responsive, responsible action is the point. The heightening of consciousness to the complexity of the reality is really intended to help us focus our energies in the most appropriate, simple, and effective action for justice.

Finally, the ultimate ground of encouragement and confidence is the God who has proven capable of using, redeeming, and overcoming our ignorance or mistakes—and loving us toward a more just and gracious future.

NOTES

1. Further discussion of the importance of involvement and passion in this type of theological reflection can be found in the chapters by Robert Kinast and Larry Rasmussen in this volume.

2. The importance of prayer for theological reflection is axiomatic. For more extensive reflection on the types and roles of prayer in this activity, see John Haughey's chapter in Part II and consult the section on worship and missionary action in John Godsey's chapter in Part III.

3. For a related discussion, see Chapter 6 by Monika Hellwig on the hermeneutic privilege of the poor.

4. The "Myers-Briggs Type Indicator" developed by Katharine C. Briggs and Isabel Briggs Myers along with materials for administering, scoring, and interpreting it can be obtained from the Consulting Psychologists Press, Inc., in Palo Alto, California.

5. The primary source is Carl Jung's volume *Psychological Types* (Bollingen Series XX, *The Collected Works of C. G. Jung,* Volume 6: Princeton University Press paperback, 1976), pp. 330–407. Helpful secondary sources include June Singer's *Boundaries of the Soul: The Practice of Jung's Psychology* (Garden City, New York: Doubleday, Anchor Press paperback, 1972), Chapter 7; and David Keirsey and Marilyn Bates' *Please Understand Me: An Essay on Temperament Styles* (Del Mar, California: Prometheus Nemesis Books, 1978).

6. The literature on stages of psychological development continues to grow. A brief sampler for an introduction to the field might include Erik Erikson's *Childhood and Society* (New York: W.W. Norton & Co., 1963) and *Insight and Responsibility* (New York: W.W. Norton & Co., 1964); Lawrence Kohlberg's article "The Cognitive-Developmental Approach to Moral Education" in the June 1975 issue of the *Phi Delta Kappan;* Carol Gilligan's articles "In a Different Voice: Women's Conceptions of Self and of Morality" and "Woman's Place in Man's Life Cycle" in the *Harvard Educational Review* (Vol. 47, No. 4, November 1977, and Vol. 49, No. 4, November 1979); James Fowler's *Life-Maps: Conversations on the Journey of Faith* (with Sam Keen: Waco, Texas: Word Books, Publishers, 1978) and *Stages of Faith: The Psychology of Human Development and the Quest for Meaning* (New York: Harper and Row, Publishers, 1981); Daniel Levinson's *The Seasons of a Man's Life* (New York: Knopf, 1978), and *Toward Moral and Religious Maturity: The First International Conference on Moral and Religious Development* (Morristown, New Jersey: Silver Burdett Company, 1980).

7. This development has triggered a return to classical sources of social analysis such as the work of Weber, Durkheim, and Marx. Contemporary work in the sociology of knowledge by people such as Peter Berger and Thomas Luckmann has also had great importance. More popular materials have been developed and distributed recently by the Center of Concern (*Social Analysis: Linking Faith and Justice* by Joe Holland and Peter Henriot,

S.J.: 3700 13th St., N.E., Washington, D.C., 20017, 1980), Maryknoll (*Social Analysis and Research with Grassroots Groups: Basic Models and Approaches* and *Social Analysis According to Gospel Values: A Resource Manual for Planners:* Maryknoll, N.Y., 10545, 1981, 1979), and the Jesuit Conference (*The Context of Our Ministries: Working Papers:* 1717 Massachusetts Ave., N.W., Washington, D.C., 20036, 1981).

8. For a much fuller treatment of issues related to economic influences, I refer again to Monika Hellwig's chapter in this volume, "Good News to the Poor: Do They Understand It Better?"

9. This program is described briefly in Chapter 2.

10. The categories in this general social analysis could be organized as follows:

Historical Dimension (Diachronic Analysis)

	Past	Present	Future
Physical			
Psychological			
Sociological			
Political			
Economic			
Cultural			

Structural Factors

(Synchronic Analysis)

11. See Chapter 9 of this volume, "Theological Reflection: New Testament Antecedents and Models."

12. This account relies heavily on the work of James M. Gustafson. See *Can Ethics Be Christian?* (Chicago: University of Chicago Press, 1975), pp. 82–116; *Christ and the Moral Life* (New York: Harper and Row, 1968); and *Ethics from a Theocentric Perspective: Theology and Ethics* (Chicago: University of Chicago Press, 1981).

13. For related material, see John Haughey's discussion of the tension between the transcendent and the immanent in Christian life in Chapter 4.

14. Jn 1:2; Col 1:15; 2 Cor 5:17.

15. Col 3:15.

16. Lk 23:34. For the other texts alluded to in this and the preceding section, cf. Lk 12:22–32; Mt 5:43–48; Mk 1:14–15; Jn 8:1–11; Lk 5:17–26.

17. Many are reluctant to agree that contemporary religious experience can and sometimes should expand and modify the tradition. Thomas Clarke's suggestion for dealing with this difficult issue is very helpful. See the section of Chapter 1 of this volume entitled "Ecclesial Space and Time" where he sketches a process called "the traditioning of experience and the experiencing of tradition."

18. There are a number of helpful discussions of the uses of Scripture in ethics. For example, see James Gustafson's *Can Ethics be Christian?*, pp. 117–168. Larry Rasmussen and Bruce Birch provide a good survey of the literature and the issues in *Bible and Ethics in the Christian Life* (Minneapolis, Minnesota: Augsburg Publishing House, 1976). For a summary of the more recent periodical literature, see "Notes on Moral Theology: 1980" by Richard A. McCormick, S.J., in *Theological Studies* (Vol. 42, No. 1, March 1981).

19. The issue of authority in the Church is obviously a very complex and difficult one. It touches Catholic Christians from one angle and Protestant Christians from a number of others. It is not possible or appropriate for me to deal with that issue in any detail here. I would only suggest that prayerful discerning attention to one's own individual and communitarian religious experience will provide the best witness to the appropriate expression of Church authority in any particular situation. For more reflection on the resolution of the tensions possible between local groups and the larger Church community, see the chapters by Avery Dulles and Thomas Clarke in this volume.

20. NETWORK, Sojourners, the Friends' Committee on National Legislation, and the New Jerusalem Community each speak of working toward consensus. The New Jerusalem Community uses explicitly Ignatian meth-

ods. A description of those can be found in John C. Futrell's pamphlet, "Communal Discernment: Reflections on Experience," in *Studies in the Spirituality of Jesuits,* Vol. IV, No. 5 (November 1972). The other groups developed their own processes out of their own traditions. Further information can be obtained by contacting the individual groups.

Biographical Data

Jouette Bassler is assistant professor of theology, Georgetown University.

Thomas E. Clarke, S.J. is a writer and lecturer working out of New York City.

Avery Dulles, S.J. is professor of theology, The Catholic University of America.

John D. Godsey is professor of systematic theology, Wesley Theological Seminary.

John C. Haughey, S.J. is a research fellow, Woodstock Theological Center.

Monika K. Hellwig is professor of theology, Georgetown University.

Alfred T. Hennelly, S.J. is a research fellow, Woodstock Theological Center.

Joe Holland is a staff associate, Center of Concern.

James E. Hug is a research fellow, Woodstock Theological Center.

Robert L. Kinast is assistant professor of theology, The Catholic University of America.

John Langan, S.J. is a research fellow, Woodstock Theological Center.

William L. Newell is a former teacher of theology at the Gregorian Pontifical University and Loyola Marymount University.

Larry L. Rasmussen is professor of Christian social ethics, Wesley Theological Seminary.

Index

311